Digital Diplomacy

Digital Diplomacy

U.S. Foreign Policy in the Information Age

Wilson Dizard, Jr.

Published with the cooperation of the
Center for Strategic and International
Studies, Washington, D.C.

PRAEGER

Westport, Connecticut
London

Library of Congress Cataloging-in-Publication Data

Dizard, Wilson.
    Digital diplomacy : U.S. foreign policy in the information age / Wilson Dizard, Jr.
        p. cm.
    "Published with the cooperation of the Center for Strategic and International Studies,
Washington, D.C."
    Includes bibliographical references and index.
    ISBN 0–275–97227–5 (alk. paper)—ISBN 0–275–97228–3 (pbk. : alk. paper)
    1. United States—Foreign relations—1989–   2. Telecommunication policy—
United States.   3. Telecommunication policy—United States—History.
4. Telecommunication—International cooperation.   5. Digital communications—
Political aspects—United States.   6. Technology and state—United States.   I. Title.
E840.D5   2001
384—dc21   00–064956

British Library Cataloguing in Publication Data is available.

Library of Congress Catalog Card Number: 00–064956
ISBN: 0–275-97227–5
        0–275-97228–3 (pbk.)

First published in 2001

Praeger Publishers, 88 Post Road West, Westport, CT 06881
An imprint of Greenwood Publishing Group, Inc.
www.praeger.com

Printed in the United States of America

The paper used in this book complies with the
Permanent Paper Standard issued by the National
Information Standards Organization (Z39.48–1984).

10 9 8 7 6 5 4 3 2 1

For Lynn, again.

Contents

Preface		ix
1.	Foreign Policy in the Information Age	1
2.	The Origins of Digital Diplomacy	19
3.	Communications Satellites: The Policy Challenge	37
4.	The Spectrum Wars	59
5.	The Threat to Global Information Flows	73
6.	Restructuring Diplomatic Communications	99
7.	Organizing Digital Diplomacy	113
8.	Negotiating Electronics Trade	135
9.	The Future of Digital Diplomacy	165
Selected Bibliography		193
Index		207

Preface

This survey is an account of how American diplomacy is being reshaped by forces that are moving the United States from an industrial democracy to a new form of postindustrial, information-intensive society whose outlines are still unclear.

Foreign policy is only one piece in the mosaic of changes propelling us into a new era. It has, however, a special importance in defining and carrying out U.S. strategic relations with the world outside our borders. The digital revolution touches on every aspect of American interests in the transition to a global information age.

The shift began over 150 years ago with the invention of the Morse telegraph. My focus, however, is on recent decades, which have seen the development of advanced computers, communications satellites, semiconductor chips and the other building blocks of a new information infrastructure. The latest addition to this list, the Internet, may bring about the most profound changes of all. What is certain is that these technical breakthroughs have far outpaced our political, economic and social attempts to deal with them effectively.

I have had occasional qualms about suggesting a new name for the subject under discussion here—*digital diplomacy*. For the present, it may be a useful, if temporary, addition to a long tradition that has seen such predecessors as gunboat diplomacy, dollar diplomacy, quiet diplomacy, shuttle diplomacy, ping-pong diplomacy and, more recently, public diplomacy.

By way of full disclosure, I was involved in many of the events described in this work. This began in December 1966 when, as a foreign service officer, I was assigned to the White House as manager of a survey of the political implications of the then-new communications satellite technology. My involvement in digital matters continued through the rest of my government career and, later, at the Center for Strategic and International Studies (CSIS). This book is not, however, a personal memoir. It is the story of hundreds of men and women, in and out of government, who have contributed to the work of integrating digital realities into traditional foreign policy concerns and practices.

I have had a great deal of help from many people in putting together this account of the early years of a new kind of diplomacy. Special thanks go to colleagues at CSIS and at Georgetown University, in particular to Diana Lady Dougan, chief of the center's communications policy program, and to Peter Krogh, former Dean of the School of Foreign Service at Georgetown, both of whom gave me the space, time and other resources to undertake this survey.

The staff of the Association for Diplomatic Studies and Training, where I had an appointment as a research fellow, was helpful, with special mention to the encouragement given to me by Edward Rowley, the association's president, and by Margery Boichel-Thompson, its publications director.

Finally, a special acknowledgment to my resident chief editor and thoughtful critic on works in progress, Lynn Wood Dizard.

Digital Diplomacy

Chapter 1

Foreign Policy in the Information Age

Of the four great instrumentalities available to nations for influencing the world around them—diplomacy, armed forces, money and
information—the last is both the most powerful and the least
understood.
                      —Ithiel de Sola Pool, MIT political scientist[1]

These words were written a generation ago in a technologically simpler
time, before the large-scale expansion of computer power and global
information networks. Professor Pool's emphasis on information as a
strategic resource takes on new meaning in the current millennial environment. His insights foreshadowed a larger transformation of American
society as it moves beyond the industrial age into an information-
intensive postindustrial environment.

This survey examines a small but important aspect of this shift, namely
how the U.S. diplomatic establishment is adjusting to information age
realities. Electronic communications and information resources are influencing foreign policy, not only by raising a new set of strategic issues
but also by altering the ways in which we deal with them. The result is
a distinctly different type of relations between nations—one that calls
for a responsive *digital diplomacy*.

The change is substantial enough to suggest that it is the most important innovation affecting diplomatic practices since the fifteenth century,
when permanent ambassadors were first exchanged among the royal
courts of Europe. In his magisterial study of Renaissance diplomacy, historian Garrett Mattingly noted that the role of an ambassador then was

to uphold "his majesty's honor at a foreign court, aided by no more than his wit, courage and eloquence."[2]

These are still useful diplomatic qualities. More recently, however, ambassadorial resources have been dramatically enhanced by access to computers, satellites and other information technologies. These latter-day capabilities are having a subtle but profound effect on diplomatic traditions. They mark the final demise of diplomacy as a profession carried out by an elite group of officials dealing with like-minded colleagues in foreign chanceries. The U.S. foreign policy establishment has moved faster and further away from this tradition in recent years than have most of its counterparts abroad.

The transition is, however, incomplete. American diplomacy lags behind the rest of U.S. society in adopting new electronic practices.[3] Lingering elitist attitudes in the foreign service are not the only restraint. The pace has also been slowed by perennially underfunded foreign affairs budgets, particularly for the expensive equipment needed to keep diplomatic operations in step with changing information technologies. That said, there is still resistance to accepting the new digital realities by tradition-bound officials within the diplomatic community. Old habits die slowly.[4]

These barriers are being lowered, particularly with the recruitment of a generation of professionals who are at ease with computers and other digital resources. However, the tendency to move slowly in adapting digital technologies to foreign policy operations persists.[5] It was not until March 1998 that the State Department took the overdue step of consolidating management of its electronic information resources in a central office.[6]

Meanwhile, a minority view has emerged that calls for a radically stepped-up pace of computerizing foreign policy operations. In their more imaginative moments, this minority proposes a diplomacy conducted increasingly by remote control. Their plan for telediplomacy involves "virtual embassies" serving as electronic data-gathering outposts for computerized decision making in Washington. This would be technocracy run amuck. Machines cannot replicate the essential personal skills of diplomacy, particularly what British diplomat Harold Nicolson has defined as moral precision, the willingness to confront foreign policy realities directly and with conviction.

The point is made in a Georgetown University study of the future of diplomacy:

There will be no such thing as remote-control diplomacy. The "global village" is a deceptively attractive term which obscures the real differences in peoples and governments. Foreigners will continue to live, think, and view events in ways that are foreign to us. We will continue to need diplomats pounding the pavements, talking to all sorts of people in foreign countries and analyzing the significance of what they have learned.[7]

This survey examines the practical consequences of digital diplomacy, from its origins to its present potential for strengthening the content and conduct of U.S. foreign policy in a changing world order. Political scientists Joseph Nye and William Owens see "America's information edge" as the critical factor in this new environment:

Knowledge, more than ever, is power. The one country that can best lead the information revolution will be more powerful than any other. For the foreseeable future, that country is the United States. America has apparent strength in military power and economic production. Yet its more subtle comparative advantage is its ability to collect, process, act upon and disseminate information, an edge that will almost certainly grow in the next decade.[8]

Other observers challenge this viewpoint as overly simplistic. They question whether information technology as such can project decisive power. However useful the new digital resources, they do not displace the traditional measures of strength such as physical territory, industrial production and military force.

Moreover, the doubters point out, information resources rely on fragile structures (e.g., data banks and communications circuits) that are vulnerable to physical destruction or are capable of being disabled electronically by a new breed of computer-savvy political terrorists or even by teenage hackers. The foreign policy establishment itself is not immune to such attacks: in 1998, General Accounting Office officials surveying the vulnerability of government computers were able to gain easy access to classified documents in State Department computers.[9] Finally, these critics argue that information resources by themselves fail the ultimate test of national security—the ability of a society to impose its will over another.[10]

The debate over the strategic role of information resources is ongoing, supporting a growing cottage industry within the foreign policy community. No consensus has emerged, nor will it soon, given the complexities of the subject. There is, however, general agreement that American strategic interests will be increasingly defined by the ability to maintain a strong lead in information resources.

In this area, America is first among unequals. Its digital strength ("soft power" in the new lexicon) consists of uncountable trillions of invisible electronic impulses, bits and bytes stored in computers and moved silently through high-speed communications networks.

The most visible example of this trend is the Internet. From small beginnings in the early 1970s, the Net has leapfrogged over older technologies to become the working model for a global information utility. Moreover, it is uniquely American in spirit. "The Internet is profoundly disrespectful of tradition, established order and hierarchy, and that is very American," says Fareed Zakaria, managing editor of *Foreign Affairs*. Don Heath, president of the Internet Society, adds: "If the United States government had tried to come up with a scheme to spread its brand of capitalism and its emphasis on political liberalism around the world, it couldn't have invented a better model than the Internet."[11]

At the turn of the new century, about half of the world's Internet users were American.[12] All but 6 percent of the most-visited World Wide Web sites were in the United States. Forty percent of these sites were in California.[13]

The United States is both the prime generator and distributor of all digital information resources. Currently, about 35 percent of global communications traffic originates or terminates in the United States, a country with less than 6 percent of the world's population. A useful measure of "bit power" is the number of databases a nation possesses. Here America handily outdistances the rest of the world with 5,000 major data banks. In the late 1990s, this was double the number installed in all other countries combined.[14]

This database gap is narrowing but, for the present, America exercises what amounts to a new kind of hegemony.[15] This digital lead results from what Harvard economist Joseph Schumpeter once called creative destruction, the ability of a society to adjust successfully to technological and economic changes.

As economic analyst Cornelia Small has noted,

To move into the postindustrial cycle, a country must permit old wealth based on industrial technology to be destroyed, while accepting a new source of wealth creation based on information technology. The ability to jump from the old curve to a new curve requires a country to be flexible enough to reinvent itself. As this happens there will be a change in the way the economy works, in the political power base, in society, in the concept of what we think a country is.[16]

This survey will focus on three trends that define diplomacy's role in this process. In turn, they involve policy, operations and public advocacy:

1. *The emergence of a new set of foreign policy issues involving advanced communications and information resources.* This change has been driven largely by a technological imperative—the need to adjust to the impact of advanced electronic resources that have been created largely in U.S. research institutions in recent decades. These technologies have set in motion political and economic forces that redefine American geopolitical interests.

This digitally driven agenda increasingly affects all other foreign policy issues. The most visible of these is trade. Information technology in all its forms—both hardware and software—has become the leading American export sector.[17] As such electronics is a critical element in maintaining U.S. economic growth in an increasingly globalized economy. Digital technologies affect other strategic areas. One is what the Defense Department calls the revolution in military affairs (RMA), with its emphasis on the role of advanced information resources in twenty-first-century conflicts, from Pentagon strategic planning to tactical battlefield situations. Other policy areas—from energy to human rights—are similarly influenced by the new electronics.

2. *Changes in the organization of information resources within the State Department and other foreign affairs agencies.* Information has always been the raw material of two of diplomacy's basic tasks—reporting and negotiating. In both cases, the advantage lies with the side which is better at using advanced technologies to collect and process the data needed for decision making.

Diplomats have always been wary of new information technologies. When the first telegram arrived on the desk of the British foreign minister, Lord Palmerston, in the 1840s, he reportedly declared: "My God, this is the end of diplomacy." In a way, he was right. The telegraph and the innovations that followed changed the gentlemen's trade Palmerston knew. Despite his misgivings, telegraphic traffic became an important working tool in the British Foreign Office and in its counterparts around the world.[18]

Incredibly, the U.S. State Department was a latecomer to this process. Its officials did not hire a communications clerk for a dozen years after the first Morse telegraph network began operations. His duties were to pick up telegrams addressed to the department at the Western Union office in downtown Washington. It was another decade before telegraph connections with the State Department's overseas missions were established.[19]

Diplomatic cable traffic has since been largely displaced by messages stored in computers and distributed by high-speed communications circuits. The State Department's operations would be hopelessly bogged down without the electronic resources that connect its Washington operations with over 170 embassies and other posts abroad. Despite considerable improvements, the department still faces a massive upgrading of its entire electronic facilities in the coming years. In the late 1990s, it was still saddled with four separate and incompatible internal communications networks, none of which could "talk" with the others.

3. *The rise of "public diplomacy," and specifically the use of digital technologies to influence public opinion.* Public diplomacy is a catchall phrase for a broad range of information and cultural programs aimed at audiences

at home and abroad. Controversial when they were first introduced during World War II, these programs are now an integral part of U.S. foreign policy operations. Beginning with the Voice of America radio, public diplomacy has expanded in recent decades to include a wide range of electronic operations, from the Internet to satellite broadcasting.

During the cold war years, organizational responsibilities for public diplomacy programs were split between the State Department, which dealt with domestic opinion, and an independent U.S. Information Agency, whose programs were directed at overseas audiences. In October 1999, the two programs were combined in a single unit within the State Department. It is one of the largest bureaus in the department, with over 4,000 employees in Washington and overseas, using the Internet and other information resources to get its messages out.[20] As such, its activities are part of this survey of digital diplomacy.

Policy, operations and public diplomacy—these are the three strands we will follow in measuring the foreign policy impact of advanced information technologies. The survey will focus primarily on the State Department, the senior foreign affairs agency. As we shall see, the department has gone through a series of internal reorganizations to deal with digital issues. In addition, two "outside" groups have influenced its activities in this area. They are domestic federal agencies and nongovernmental organizations, the so-called NGOs.

Recent decades have seen a vastly expanded role for other federal agencies in foreign policy in general and digital issues in particular. Before World War II, foreign policy management was almost exclusively the province of the State Department. After Pearl Harbor, other agencies became more directly involved in the diplomatic complexities of a global war.

This change was institutionalized in 1947 with the creation of a national strategy coordinating group at the White House level, the National Security Council. The Defense Department and the Central Intelligence Agency, both then newly created, achieved strategic planning equality with the State Department.[21] As a result, the State Department found itself confronted by two powerful rivals for White House attention, each with responsibilities for the management of ongoing programs that impinged, in varying degrees, on traditional diplomatic responsibilities.

In today's more complex world, this pattern of collaborative foreign affairs management occurs at many levels. Dozens of federal agencies are involved, often with their own extensive overseas operations, including representatives assigned to American embassies abroad. The Paris embassy staff in 2000 included over 200 employees from 15 Washington agencies, outnumbering State Department personnel.

Inter-agency coordination is particularly important in managing communications and information policy. Issues in this area are often highly technical, involving expertise that the State Department lacks. Moreover, digital diplomacy issues almost always have domestic policy implications, involving responsibilities assigned to other agencies. As a result, the Treasury, the Defense and Commerce Departments, the Federal Communications Commission and the White House Office of the U.S. Trade Representative, among other agencies, are permanent participants in planning and managing overseas communications policy. As we shall see throughout this study, this interplay of domestic interests and foreign policy concerns is one in which State Department viewpoints are often overridden.

In addition to domestic federal agencies, non-governmental organizations—the NGOs—increasingly exert their influence over the State Department's digital diplomacy. NGO involvement in foreign affairs was once limited to a small group of elite organizations. One of them, the Council on Foreign Relations, has had a long record of influencing State Department policy, in part because its membership in the past overlapped the department's Eastern-establishment leadership. The Council still has special standing among the foreign policy NGOs, but its advisory role is overshadowed by a new wave of special interest organizations, representing business, labor, professional, technology and consumer interests.[22]

With their focussed agendas, these groups are now an omnipresent force in foreign policy. Their influence stems in large part from their ability to influence public opinion through electronic channels, from faxes to Internet Web pages. This capability alone makes them an increasingly important part of the diplomatic process. Their new prominence is, moreover, a global phenomenon. A United Nations survey has identified 28,900 international NGOs, including outsized representation by American groups.[23]

In many ways, this strong U.S. presence among global NGOs reflects a long-standing characteristic of American foreign policy. No other diplomatic establishment is more directly affected by public opinion in general and by pressures from specific constituencies in particular.[24] Alexis de Toqueville famously commented on this over 150 years ago when he observed that a democratic society lacked the discipline to carry out an effective diplomacy: "Foreign politics demand scarcely any of those qualities which are peculiar to a democracy; they require, on the contrary, the perfect use of almost all those in which it is deficient."[25]

Today's NGOs and their contentious agendas are a logical extension of de Toqueville's observation. They have moved beyond the genteel advisory activities of a Council on Foreign Relations to aggressive lobbying across the spectrum of diplomatic issues, from trade agreements to preserving the Amazon rain forest.[26]

The new NGOs work both inside and outside the formal diplomatic system. They are represented on a wide range of government advisory committees, working groups and other forums on foreign policy issues. Moreover, Congress has mandated since the late 1970s that NGOs be represented as advisers to American delegations to international meetings where their interests are being discussed.

At times, the NGOs can lay claim to being a decisive influence in diplomatic negotiations. In one example, executives from large U.S. banks were advisers to the American delegation at a 1997 World Trade Organization (WTO) conference considering ways to lower barriers to cross-border financial flows. In a moment of candor, one of the bank executives declared: "We were the most powerful delegation there—including the American delegation." More neutral observers at the conference did not challenge his claim.

In other instances, NGOs can put pressure on international negotiations from the outside. Over 230 public interest NGOs lobbied their opinions in the corridors of a 1998 Rome conference to set up an international court for war crimes.[27] They also used Internet Web sites to spread their views. The war crimes tribunal was approved, but American NGOs failed in their attempts to get a favorable U.S. vote.[28]

Other NGOs were more successful in influencing the outcome of a December 1999 WTO ministerial conference in Seattle. Called to approve an agenda for future WTO actions, the conference was disrupted by 30,000 street demonstrators, representing a wide range of labor, environmental, church and human rights groups. The meeting adjourned without taking action on its proposed agenda.[29]

NGO influences are particularly strong in trade policy, given the new dominance of information technologies, both hardware and software, as the single largest U.S. business sector. NGOs apply continuing pressure to influence policies that affect U.S. commercial interests in a global sector that accounted for a trillion dollars in annual revenues at the turn of the century.[30]

Electronics-based trade decisions are tracked by the industry's major lobbyists, including the National Association of Manufacturers, the U.S. Chamber of Commerce and specialized trade associations. Their activities are often challenged by other lobbyists—environmentalists, human rights groups, and labor unions with specific worries about the loss of jobs to low-cost overseas industries.

As noted above, the effectiveness of these groups stems from the fact that they are often better informed about the issues involved than are government agencies. A generation ago, the primary information source on export trade issues was the federal government. This role has been largely taken over by commercial firms. In the critical area of economic data, business relies on Reuters, Dow Jones, Bloomberg and other financial news services. Washington agencies cannot match their speed and efficiency in providing the information business needs to operate at home and abroad.

The big corporations have their own advanced information resources. Cargill International, a major player in agricultural exports, has a massive electronics-filled "situation room" at its Minneapolis headquarters which processes computerized data on global currency movements and crop conditions around the clock. IBM, AT&T, Microsoft and other information technology giants have similar arrangements for tracking developments affecting their overseas operations.

Smaller NGOs lack such elaborate facilities. In recent years, however, they have benefited from the worldwide expansion of the Internet and its World Wide Web. Among other uses, the Web is an advocacy channel for them, making their views known to a global audience. The Internet allows NGOs to set up and operate their own Web pages at relatively small cost. Moreover, the Web is a two-way electronic street, which permits audiences to react via e-mail and other channels. Human rights groups, usually small and underfunded, have made effective use of Web facilities to identify and publicize rights violations around the world.[31] At another level, Web sites were used both by the Yugoslav government and local opposition groups to spread their disparate views instantaneously during that country's political turmoil in the late 1990s.[32]

American-funded digital resources played a special role in bringing about the downfall of the dictatorial Milosevic regime in Yugoslavia in September 2000. This involved assistance to the democratic opposition in the run-up to national elections that resulted in Slobodan Milosevic's ouster. The aid, which reportedly cost $77 million, involved heavy reliance on electronic goods and services, including computers, fax machines and voter-survey databases. These resources were turned over to labor unions, student groups and independent media outlets, which made up the country's famously fractured democratic opposition. Much of the assistance was channeled through non-governmental organizations such as the Washington-based National Democratic Institute for International Affairs.[33]

In summary, the Internet has become a newly potent adjunct to electronic diplomacy, particularly in advocating alternatives to official policies. Terrorist groups use it as a channel to attract support: Shining Path guerrillas in Peru have had a Web page touting their message for many years.

At a more benign level, other advocacy groups have turned to the Web to promote policies that often clash with U.S. policy objectives. The American government has also used the Web to support U.S. private groups mediating local disputes in Northern Ireland, Sri Lanka and the Middle East.[34] Web sites are one of the resources funded by the U.S. Agency for International Development (AID) in a small but effective program supporting local human rights groups in more than 25 countries around the world.[35]

The Internet's ability to influence American foreign policy was confirmed in the late 1990s during a global debate over a U.N.-sponsored treaty to ban the use of land mines. A Vermont-based advocacy group, the Campaign to Ban Land Mines, played a critical role in supporting the treaty, which was opposed by the U.S. government. The Vermont group relied primarily on the World Wide Web to organize over a hundred advocacy organizations at home and abroad to back the agreement, which was adopted in December 1997. Jody Williams, who managed the campaign, won the Nobel Prize the following year for her work.[36]

The land mine campaign involved a temporary Web page alliance by like-minded groups to deal with a single event. More recently, such networking has taken on a more permanent institutional cast. The trend is towards forming ongoing public policy networks covering a wide range of cross-border issues, from the eradication of malaria to the depletion of global fishing grounds. At the turn of the century, the World Bank identified about 50 major policy-oriented networks. They are run by groups that thrive in a borderless environment, capitalizing on the World Wide Web's interactive capabilities.

The organizations that make up these networks are an eclectic mix of government agencies and non-government groups. In a sense, these networks represent a new kind of diplomacy, operating in neutral cyberspace, in which the interests of a wide range of groups are put forward, debated, and acted upon. "Although their objectives and budgets are still relatively modest, their record of success holds the promise not only of untangling a knot of global problems, but of improving the principles and methods of global governance," according to Wolfgang H. Reinicke, director of the U.N. Vision Project on Global Public Policy Networks.[37]

The mass media have a special role in this new mix of electronic influences on American foreign policy. Television images, in particular, define the subject for most viewers at home and abroad. During her tenure as ambassador to the United Nations, Madeleine Albright referred to the Cable News Network (CNN) as the sixteenth member of the Security Council.[38] It was a wry acknowledgment of the network's influence on both diplomats and the general public through its ability to provide vivid accounts of fast-breaking news.[39]

Television is part of a larger trend in which digital networks collapse both time and distance to make information resources available to everyone. The implications of this change are only beginning to be understood. Communications researcher Gregory Staple has given a name to the phenomenon. He calls it telegeography:

For most of the world's history, geography has provided something of a cultural buffer between the values of the city and countryside and between one religious community and another. Yet in much of the world, the network threatens to leapfrog this barrier. Telegeography transports every villager's home into the metropolis and settles the atheist next door to the true believer.[40]

Direct broadcasting satellites have dramatically expanded the availability of round-the-clock information. One such satellite, owned by Rupert Murdoch's News Corp., transmits news and entertainment programs to millions of small earth stations in over 30 countries stretching from Japan to the Persian Gulf. Meanwhile, in Washington, White House and State Department officials scurry to react to what are often superficial sound bite reports of complex events.[41]

The most pervasive electronic influences on U.S. diplomacy come from the big international corporations. Their role is often overstated: most of them still produce and trade mainly within their home economies. Nevertheless their global influence grows: by the mid-1990s, they were earning $7 *trillion* in annual sales through their foreign affiliates, an amount greater than the world's total exports at the time.[42]

The multinationals' interest in digital issues can be traced to the advanced networks that give them a worldwide reach, allowing them to control production and distribution facilities on all continents. One example among many is the Ford Company's "world car," a basic module created in a half-dozen design labs around the globe, manufactured on three continents and sold under various trade names in over 100 countries.[43]

Ford's success in using advanced communications networks to integrate its worldwide operations has been replicated by many other firms. These companies have, in effect, untethered themselves from their national origins in ways that are changing traditional foreign relations. As Jessica Mathews, head of the Carnegie Endowment, notes, these firms "are disconnecting from their home countries' national interests, moving jobs, evading taxes, and eroding economic sovereignty in the process."[44]

The global financial community, led by the Americans, plays a special role in this shift. Its worldwide networks undermine the traditional role of governments in regulating the flow and value of their currencies. National controls are largely bypassed when currencies are traded as electronic digits in the noisy money bazaars of New York, London and other financial centers.

This digitization of money is a relatively new phenomenon. For most of the post–World War II era, the United States and other industrial powers were able to manage and control money flows and values through international agreements, in particular the 1944 Bretton Woods agreement that set out rules for national control of exchange rates. New pressures on the system, including the beginnings of cross-border electronic transfers, ended the Bretton Woods system in the 1970s. Control has since shifted to private financial groups whose assets, measured in bits and bytes, move at the speed of light over high-capacity circuits.

Daily turnover in currency markets today often exceeds the global stock of official foreign exchange reserves. International banks move where the money is. By the mid-1990s there were more American banks in London than in New York.[45] They are links in a foreign exchange network whose average daily volume often exceeds $1.5 trillion. Attempts by government central banks to intervene in the market to protect their currencies have relatively little effect against this torrent of private transactions. As British financial analyst Philip Coghlan notes, they might as well attempt to repeal the laws of gravity.[46]

This new financial order is only one part of the ripple effect of global digitization that is undermining long-standing sovereign prerogatives. As Nicholas Colchester of the The Economist Intelligence Unit points out:

Educated elites no longer advance within their nations: they move in galaxies—of film, finance and fashion—that bestride nations. . . . The supranational challenge goes beyond the economic. The rise of the electronic media is changing a basic tenet of the post–Second World War order—that nations are inviolable, however they may behave within their own frontiers, provided that they do not misbehave across them. Goodbye nation state, hello . . . what?[47]

These trends raise the prospect of the withering away of the nation-state in the face of powerful transnational forces, including the new electronic networks. Its basic premise is that the balance of power and authority is tipping away from governments towards big global corporations and other borderless institutions. The explanations for this shift vary, but the main thrust is the same: the global economy rules. Information-driven globalization adds to the reach and power of the market. Sovereign rights, the bedrock of traditional diplomacy, seem to be retreating before the new corporate masters of global competition.[48]

It is an intriguing proposition, backed with enough anecdotal evidence to make it credible. But an equally persuasive case can be made that, overall, governments are holding their own in the new reshuffling of resources and the power they confer. They are doing this by selectively ceding control to corporate interests. "In other words," the London *Economist* notes, "governments have freely chosen to give market forces more sway in the hope that this will raise living standards. It is odd therefore to say that the global economy has seized power from the state and it is plain wrong to say that democratic rights have been trampled on."[49]

This is particularly true of how most governments have begun to deal with digital resources in their national strategies. They are surrendering control over their telecommunications systems—a long-standing sovereign imperative—in favor of more open market competition, including foreign investment in these systems. Until very recently, these resources were strict national monopolies in most countries.

Deregulation and privatization of these facilities is now the order of the day as part of a larger trend by governments to allow their economies to compete openly and effectively at home and abroad. By and large, this policy has had positive effects in strengthening national economies around the world. Digital communications have not hastened the end of the nation-state or the need for diplomacy. They have, however, altered the functions of both.

In giving up their communications monopolies, many governments are following, with variations, the American lead. The United States was the first country to open its national network to competition in a 1982 decision that ended AT&T's dominant monopoly. The result has been the explosive growth of domestic communications resources since then— the digital infrastructure of American society.[50]

The AT&T breakup had a powerful impact overseas. At the turn of the century, governments in over 100 countries have taken similar steps, giving up full or partial control of their telecommunications resources. This trend now dominates over 90 percent of all communications networks worldwide. The holdout governments are in the developing world. Even here the so-called big emerging markets—India, Brazil, Mexico and Indonesia, among others—have opened their systems to competition. By 2010, only a handful of smaller countries will have government communications monopolies.[51]

These developments have altered the policy landscape in which American digital diplomacy now operates. As we shall see throughout this survey, the U.S. government's major policy thrust in recent years has been to encourage the opening up of overseas communications and information markets in ways that benefit U.S. business. In particular, American negotiators were successful in the mid-1990s in pressing for two WTO agreements which have steadily reduced cross-border barriers to telecommunications and information trade.[52]

In summary, a new political pattern is emerging in the world's electronic resources. It involves a very different relationship between government and private interests, one whose eventual form is still to be defined. In communications as in other areas, as British commentator John Browning points out: "Government isn't disappearing. It's being disintermediated."[53] In the process, the definition of national sovereignty in the information age is being rewritten. Governments must adjust to this new mix in which private sector groups preempt, in whole or in part, powers that had long defined national authority in communications and other sectors. The process is encapsulated in a newly minted bureaucratic phrase: sovereignty repositioning.

As a result, American diplomacy now deals with a different set of policy realities, beginning with a new relationship between government and private institutions at home and abroad. This change is having a major impact on U.S. national interests as we move more deeply into an information-intensive postindustrial age. In the process, it is restructuring strategic policy—both the issues it confronts and the ways in which it uses advanced electronic facilities to deal with them.

Dean Acheson, one of the great secretaries of state of the past century, described the popular perception of diplomacy as an alien business. He believed that this perception had to change:

Foreign policy is the whole of national policy looked at from the point of view of exigencies created by the "vast external realm" beyond our border. It is not a jurisdiction. It is an orientation, a point of view, a measurement of values—today, perhaps, the most important one for our national survival.[54]

This vision takes on new meaning in the information age, in which American global interests are expanding beyond what even such an astute observer as Acheson could have imagined. Foreign policy in his day was still the province of a small cadre of professionals, a group apart, who carried out their day-to-day work largely insulated from outside domestic pressures. This is much less true now, and it will be even less so in the future. The reason is that U.S. strategic interests will be increasingly defined by information resources.

A German observer, journalist Josef Joffe, notes that historically when one country's control over a key resource is so preponderant, other countries try to team up to challenge it. Why has this not happened in any significant way with American information power? The reason, Joffe suggests, is that most foreigners, in and out of government, see these resources less as a threat than an attraction. Nevertheless, some players in international politics are issuing warnings (most explicitly voiced by the French) about the baleful influences of America as an "information hyperpower."[55]

These are the stakes as we begin to look at the origins of digital diplomacy, its current status and how it fits in with larger national purposes. It is a story that begins over 150 years ago with Samuel F. B. Morse and his new-fangled telegraph machine.

NOTES

1. Ithiel de Sola Pool, "Information goals," *Foreign Service Journal*, July 1963, p. 24.

2. Garrett Mattingly, *Renaissance diplomacy* (Boston: Houghton Mifflin, 1955), p. 211.

3. "U.S. diplomacy behind the times, studies say," *Washington Post*, 28 October 1998, p. A-17.

4. Yaacov Y. I. Vertzberger, *The world in their minds: Information processing, cognition and perception in foreign policy decision making* (Stanford, CA: Stanford University Press, 1990).

5. "U.S. diplomacy behind the times, studies say," op cit.

6. "Information resource management: A new bureau for a new era," *State Magazine*, October 1998, pp. 36–40.

7. *The Foreign Service in 2008: A report on 21st century diplomacy* (Washington, DC: Institute for the Study of Diplomacy, Georgetown University, August 1992), p. 6.

8. Joseph S. Nye, Jr. and William A. Owens, "America's information edge," *Foreign Affairs*, March/April 1996, p. 20. See also Daniel F. Burton, Jr., "The brave new wired world," *Foreign Policy*, No. 106, Spring 1997, pp. 23–37.

9. "Computers in 2 agencies found vulnerable," *New York Times*, 20 May 1998, p. A-15.

10. Stephen S. Cohen and John Zysman, *Manufacturing counts: The myth of the post-industrial society* (New York: Basic Books, 1987). See also Patrick M. Cronin, *2015: Power and progress* (Washington, DC: National Defense University Press, 1996).

11. "Welcome to the Internet: The first global colony," *New York Times*, 9 January 2000, p. WK-1.

12. "Worldwide online growth," in *The digital economy: Convergence and regulatory boundaries* (Washington, DC: Office of Plans and Policy, Federal Communications Commission, November 1999), p. 3.

13. "Why it is slow going on the Net," *Washington Post*, 24 May 1999, p. 20.

14. *The U.S Global Trade Outlook 1995–2000* (Washington, DC: Department of Commerce, March 1995), p. 182.

15. For a survey of this prospect, see Stuart J. D. Schwartzstein (ed.), *The information revolution and national security: Dimensions and directions* (Washington, DC: Center for Strategic and International Studies, 1996).

16. "A kaleidoscope view of the 21st century" (New York: Scudder, Stevens & Clark, November 1993), p. 3.

17. "Free trade in information technology goods," *Industry, Trade and Technology Review* (Washington, DC: U.S. International Trade Commission, Publication 3084, January 1998), p. 1.

18. The British Foreign and Commonwealth Office has been a leader in adapting information technology resources in its operations. See Stewart Elder, *From quill pen to satellite* (London: European Program, Royal Institute of International Affairs, 1994).

19. Daniel R. Headrick, *The invisible weapon: Telecommunications and international politics 1851–1945* (New York: Oxford University Press, 1991), p. 74.

20. "USIA merger moves public diplomacy closer to policy center," *State Magazine*, September 1999, pp. 23–25.

21. Stanley L. Falk, "The National Security Council under Truman, Eisenhower

and Kennedy," *Political Science Quarterly*, Vol. 79, No. 3, September 1965, pp. 403–433.

22. Margaret E. Keck and Kathryn Sikkink, *Activists beyond borders: Advocacy networks in international politics* (Ithaca, NY: Cornell University Press, 1998).

23. "The 'firemen' of Africa feel the heat of scrutiny," *Financial Times* (London), 19 August 1999, p. 4.

24. Philip J. Powlick, "The sources of public opinion for American foreign policy officials," *International Studies Quarterly*, No. 39, 1995, pp. 427–451.

25. Alexis de Toqueville, *Democracy in America*, Vol. 2 (New York: Vintage Books, 1990), p. 243.

26. P. J. Simmons, "Learning to live with NGO's," *Foreign Policy*, No. 110, Fall 1998, pp. 82–96.

27. "UN conference to draft war crimes treaty," *Washington Post*, 14 June 1998, p. A-22.

28. The overall influence of lobbies within the United Nations system is discussed in Peter Willetts, *The conscience of the world: The influence of non-governmental organizations in the U.N. system* (Washington, DC: Brookings Institution, 1996).

29. "Protest's architect 'gratified'," *Washington Post*, 2 December 1999, p. 1.

30. "Free trade in information technology goods," op cit., p. 1.

31. "The Internet, satellites and human rights," *On the Internet*, April 1999, pp. 19–29.

32. "War on the Web," *The Economist* (London), 15 May 1999, p. 8.

33. "U.S. funds help Milosevic's foes in election fight," *Washington Post*, 19 September 2000, p. 1.

34. David Smock (ed.), *Private peacemaking: USIP-assisted peacemaking projects of nonprofit organizations* (Washington, DC: U.S. Institute for Peace, May 1998).

35. "U.S. has spent $26 million since '95 on Suharto opponents," *New York Times*, 20 May 1998, p. A-11.

36. "U.S. activist receives Nobel peace prize for land mine campaign," *Washington Post*, 11 November 1997, p. 1.

37. "The other World Wide Web: Global public policy networks," *Foreign Policy*, No. 117, Winter 1999–2000, pp. 44–57.

38. "A vote for loyal service," *Financial Times* (London), 7 December 1996, p. 9.

39. "Ted Turner's CNN gains global influence and 'diplomatic' role," *Wall Street Journal*, 2 February 1990, p. 1. See also: Johanna Neuman, *Lights, camera, war: Is media technology driving international politics?* (New York: St. Martin's Press, 1996); "The mass media's impact on managing international affairs," in *Diplomacy and conflict resolution in the information age* (Washington, DC: U.S. Institute for Peace, June 1997), p. 3; Warren Strobel, *Late-breaking foreign policy: The news media's influence on peace operations* (Washington, DC: USIP Press, 1997).

40. Gregory C. Staple, "Telegeography and the explosion of space," remarks at the Columbia Institute of Tele-information, Columbia University, 29 October 1993.

41. Nik Gowing, *Media coverage: Help or hindrance in conflict prevention?*, report to the Carnegie Commission on Preventing Deadly Conflict, Carnegie Corporation of New York, September 1997.

42. "Worldbeater Inc.," *The Economist* (London), 22 November 1997, p. 92.

43. For other examples of product globalization, see Wilson P. Dizard, *Meganet: How the global communications network will connect everyone on earth* (Boulder, CO: HarperCollins/Westview Press, 1997), p. 107.

44. Quoted in Leo J. O'Donovan, "A dialogue in hope," *America*, 11 September 1999, p. 18.

45. The Chancellor on the City," *The Banker* (London), 27 November 1997, p. 1.

46. These implications are discussed in "The future of the state," Special supplement, *The Economist* (London), 20 September 1997.

47. "Goodbye, nation state—Hello what?" *New York Times*, 17 July 1994, p. WR-16.

48. Richard Rosecrance, "The rise of the virtual state," *Foreign Affairs*, July/August 1996, pp. 45–61. See also: Michael Nelson, "Sovereignty in the networked world," *Annual Review* (Washington, DC: Institute for Information Studies, Aspen Institute, 1998), pp. 1–22.

49. "Bearing the weight of the market," *The Economist* (London), 6 December 1997, p. 88.

50. For an overview of the intricate politics and economics of this development, see: William J. Drake (ed.), *The new information infrastructure: Strategies for U.S. policy* (New York: Twentieth Century Fund Press, 1995).

51. This development is described in *Meganet*, op cit., chaps. 4 and 9.

52. Gary Hufbauer and Clyde and Erica Wade, *Unfinished business: Telecommunications after the Uruguay Round* (Washington, DC: International Institute of Economics, 1997).

53. "Power to the people," *Wired*, January 1998, p. 88.

54. Quoted in *Report of the Commission on the Organization of the Government for the Conduct of Foreign Policy* (Washington, DC, June 1975), p. ix.

55. Joseph S. Nye, "The power we must not squander," *New York Times*, 3 January 2000, p. A-27.

Chapter 2

The Origins of Digital Diplomacy

When Cyrus Field planned the first transatlantic cable in the 1850s, he and his partners had to rely on European investors to finance the project. This incident was a telling example of American attitudes towards electrical communications with the rest of the world in the decades following the invention of the Morse telegraph.

The national focus at the time was on the domestic expansion of telegraph and telephone networks. The potential value of overseas links was largely ignored. In Washington, the government's concerns were centered on fears of foreign control over internal communications. The first congressional legislation dealing with telecommunications, the Radio Act of 1912, touched on cross-border issues in only one provision, restricting foreign ownership of American networks.[1] The United States refused to join the International Telegraph Union, created in 1865 to set technical standards for cross-border telegraph traffic, fearing that the organization might attempt to regulate domestic networks.

Until the 1940s, the major players in international communications were the Europeans, led by the British and the French. The latter saw telegraph networks as vital links for maintaining control over their colonies in Asia and Africa. As a result, the British and French governments had an effective monopoly of global telegraph circuits before World War II. U.S. companies such as AT&T and ITT played a minor role, largely by default, in Central and South America.[2]

In 1900, the American government faced its first major foreign policy issue in electronic communications. It involved a British attempt to set up a worldwide monopoly in wireless communications, based on the successful experiments of Guglielmo Marconi, who was a British citizen.

The London-based Marconi Co., with strong government backing, proposed to maintain global control of the new technology through exclusive licensing arrangements.[3] In Washington, President Theodore Roosevelt and his military advisers saw the British move as a threat to U.S. security interests. In 1904, Roosevelt set up a White House group—the Interdepartmental Board of Wireless Telegraphy—to deal with the issue. It was the first American attempt to develop an international communications policy.[4]

The lead agency in this diplomatic exercise was not the State Department but the U.S. Navy. Its interest was triggered by the Japanese navy's successful use of wireless radio in defeating the Russian fleet at the Battle of Tsushima in May 1905. Eager to equip its ships with similar capabilities, the navy opposed the Marconi licensing proposals. One result was that the United States joined the International Telegraph Union. With help from the union's European members, it was successful in turning back the Marconi plan.

The First World War confirmed the strategic advantage of electronic communications in general, and wireless networks in particular. Building on its success in preventing the British wireless monopoly, the United States proposed the ending of all restrictions on cross-border communications at the 1919 Versailles peace conference. Although this initiative was rejected by the other delegations, the principle of open global communications was established as the cornerstone of American policy in global negotiations on the subject ever since.[5]

During the inter-war years, U.S. communications policy was shaped mainly by the military services, and particularly by the navy. Their concern was to encourage a robust domestic industry, both in manufacturing and services, as a strategic resource which would eventually match the superior facilities of European firms. The navy played a discrete but direct role in creating the Radio Corporation of America (RCA). Internationally, AT&T and other American communications companies were encouraged to extend their cross-border networks, particularly into Latin America. Although the State Department provided some support in negotiating these arrangements, its role continued to be distinctly subordinate to that of the military.

As the threat of a European war increased, this marginalization of civilian diplomacy continued. In the late 1930s, the State Department was represented on a new Defense Communications Board, headed by a Federal Communications Commission (FCC) official. The board, dominated by the military, established policies and recommended actions which resulted in the massive global networks supporting U.S. troop and naval operations after the attack on Pearl Harbor.[6] These networks were the first large-scale projection of American electronic communications power on a global scale, replacing previously dominant European resources, most of which were destroyed or disabled in combat operations.

The State Department continued to play a relatively minor role in the events surrounding this wartime expansion. Its primary involvement in communications issues at the time took place in another area—countering the propaganda offensive of the Axis powers. It was the beginning of an important aspect of modern electronic diplomacy, namely the use of radio broadcasting and other electronic technologies to influence public opinion at home and abroad—what is known today, somewhat benignly, as public diplomacy.

Begun on a small scale in the late 1930s, the department's activities in this area were expanded to the point that, by the end of the war in 1945, it was in charge of the largest network of global information resources seen until that time, including Voice of America shortwave radio. As such, these World War II efforts, and those that followed during the cold war, are an important part of this survey of digital diplomacy.

The beginnings of the State Department's involvement in overseas information programs can be traced back to the late 1930s. At the time, there was increasing evidence of a successful German propaganda effort targeted at Latin American audiences. Berlin's purpose was to undermine support for Britain and the other West European democracies.[7] The Roosevelt administration faced a dilemma in dealing with this threat within a domestic strategy of appearing neutral in the European conflict.[8]

The result was a convoluted set of policies and actions designed to accommodate both domestic and international policy interests. In November 1940, the White House authorized a planning committee, headed by Secretary of the Interior Harold Ickes, to develop an information strategy for dealing with public opinion as the United States moved closer to involvement in the European war. The State Department was represented on the committee, but the emphasis was on domestic programs. The group's primary accomplishment was to propose a pragmatic division between domestic and international information activities. Domestic programs were assigned to an Office of Civil Defense, headed by New York Mayor Fiorello La Guardia.[9]

Setting up a bureaucratic framework for overseas information activities was more complicated. As early as 1938, the State Department had created a Division of Cultural Cooperation, primarily to support the Roosevelt "good neighbor" policy in Latin America. The division's main project was to create binational cultural institutes throughout the region.[10]

This initial effort at public diplomacy was soon to be expanded dramatically by a Washington newcomer, Nelson A. Rockefeller. Young, rich and well-connected in the Eastern establishment, Rockefeller had made a name for himself as president of Rockefeller Center. He also had political ambitions, focussed on Latin America, where he had established business ventures. Rockefeller combined these interests in a campaign to change what he regarded as the government's inadequate response to the German threat in Latin America. He lobbied successfully for the creation of a semi-autonomous organization within the State Department— the office of the Coordinator for Inter-American Affairs (CIAA).[11]

Not surprisingly, the coordinator was Nelson Rockefeller. He proceeded to organize economic, information and cultural programs designed to strengthen American (and indirectly Allied) influence south of the border. The CIAA was the department's first significant experience with overseas information and cultural programs. The new organization became involved in electronic operations when it contracted with two radio networks, NBC and CBS, to beam shortwave news broadcasts to Latin America.[12] Meanwhile, department officials were put off by such Rockefeller-inspired projects as an Orson Welles film about a Brazilian carnival, Disney cartoons, and expansion of the shortwave news to include entertainment programs.

The department also became more involved with information operations on the domestic front. This was prompted by the need to promote President Roosevelt's ambiguous policies on the widening European war to the American public. The department's domestic public information activities at the time were minimal, consisting largely of Secretary of State Cordell Hull's daily informal meeting with a few newspaper reporters who covered foreign policy developments.[13] As the threat of U.S. involvement in the war increased, department officials saw the need for a more structured media program, one that would recognize, in particular, the growing role of radio stations as news outlets.[14]

Planning was begun to expand the State Department's domestic information operations. Among other proposals, the department's press chief, Michael McDermott, recommended in October 1941 consolidating these activities into what he called "an American version of a Ministry of Information," headed by a cabinet-rank chairman. The proposal was forwarded to the White House where it was tartly dismissed by President Roosevelt as "an impossible suggestion."[15]

The attack on Pearl Harbor changed all this. After some organizational confusion, most public information activities, both domestic and overseas, were assigned to an Office of War Information (OWI) in June 1942. Covert psychological warfare operations were lodged in the Office of Strategic Services (OSS), the forerunner of the Central Intelligence Agency. A crash program to build a global shortwave radio network, the Voice of America, was undertaken under OWI direction. In this and other mass media efforts, OWI bureaucratized the public diplomacy function in American foreign relations.

A War Information Board was created to coordinate these activities, with representation from the State Department, the military and the

OWI. Meanwhile, the OWI was nominally independent of the State Department, except for a loosely written requirement to abide by the department's guidance in materials prepared for overseas audiences. The OWI's reliance on such guidance was fitful at best. Mistakes were made, some of them serious. The most famous example of this was the Voice of America's 1943 characterization of Italy's King Victor Emmanual III as a moronic little king just as the Allies were conducting sensitive surrender negotiations, including the future status of the Italian monarchy.[16] Despite such gaffs, the OWI succeeded in reaching out to foreign audiences through a variety of media programs, from Voice of America news to propaganda messages on matchbook covers airdropped into enemy territory. The agency relied heavily on American advertising techniques, which attracted attention, primarily because its audiences were curious about a far-off country and its role in the war.[17] The United States government ended the war with a formidable collection of overseas information resources—including a global radio network and local offices (the United States Information Service) in over 20 countries.

As with most wartime projects, there was strong pressure to dismantle these facilities after the defeat of Japan in August 1945. The OWI was a particular target. Plans were drawn up for closing down its overseas operations. They were soon changed. Faced with Soviet expansionist pressures, Washington slowly recognized the need for continuing its overseas information programs, redirecting them to counteract Soviet propaganda. At another level, World War II dramatically transformed America's standing in global communications. The United States emerged from the war as the unchallenged telecommunications power. Its base was the worldwide military network built by the Army Signal Corps and the navy, with extensive help from AT&T. The prewar networks controlled by European countries had meanwhile suffered heavy damage in the hostilities.

European dominance had been further reduced in 1943 when Washington pressured the British government to end the practice of routing all wireless messages to its colonies via London—a wartime measure that was extended after the Japanese surrender.[18] This action was a critical factor in opening up the postwar communications market overseas for American telephone and cable companies.

The expansion of American global communications influence in the early postwar years had a limited effect on the State Department's involvement in communications issues. Policy control remained largely in the hands of the newly created Department of Defense, whose interest was in preserving and expanding its new global networking capabilities. Within the State Department, communications issues were handled by a small office in the economics bureau. Its primary function was as a liaison with the International Telecommunications Union (ITU), successor to the International Telegraph Union. The ITU became a United Nations specialized agency in 1947.[19] Before the war, the organization had been an old boy's club, controlled by the United States and other industrial powers through weighted-voting rules. Its primary mission was to assure the orderly management of the radio spectrum, the basic resource for electronic communications.

The prospect of accelerated expansion of global networks after 1945, stimulated by wartime advances in communications technologies, called for changes in the way the ITU operated. The United States took the lead in organizing four consecutive conferences to reorganize the ITU and its activities in the late 1940s.[20] It was, among other outcomes, the beginning of a tangled relationship within the ITU, involving the United States as the dominant communications power and other ITU members, notably the more than one hundred newly independent countries that joined the organization in the postwar decades.

Meanwhile, the State Department found itself deeply involved in the bureaucratic struggle over the future of the Office of War Information. Proposals to extend its activities ran up against congressional pressures to close down all civilian wartime programs. In the OWI's case, this attitude was reinforced by Republican suspicions that the agency was a haven for left-wing liberals or, at the very least, Democrats.[21] Within the State Department, many officials, irritated by the OWI's free-wheeling practices, hoped to get rid of the agency. The exception was Nelson Rockefeller, who lobbied for a permanent peacetime information operation as early as 1943.[22]

The OWI's overseas operations, although severely curtailed, were given a reprieve—and a new home. Within weeks after the Japanese surrender, President Truman signed an executive order transferring the OWI to the State Department as the International Information Administration (ITA). The order also called for a study of the future of overseas information operations.

For the first time, the State Department found itself directly managing a global information operation. A new bureau was created to handle these responsibilities. The bureau, initially headed by poet Archibald MacLeish, included two separate divisions—one for administering the remnants of the OWI's wartime operations and the other for dealing with the department's domestic information programs.

The latter effort had expanded rapidly in the war years. As hostilities wound down, department officials saw the need for a more structured public affairs effort aimed at gaining domestic support for postwar policy changes.[23] Late in the war, Secretary Edward Stettinius ordered a special effort to allay domestic suspicions about plans for a United Nations organization. Department officers were assigned to do radio interviews and to make speeches supporting the proposed organization.

Two million copies of a pamphlet about the United Nations were distributed—an unprecedented move for the department at the time.[24]

Meanwhile, department officials were uncomfortable with their new responsibilities for overseas information and cultural programs. Their unease was confirmed when they found themselves embroiled in a dispute over a cultural exhibition in Paris. The event was part of a festival organized around the inaugural meeting of the new United Nations Educational, Scientific and Cultural Organization (UNESCO).

The U.S. contribution to the festival was an exhibit, "Advancing American Art," consisting of modern paintings bought with leftover OWI funds. The exhibit was well received by critics at a preliminary showing at New York's Metropolitan Museum of Art. By the time it had opened in Paris, however, the exhibit had become subject to a barrage of criticism by some American media organizations, led by the right-wing Hearst newspapers. Their criticisms focussed on allegations that the paintings portrayed a decadent America.

The department's sponsorship of the paintings was not helped by President Truman's off-the-cuff remark about the paintings. "If that's art," he declared, "then I'm a Hottentot." Congressional critics chimed in with equally caustic comments. One congressman described the paintings as "Communist caricatures . . . sent out to mislead the rest of the world of what America is like." A senator suggested that the department's art programs should stick to images of George Washington and Abraham Lincoln.[25] The Paris art show controversy soon blew over, but it was a forerunner of a more serious assault on alleged subversion in the State Department by Senator Joseph McCarthy a few years later.

Meanwhile, the new International Information Administration, cobbled together from the remnants of the wartime OWI, began its uneasy existence inside the State Department.[26] In personnel terms, IIA was the department's largest single operation at the time. However, its annual budget had been drastically reduced by a Congress suspicious of a peacetime propaganda agency. The IIA's integration into the State Department did little to add a public diplomacy component to overall policy planning. Its influence in the department's policy counsels remained weak.

Despite these organizational handicaps, IIA operations were sustained by two postwar imperatives. The first was the need to conduct what became known as democratization programs in occupied Germany and Japan. The programs' aims were to counter the lingering influence of totalitarian attitudes and practices in both countries, primarily through the introduction of a free press and other democratic resources. IIA officers worked closely with occupation authorities in Germany and Japan, using a full range of mass media to influence public attitudes. Although the process was one of trial and error, these efforts laid the groundwork for the development of free media institutions in both occupied countries.[27]

The second event which gave renewed prominence to the IIA's overseas operations was the challenge to American security interests by the forcible incorporation of East European nations into the Soviet orbit. The shift from an uneasy wartime partnership with the Soviet Union to a so-called cold war soon dominated every aspect of American foreign policy. Although the cold war's primary emphasis was on military confrontation, the American response to the Soviet challenge also involved a large component of what can be described as communications warfare.

It was an unequal contest. As noted earlier, the United States emerged from World War II as the leading global communications power. The Soviet Union was an also-ran. Although it expanded its telecommunications facilities significantly during the cold war years, Moscow never caught up with the West. Soviet communications warfare strategy was narrowly conceived, limited largely to psychological warfare operations. As we shall see throughout this survey, Western, and particularly American, strategies had a wider focus, including the need to remain on the technological cutting edge in developing advanced electronic communications and information facilities on a worldwide basis.

Electronic facilities played a major role in both American and Soviet propaganda efforts, beginning with shortwave radio and later expanding to include satellites, computers and other technologies. This development turned electronic resources into political weapons on a scale never before attempted. As such, this aspect of the 40-year cold war has a distinct role in the evolution of American digital diplomacy.

The Soviet leadership had the advantage of a well-honed doctrine of political communications. In the early 1920s, V. I. Lenin recognized the value of the then-new technology of radio broadcasting as an organizing weapon, describing it as newspapers without walls. Before he died in 1922, he ordered the construction of radio stations throughout the country.[28] The USSR later pioneered transborder shortwave broadcasting; by the end of World War II, Radio Moscow had a global presence. The station accounted for a considerable portion of the country's estimated $1.4 billion propaganda budget in the late 1940s.[29]

Slowly, then swiftly, the American government reacted to this Soviet challenge. In 1948 Congress passed legislation, known as the Smith-Mundt Act, which authorized permanent overseas information and cultural programs as an element of American foreign policy. The bill's emphasis was on activities which provided "a full and fair picture of the United States" to overseas audiences, a curiously bland mandate at a time when U.S. policy was increasingly focussed on a militant response to Soviet propaganda operations.[30]

The White House later took a tougher stance. In April 1950, President

Truman announced a "Campaign of Truth" to counter the Soviet propaganda offensive.[31] Its most immediate effect was to increase support for the State Department's International Information Administration programs. The unit's annual budget was raised to $121 million, a six-fold increase over previous years. These changes raised both the IIA's visibility and the effectiveness of its information programs abroad. VOA radio programming was expanded to over 40 languages. U.S. Information Service offices and libraries were opened in dozens of new countries, particularly in Asia and Africa.

Meanwhile, State Department officials were more focussed on another role for information operations in foreign policy. It was their use as a resource in covert psychological operations against the Soviet Union. This activity had its origins in World War II experience with so-called "black propaganda" operations designed to undermine enemy morale. The OSS and military "psywar" units were generally successful in using clandestine radio broadcasts, attributed to the enemy, to spread false rumors.[32]

In the late 1940s, there was renewed interest in adapting psywar techniques to cold war needs. This interest was fed by a spate of academic studies that proposed formulas for scientifically infuencing mass opinion. Research units at MIT, Harvard and Columbia prepared specific scenarios to exploit Soviet psychological vulnerabilities.[33]

Within the government, interest in this subject coincided with the reorganization of the foreign policy structure in the National Security Act of 1947, which created the National Security Council (NSC) at the White House level. There was no mention of psychological warfare or propaganda in the legislation. However, it contained catchall language authorizing "functions and duties . . . affecting the national security."[34] This was a big enough loophole to accommodate psywar advocates and their proposals. A few months after it was organized, the NSC took steps to deal with what it called "the vicious psychological effects of the USSR to undermine U.S. national security."[35] A "Special Procedures Group" within the CIA was assigned the task of developing an action plan.

The State Department was deeply involved in establishing both the doctrinal and operational underpinnings for the project. State's role was largely defined by George Kennan, the first head of the department's newly formed Policy Planning Staff. Kennan's interest in the subject drew from his general proposals on how to deal with the postwar Soviet Union, famously outlined in his "X" article, "The sources of Soviet conduct" in the July 1947 issue of *Foreign Affairs*.

Kennan's views have usually been summarized as advocating containment of Soviet expansion, an essentially defensive approach. But the "X" article saw drawing the line on Moscow's aggressive moves as only the first stage of a longer-range strategy. Kennan proposed a second stage in which the pull of Western cultural and economic forces would undermine Soviet domination of Eastern Europe. Dissension and unrest would follow, forcing Moscow to modify its international behavior or face internal collapse.

Kennan expanded this second-stage theme in a December 1947 lecture at the National War College. He cited the Marshall Plan, then being debated in Congress, as part of an overall strategy that could lead to the liberation of Eastern Europe. He then outlined a scenario for a "psychological dissolution of Soviet power" in Poland and other satellites through the establishment of what he called a "salient of free political institutions in the region."[36]

Kennan did not mention psychological warfare specifically as part of his scenario, but he was clearly seized with the prospect. Moreover, as head of the Policy Planning Staff (PPS), he had a bureaucratic base for carrying out his ideas. Two months after the War College lecture, the PPS staff made its initial recommendation that covert actions, including information programs, be extended to Eastern Europe. Among other proposals, it suggested recruitment of Soviet-bloc refugees for "political-psychological operations," organized in part through "freedom committees" in the West.

The proposed psywar campaign put heavy emphasis on radio broadcasting. Planning began for a network of stations which would be allegedly supported by contributions from the American public. By 1950, two Munich-based networks, Radio Free Europe and Radio Liberation, clandestinely funded and run by the CIA, were broadcasting respectively into Eastern Europe and the Soviet Union.[37] The two radio networks attracted large audiences, making them the most successful of the psychological operation plans advanced by Kennan and others in the late 1940s. There were other projects, most of them impractical or preposterous—including the sending of small helium-filled balloons into Eastern Europe carrying liberation messages.[38]

The general ineffectiveness of most of the early psywar operations was due, in part, to dissension among the Washington agencies over who would control the operation. The result was a bureaucratic tug-of-war involving the State Department, the CIA and the military. The outcome was a compromise, brokered at the National Security Council. An Office of Special Projects was established at the CIA with a State officer, Frank Wisner, a close Kennan associate, as director.[39]

For the time being, the department's policy planning staff was in control of covert psywar plans and operations, with a veto power over projects. It was to be, in Kennan's phrase, a directorate of political warfare.[40] This arrangement soon broke down. The CIA had superior assets, including the funds, to mount its own operations. Moreover, Kennan's incursions into psychological operations did not sit well with many State

officials. This attitude emerged more strongly after Dean Acheson became secretary of state in January 1949.

George Kennan's emphasis on a long-range political strategy ran
counter to the new secretary's hard-line containment policies, including
a military buildup along the ideological faultline separating Western and
Eastern Europe. As a leading architect of the NATO alliance, Acheson
established a permanent U.S. military presence in Europe, along with a
rearmed West Germany as the fulcrum of a structure to maintain Western unity and contain Soviet expansionism.[41] Kennan saw this as the
militarization of American policy. He left the department a year later to
take up an appointment at Princeton's Institute for Advanced Study.[42]
His later writings reflected his struggle to resolve his dual role as both
an architect and critic of cold war strategy.

Secretary Acheson's strategic vision was summarized in the most important statement of U.S. policy goals in the early cold war era—the
National Security Council's NSC-68.[43] It called for a massive mobilization
of U.S. military power to match Soviet efforts. It also outlined a more
aggressive political warfare strategy, including information operations.
The aim, the document declared, was "the intensification of affirmative
and timely measures and operations by covert means in the fields of
economic warfare and political and psychological warfare with a view
to fomenting and supporting unrest and revolt in selected strategic satellite countries."[44]

NSC-68 endorsed the creation of a Psychological Strategy Board to
coordinate psywar operations. The board proceeded to develop an operations strategy for covert operations. After eight months of examining
the options, it concluded that there were no quick-fix solutions to ending
Soviet aggressive policies and actions. The board suggested a more mod-
erate long-range psyops plan to counter Soviet aggressiveness.[45]

This approach did not satisfy the administration's foreign policy critics. As historian Arthur Schlesinger, Jr. noted at the time:

For the Truman Administration, psychological warfare was essentially an auxiliary weapon—auxiliary both to diplomatic policy and to military power. But
to an increasingly vocal minority during the last years of the Truman administration, psychological warfare came to be seen as an independent weapon, powerful in its own right, whose uninhibited use could take the place of diplomacy
and rearmament and change the whole atmosphere of the cold war.[46]

The challenge came primarily from the Republican party, anxious to
recapture the White House in the 1952 presidential election after 20 years
in the political wilderness. Party leaders accused the Truman administration of being "soft" in reacting to Soviet aggression. Led by the party's
chief international adviser, John Foster Dulles, the Republicans advo-

cated a "rollback" strategy, including military pressure aimed at forcing a Soviet retreat from Eastern Europe.

Once in office, the Eisenhower administration reviewed the options for implementing its election campaign promises of a muscular liberation strategy. Dulles, the new secretary of state, set the tone for the new policy. "Surely what they can accomplish, we can accomplish," he announced. "Surely if they can use moral and psychological force, we can use it."[47] A week after his inauguration, the new president appointed a Committee on International Information Activities, headed by William H. Jackson, a former CIA deputy director. Time Inc. executive C. D. Jackson was named a presidential assistant to deal with psywar activities.

The administration's first psywar challenge took place a month later, following the death of Josef Stalin. This event, which had been anticipated for over a year, led to expectations that there would be a succession struggle within the Kremlin, which could be exploited in ways that would weaken overall Soviet power. The succession struggle took place but U.S. efforts to exploit it never materialized. White House public reaction to the event was limited largely to an ambiguous presidential statement to the Soviet people, suggesting that they put their faith in God and in an "abiding political system." It was not a message designed to send disaffected Soviet citizens into the streets calling for an end to Communist rule. In Washington, discretion, based on imperfect information about the succession struggle, had ruled out militant calls for liberation.

Similar cautions limited most other psywar operations. The high-water mark in the use of electronic resources in the liberation crusade occurred during the uprising of East German workers against their Soviet-installed rulers in June 1953. It began as a strike by construction workers protesting stringent new work rules. Although the offending rules were quickly cancelled, the demonstrations spread to hundreds of towns and villages.

In Washington, the Psychological Strategy Board informed the president that the event created "the greatest opportunity for initiating effective policies to help role back Soviet power that has yet come to light."[48] Proposals were drawn up for covert operations designed to encourage the protesters, including the use of balloons to distribute leaflets in Soviet-occupied territories. Most of the plans were eventually shelved, as higher political priorities, notably the pending integration of West German armed forces into NATO, dictated restraint.

The one success in influencing the East German uprising involved a U.S. government radio station in Berlin—RIAS, Radio in the American Sector. RIAS broadcasts had strong credibility among the East Germans during the tense weeks of confrontation, informing them of what was happening and, eventually, letting them know that the West would not intervene in the uprising.[49]

Meanwhile in Washington, plans were under way to reorganize the State Department's international information programs. These proposals reflected Secretary Dulles' intention to reduce the department's size in ways that would focus its operations on what he regarded as its traditional diplomatic functions. In particular, he wanted to move the International Information Administration out from under the department's jurisdiction. It also marked his general disdain for international public opinion as a factor in foreign policy.[50] Dulles summarily dismissed the IIA's director, Wilson Compton, a distinguished academic and a Republican who had been appointed by Dean Acheson to shore up the department's bipartisan image.

The job of managing the IIA's departure from the department was assigned to Compton's successor, Robert L. Johnson, president of Temple University and a certified Republican conservative. Johnson's task was complicated by the Senate investigation into alleged subversive activities in the department, led by Senator Joseph McCarthy, Republican from Wisconsin. He had begun his investigation several years earlier with charges that 205 department employees were Communists.

By the spring of 1953, McCarthy had shifted his search for subversion in the department to the IIA's information programs. This included allegations that U.S. Information Service libraries abroad included books by Communist authors. The department responded by issuing a directive prohibiting books by "Communists, fellow travellers, etc." in the libraries. It then faced the job of identifying Communists (as well as fellow travelers and "etc.") among the authors of the library system's 2 million volumes, plus those who wrote the 3,000 new books ordered every month.[51] The department's task was not helped by an offhand press conference remark by President Eisenhower that he would have left the works of one of the banned writers, left-wing novelist Dashiell Hammett, on the shelves.

The circus-like McCarthy hearings wound down slowly in the summer of 1953, ending with a Senate censure of McCarthy several months later. Meanwhile, the reorganization of overseas information operations continued. On June 1, the White House announced a plan for shifting the IIA information program to an independent U.S. Information Agency (USIA). The department's role was reduced to providing policy guidance for the new agency. The IIA's cultural and exchange operations were turned over to a newly organized cultural affairs bureau in State.[52] The USIA had the advantage of strong congressional support, including a report by the Senate Foreign Relations Committtee that the needs of an effective information program "could hardly be met within the confines of a cautious, tradition-bound, bureaucratic foreign office."[53]

Meanwhile, at the White House, the Jackson Committee issued its assessment of psychological warfare options. Its conclusions signaled a retreat from the Eisenhower administration's previous assumptions about psywar's role in foreign policy. The Jackson report called for the abolition of the Psychological Strategy Board, and added this sobering note:

"Cold war" and "psychological warfare" are unfortunate terms. . . . In reality there is a "psychological" aspect or implication to every diplomatic, economic or military policy and action.

This implication should receive more careful attention both in the planning and execution state of policy, but not to the exclusion of other vital factors. Except for propaganda, there are no "psychological warfare" instruments distinct from traditional instruments of policy.[54]

The Jackson report's recommendations defined the general tone and organization of U.S. strategic information policy throughout the cold war period. The more strident aspects of psywar operations in countering Soviet power were quietly dropped. The CIA was given responsibility for covert operations, with loose supervision by the National Security Council.[55] Meanwhile, USIA expanded its overseas public programs, with particular attention to establishing a presence in over 75 newly independent countries in Asia, Africa and the Middle East. The ability of its radio operation, the Voice of America, to reach audiences in these regions was enhanced by the construction of powerful relay transmitters in Greece, Liberia, Thailand and the Philippines.

With the stabilization of these cold war information programs, the focus of digital diplomacy shifted to other issues in the late 1950s. In large part this was the result of technological breakthroughs that made possible a major expansion of global communications. One such innovation involved raising the capacity of telecommunications cables. For over a century these cables had been limited largely to transmitting telegraphic messages. By 1950, this capability had been dramatically upgraded by the introduction of coaxial submarine cables which could handle telephone and television traffic. The new technology had a special impact on international communications. The first long-distance submarine cable for overseas phone calls went into operation in the North Atlantic in 1956, followed quickly by a transpacific cable. Both cables were heavily used from the beginning for business communications, giving American corporations an important new tool for managing their expanding overseas operations.[56]

At the time, the new submarine cables represented a relatively minor policy concern for the State Department. The primary responsibility for authorizing the cables lay with the Federal Communications Commission as an extension of its regulatory oversight of domestic networks. All of the early ocean cables were operated by AT&T as joint ventures with foreign telecommunications monopolies.

By the early 1960s, the State Department's involvement in digital diplomacy issues became more complex with the launching of the first communications satellites ("comsats"). Three satellites, floating 22,000 miles in space, could provide voice, data and television services to every part of the earth. Building and operating a global network to deliver such services required a degree of political, economic and technical cooperation on a scale never before attempted in international diplomacy. A major barrier was the tangle of regulatory laws that governed communications in all countries. Who would finance and build the network? Who would own and operate it?

The United States held the key to resolving these questions. It had a virtual monopoly over comsat technology. It was also the only country with the economic resources to build the network. Moreover, Washington had a strong political motive for undertaking the project. Intelligence reports at the time indicated that Soviet research labs would soon be able to match American comsat technology. A USSR-sponsored satellite network would be a stunning political achievement, with potentially greater psychological impact than the 1957 launching of Sputnik, the first earth-circling satellite. This prospect was a critical element in Washington's decision to build an American-sponsored comsat network as quickly as possible.

The project represented a coming of age for U.S. digital diplomacy. Before the comsats, communications policy had been a low-level concern, limited largely to occasional bilateral dealings with individual countries. The satellites called for a new approach: a global policy that involved political, economic and technical negotiations across the board.

As we shall see in the next chapter, this exercise in digital diplomacy stretched out over 10 years. In the end, it was successful, not only in creating a global network but also in confirming America's position as the preeminent communications power.

NOTES

1. J. Gregory Sidak, *Foreign investment in American telecommunications* (Chicago: University of Chicago Press, 1997), pp. 9–10.

2. William Pletcher and Nicholas Jequier, *The diplomacy of trade and investments: American economic expansion in the hemisphere 1865–1900* (Columbia: University of Missouri Press, 1998).

3. Daniel R. Headrick, *The invisible weapon: Telecommunications and international politics 1851–1945* (New York: Oxford University Press, 1991), pp. 119–121.

4. Sidak, op cit., p. 17.

5. Headrick, op cit. pp. 174–176.

6. Headrick, op cit., pp. 261–263.

7. Clayton D. Laurie, *The propaganda warriors: America's crusade against Nazi Germany* (Lawrence: University Press of Kansas, 1996), pp. 45–66.

8. Richard W. Steele, *Propaganda in an open society: The Roosevelt administration and the media 1933–1940* (Westport, CT: Greenwood Press, 1985).

9. Laurie, op cit., p. 52.

10. Frank A. Ninkovich, *The diplomacy of ideas: U.S. foreign policy and cultural relations 1938–1950* (New York: Cambridge University Press, 1981), pp. 24–34.

11. Cary Reich, *The life and times of Nelson A. Rockefeller: Worlds to conquer 1908–1958* (New York: Doubleday, 1996), pp. 189–209.

12. Charles A. H. Thomson, *Overseas information services of the United States government* (Washington, DC: Brookings Institution, 1948), pp. 24–34. See also: Ninkovich, op cit., pp. 24–34.

13. "How Cordell Hull handled the press when he was 'at home'," *State Magazine*, May 1987, pp. 28–29.

14. Nancy T. Bernhard, "Clearer than truth," *Diplomatic History*, Vol. 21, No. 4, Fall 1997, pp. 545–547.

15. Memorandum for the Secretary of State. Box 4619, Executive papers, Franklin D. Roosevelt Library, Hyde Park, NY. For other efforts to develop domestic information programs, see: Richard W. Steele, "Preparing the public for war: Efforts to establish national propaganda agency 1940–41," *American Historical Review*, October 1970, pp. 1640–1653.

16. Holly Cowan Shulman, *The Voice of America: Propaganda and democracy 1941–1945* (Madison: University of Wisconsin Press, 1990), p. 100.

17. Alan M. Winkler, *The politics of propaganda: The Office of War Information 1942–1945* (New Haven, CT: Yale University Press, 1978).

18. Headrick, op cit., p. 264.

19. George A. Codding, Jr. and Anthony M. Rutkowski, *The International Telecommunications Union in a changing world* (Dedham MA: Artech House, 1982), p. 29.

20. Ibid., pp. 18–26.

21. Winkler, op cit., pp. 65–68.

22. Thomson, op cit., p. 195.

23. Bernhard, op cit., pp. 551–559.

24. Jonathan Soffer, "All for one or all for all," *Diplomatic History*, Vol. 21, No. 1, Winter 1997, pp. 52–53.

25. Frank Ninkovich, "The currents of cultural diplomacy: Art and the State Department 1938–1947," *Diplomatic History*, Vol. 1, No. 3, Summer 1976, p. 228.

26. Edward Barrett, *Truth is our weapon* (New York: Funk & Wagnalls, 1953). Barrett replaced Archibald MacLeish as assistant secretary for public affairs, a post which included supervision of IIA programs.

27. For a latter-day assessment of the democratization program in Germany, see: "The American occupation of Germany in cultural perspective: A roundtable," *Diplomatic History*, Vol. 23, No. 1, Winter 1999, pp. 1–77.

28. For a description of early Soviet propaganda efforts, see: Peter Kenez, *The birth of the propaganda state: Soviet methods of mass mobilization 1917–1929* (New York: Cambridge University Press, 1985).

29. The figure is cited in *Overseas information programs of the United States*, Re-

port No. 406, Senate Committee on Foreign Relations, 83rd Congress, 1st Session, 15 June 1953, p. 2.

30. Public Law 402, 22 USC 1431–1442. For the text of this and other early congressional legislation and executive branch documents affecting overseas information programs, see: *Legislation on foreign relations through 1977*, Vol. 1, Current legislation and related executive orders, Joint publication of the House Committee on International Relations and the Senate committee on Foreign Relations, February 1978, pp. 679–751.

31. Truman made his Campaign of Truth proposal in a speech to the American Society of Newspaper Editors on 20 April 1950 in Washington. The proposal's genesis is described in Barrett, op cit., chap. 6.

32. Sefton Delmar, *Black boomerang: Black radio operations in World War II* (London: Secher & Warburg, 1962).

33. These efforts are described in Gregory P. Mitrovich, *Undermining the Kremlin: America's strategy for subverting the Soviet bloc 1947–1950* (Ithaca, NY: Cornell University Press, 2000), pp. 117–120.

34. Section 102 (d) (5), National Security Act of 1997.

35. National Security Council Directive 4-a, 17 December 1947.

36. Giles D. Harlow and George C. Maerz (eds.), *Measures short of war: The George F. Kennan lectures at the National War College* (Washington, DC: National Defense University Press, 1991), p. 309.

37. Michael Nelson, *War of the black heavens: The battles of Western broadcasting in the cold war* (Syracuse, NY: Syracuse University Press, 1997).

38. Edward P. Lilly, "The development of American psychological operations 1949–1951," in *Declassified documents reference systems*, Vol. 1 (Washington, DC: Carrollton Press, 1989).

39. National Security Council directive on Office of Special Projects (NSC10/2), 19 June 1948.

40. This concept was outlined in a planning staff paper, "The inauguration of organized political warfare," 30 April 1948.

41. James Chace, *Acheson* (New York: Simon & Schuster, 1998), pp. 200–202.

42. Kennan's overall role in the formation of early cold war policies is documented in Wilson D. Miscamble, *George F. Kennan and the making of American foreign policy 1947–1950* (Princeton, NJ: Princeton University Press, 1992).

43. National Security Council directive NSC-68, *Foreign Relations of the United States*, 1950, Vol. 1, pp. 237–290. See also: Paul Nitze, "The development of NSC-68," *International Security*, Spring 1980, pp. 170–176.

44. NSC-68, op cit.

45. Samuel Wells, Jr., "Sounding the tocsin: NSC-68 and the Soviet threat," *International Security*, No. 4, Fall 1979, pp. 116–158.

46. Arthur Schlesinger, Jr., "Psychological warfare: Can it sell freedom?" *The Reporter*, 31 March 1953, p. 9. See also: Monteagle Stearns, "Democratic diplomacy and the role of propaganda," *Foreign Service Journal*, October 1953, pp. 24–25.

47. Quoted in Schlesinger, op cit., p. 9.

48. "Interim U.S. psychological strategy plan for exploitation of unrest in satellite Europe," PSBD-45, Psychological Strategy Board, 1 July 1953.

49. For a useful summary of American information operations during the East

German uprising, see: Christian F. Ostermann, " 'Keep the pot simmering': The United States and the East German uprising of 1953," *German Studies Review*, Vol. 19, No. 1, February 1996, pp. 61–89. See also: Edmund Taylor, "RIAS: The voice East Germans believe," *The Reporter*, 10 November 1953, pp. 22–32.

50. See, for instance, his views on this subject in a discussion with Abbott Washburn and Henry Loomis, staff officers on the Jackson committee in a meeting with Dulles. Loomis interview, Foreign Service Oral History Project, 25 February 1989.

51. "Order bars Reds' works on 'Voice'," *Washington Post*, 20 February 1953, p. 1.

52. White House Reorganization Plan No. 8, 22 U.S.C. 1461, 1 June 1953.

53. *Overseas information programs of the United States*, op cit., p. 8.

54. White House press statement on the report, 8 June 1953, p. 2. The full report was never made public.

55. There is a large and growing literature on the CIA's cold war psyops activities, including the use of front organizations, subsidized publications and radio broadcasting. For a useful survey of the agency's covert activities in the early cold war years, see: Trevor Barnes, "The secret cold war: The CIA and American foreign policy in Europe 1946–1956," *The Historical Journal* (London), Vol. 24, No. 2, 1981, pp. 399–415.

56. For the early history of the coaxial submarine cables, see: Arthur C. Clarke, *Voices across the sea* (London: William Luscombe Publishers, 1958).

Chapter 3

Communications Satellites: The Policy Challenge

On a hot summer night in 1962, millions of Americans were watching a run-of-the-channel CBS television drama about a Scotland Yard detective when an announcer broke in: "We interrupt this program. . . . The British are ready to bounce a program off Telstar."

On their screens viewers saw an unpretentious communications control room with three men seated at a plain table. Without introduction, one of them spoke up: "On my right is that dour Scot, Robert White," and, as he waved his hand towards the other man, "John Bray, who is in charge of our planning in the space field. . . . It is half-past-three in the morning. Good luck."

On this understated note, the first experiment in intercontinental communications by space satellite ended. The video images were being transmitted from the Goonhilly Downs space antenna in the south of England to a similar antenna in Andover, Maine and then relayed to the CBS network. It was the beginning of an enterprise that has since transformed the technology, economics and politics of global communications.

Telstar was the first active-repeater satellite, one that could provide reliable voice, data and video messages between two points on earth. It was a primitive machine, a "comsat" capable of handling only 60 simultaneous phone conversations or one television transmission. The Andover earth station weighed 380 tons and was 177 feet long. Thirty years later, international satellites were routinely capable of transmitting over 100,000 phone calls and dozens of TV transmissions into antennas as small as a pie plate. Developed by AT&T's Bell Laboratories, Telstar was the first success in a wide-ranging American research and development effort in the 1950s to exploit the prospects of space communications. The effort was so intense that, within three years after the first Telstar launch, its technology was obsolete, overtaken by more efficient machines.[1]

Before Telstar, international communications was a cautious business, involving the slow expansion of earthbound networks. In the century after the invention of the telegraph and telephone, these networks served less than 10 percent of the world's population. There were few political and economic incentives to speed up this pace. In most countries, communications networks were government monopolies. The major exception was the United States, where AT&T was comfortably entrenched as the congressionally mandated national network, linking its own local Bell systems and over 1,000 small private phone companies. Because of the efficiencies of this private sector arrangement, the United States accounted for over half of the world's telephone traffic in the 1960s.

Despite its technical limitations, Telstar created a new set of political and economic issues for the United States and other countries. Its technology promised a revolution in global communications that required a high degree of international cooperation. There was, moreover, a sense of urgency about dealing with this prospect. Telstar showed that the technology worked. Furthermore, it was evident that the network it promised could not be built piecemeal. It had been planned as a worldwide system from the start.[2]

The prospect of such a system was a critical turning point in the evolution of American digital diplomacy, both in the issues it dealt with and in its operational methods. Previously, as we have seen, telecommunications and information issues were minor concerns in U.S. foreign policy. They were largely episodic, reflecting the wide independence that American corporations had in building and managing their overseas networks. These arrangements were handled in bilateral agreements with government-controlled networks in other countries. After the first Telstar satellite was launched, most communications experts assumed that this pattern would hold for American satellite networks, namely that they would be built and operated privately, with little if any U.S. government involvement.

This did not happen, for reasons that explain why satellites opened up a new era in digital diplomacy. The American government had a strategic stake in decisions on how a global comsat network would be organized and operated. Satellite technology was heavily dependent on government resources—from research laboratories to NASA's rockets and launching facilities. The Department of Defense had an active space program, exploring the military uses of satellites for surveillance and communications, beginning with a U.S. Navy study in 1945.[3]

Despite AT&T's heavy involvement in satellite development, there were compelling political and legal obstacles (including antitrust restrictions) in any plan either for giving the company exclusive control over an American-built comsat network or for creating a consortium of U.S. companies to do the job. It soon became clear that the traditional pattern of bilateral agreements between American communications firms and their overseas counterparts would not work.

The prospect of creating a global network also had cold war implications. Five years before Telstar went into orbit, the Soviet Union had established itself in world opinion as the space technology leader with its success in launching Sputnik, the first man-made object orbited in space. Although the United States had a more comprehensive space research program, it had not achieved the kind of public impact that marked Sputnik and other Soviet efforts. The prospect of catching up with the Soviets dominated American space policy in the early 1960s. Telstar and its successors were the first spectacular breakthrough, followed by the more dramatic Apollo man-on-the-moon project.

In summary, the American government had compelling reasons to play an activist role in creating a worldwide comsat network. This urgency was underlined by persistent intelligence reports of the progress being made by Soviet scientists in comsat technology. The threat that the USSR could make a credible offer to invite other countries to join its own global network was a continuing goad to U.S. policymakers at the time.

Despite these political factors, there were strong pressures favoring the construction of an American network as a commercial project. In December 1960, before its first Telsat was launched, AT&T proposed to the Federal Communications Commission that a global comsat network should be organized as "a joint commercial undertaking among U.S. international communications common carriers and their counterparts abroad." The company offered to launch its satellites at its own expense, if NASA supplied launching and rocket facilities at cost.[4]

The proposal drew immediate fire from other U.S. communications firms, fearful that AT&T would dominate the enterprise. AT&T officials piously denied any such intention. "What we want," said James Dingman, the company's chief engineer, "is to get going now, use the present known art, and pay our own way."[5] The AT&T proposal was put on hold, in part because of opposition from the rest of the industry but also because it was made in the lame duck last month of the Eisenhower administration.

Meanwhile, Congress had weighed in on the need for what the Senate space committee, headed by Lyndon Johnson, called "a central policy" for communications satellites and other U.S. space projects. In its report, the committee said that the State Department should have "a primary role" in such a policy arrangement.[6]

It was the first time that a congressional group had acknowledged that the department had a major role to play in national communications policy. As noted in the last chapter, State's role in telecommunications planning had been minimal up to that time. A Telecommunications Co-ordinating Committee of federal agencies had been formed within the department in 1946, but its responsibilities were limited largely to monitoring the activities of the International Telecommunications Union. The department's initial foray into space communications policy took place in 1960 when it asked AT&T and other American international carriers to refrain from negotiations with foreign carriers until a U.S. national policy had been determined.[7]

Space policy was one of the more pressing issues facing the Kennedy administration when it took office in January 1961. During the election campaign, John Kennedy had promised to strengthen American space programs, including satellite communications. Meanwhile his administration had inherited an Eisenhower policy generally favoring a private enterprise approach to building a global network.[8] During the transition period between the election and the inauguration, the president-elect set up an advisory committee, headed by Dr. Jerome Weisner of MIT, to review national space policy. The Weisner committee's advice to the new president was that he authorize "organizational machinery within the Government to administer an industry-government civilian space program."[9]

Kennedy and his advisers saw the space program as a natural subject for establishing their activist New Frontier credentials. In his first State of the Union address, the president invited "all nations—including the Soviet Union" to join in developing a global comsat network as part of an effort to end what he called the bitter and wasteful competition of the cold war. He repeated the proposal in a speech to a special session of Congress in May.

Two months later, the White House issued a public policy statement which reflected the Weisner transition team's call for a joint private sector–government approach to setting up and managing a communications satellite enterprise, in cooperation with other countries.[10] The coordinating group for this policy project at the White House level was the newly established National Aeronautics and Space Council (NASC). The council had the distinction of managing the first oversight of global communications policy at the presidential level. NASC's membership included the Departments of State, Justice and Defense as well as the Federal Communications Commission, the Budget Bureau, and several smaller agencies, including the U.S. Information Agency.[11]

Communications satellite issues presented novel problems for the council. The idea of a government role in a global system, as proposed by the White House, ran against the strong U.S. tradition of private sector control of communications. Within industry itself, there were mixed feelings about the administration's proposal, with many companies concerned about AT&T's potential for dominating the network. At another level, cold war factors came into play as a countervailing force. It was clear to policy planners from the White House on down that the federal government had to assume an activist role in assuring that a global comsat network would serve American strategic interests. This view was strongly held by the president's brother, Attorney General Robert Kennedy, who played a major role in crafting national comsat policy in its early years.

The State Department's role in comsat policy was defined by the White House's commitment to an inclusive system which would be open to other countries. There were, however, differences within the department on the issue of U.S. private sector ownership of the network. The international-organizations bureau and the legal adviser favored government ownership while the economic and scientific bureaus supported a private sector solution. The issue was settled by Undersecretary George W. Ball, who ruled in favor of a private corporation under government regulation.

In the early stages of comsat policy development, the department took the position that satellite systems were not much different from existing networks operated by commercial firms, and therefore did not require any changes in the way that it handled the subject.[12] This attitude changed as comsat policy became more complex in the first year of the Kennedy administration. A foreign service officer, Philip Farley, was assigned as a special assistant for atomic energy and outer space in Undersecretary Ball's office.

Changes were also made in the small telecommunications policy office in the economic bureau headed by a courtly civil servant, Francis Colt de Wolf, since 1935. The office was expanded, primarily to provide support for Farley, who became the point man for space communications policy in the department. Another foreign service officer, William G. Carter, was named a special assistant for international space communications in the economics bureau. These changes were the beginning of a process, which stretched out over two decades, to enable the department to deal effectively with an expanded range of global telecommunications issues.

Meanwhile, the Kennedy administration encouraged stepped-up development of communications satellite technology. By 1962, four separate comsat research projects, including improvements in Telstar technology, were under way in government and private sector laboratories. Each used a different engineering approach. Although AT&T won the race to launch the first workable comsat, its executives were aware that Telstar technology would soon be challenged by other systems. In lobbying for their system, they claimed that Telstar technology would dominate the field for a decade or more.[13] In fact, Telstar was displaced as the technology of choice for the global system within three years. The

Kennedy White House meanwhile drafted legislation for a national com-sat strategy. Its proposals were outlined in a bill submitted to Congress in February 1962, six months before the first Telstar launch. The bill proposed the creation of a congressionally chartered Communications Satellite Corporation (Comsat), which would manage American interests in a global network under federal government supervision. The corpo-ration's ownership would be broadly based, with its stock owned by the general public as well as by the major U.S. telecommunications compa-nies.

As outlined in the White House submission, the proposal was an at-tempt to bridge the differences between those who favored more direct government control of the new network (in the form of a public entity like the Tennessee Valley Authority) and those who advocated owner-ship by U.S. communications companies. The congressional debate on the bill was lengthy and often acrimonious, extending over a six-month period. At one point, Senate supporters of private sector ownership of the network resorted to a filibuster, effectively closing down all business in the upper chamber. The Senate leadership filed a cloture petition to halt the filibuster, the first use of this parliamentary maneuver in over 30 years.[14] In congressional hearings on the bill, State Department offi-cials emphasized the need for a strong department role in monitoring the proposed corporation's negotiations with foreign countries. The White House draft of the bill stipulated that Comsat should not enter negotiations with any international agency, foreign government, or en-tity "without prior notification to the Department of State, which would conduct or supervise such negotiations."

This provision was criticized by industry lobbyists as an unwarranted restriction on the proposed corporation's activities. In congressional tes-timony, George McGhee, undersecretary for political affairs, seemed to back down when he argued that the department would only "conduct the preliminary negotiations covering general matters" and then leave the detailed negotiations to Comsat, subject to the State Department's general supervision.[15] This apparent retreat was not enough to satisfy opponents of the department's involvement in Comsat's dealing with foreign governments. The legislation was eventually modified to limit State's role to advising the corporation about foreign policy considera-tions in its international negotiations.

As congressional debate on the bill drew to a close in July 1962, AT&T launched its first Telstar satellite, adding a sense of urgency to the leg-islation's passage. The bill cleared both houses six weeks later, and was signed into law by the president on August 31.[16] The final legislation was less a clear statement of policy than a package of pragmatic com-promises which left room for further negotiations between government and private sector interests. In particular, the bill did not provide clear guidelines on the Comsat Corporation's role in the ownership and management of the proposed global network.

In the end, the Comsat Corporation won a large measure of autonomy in managing the new enterprise. As noted above, the State Department was relegated to an advisory role. The meaning of "advisory" was ambiguous, leading to a series of sharp exchanges between the department and the corporation. Comsat's unprecedented role in negotiating with foreign governments was the beginning of a trend which has since become one of the hallmarks of digital diplomacy, as commercial firms and other non-governmental groups become more involved in determining the organization and content of public policy in international communications.

Once the Comsat bill became law, the State Department and other federal agencies concentrated on the foreign policy implications of the legislation. The law supplied few guidelines on the subject, beyond authorizing the Comsat Corporation to "plan, initiate, construct, own, manage and operate itself, or in conjunction with foreign governments or business entities, a commercial communications satellite system."[17]

The months after the bill was passed witnessed a sharp struggle on how this mandate would be carried out. The first step toward establishing an operational system was taken in October 1962 when President Kennedy appointed an interim board of directors to be incorporators of the Comsat Corporation. The appointees were a diverse group of industry, labor, media and public service leaders. The domestic telecommunications industry was heavily represented, reflecting the Comsat bill's provision that half the stock in the corporation would be held by AT&T and other U.S. international carriers. The other half was issued as public stock, bought up by 150,000 investors.[18]

Philip L. Graham, publisher of the *Washington Post*, was named chairman of the group. He resigned shortly afterwards due to ill health and was replaced by Leo D. Welch, a former chairman of Standard Oil of New Jersey. Welch was a tough-minded businessman who believed that the new corporation could build and manage the global network without outside interference, particularly from Washington bureaucrats. In particular, Welch saw the State Department as an obstacle rather than ally. He and other Comsat officials rejected the department's view that the proposed network would have to involve some form of joint ownership, giving foreign governments an economic and managerial stake in its operations.[19]

Meanwhile, the White House did not intend to back down from a direct role in monitoring Comsat's activities. To coordinate this project, President Kennedy authorized an Ad Hoc Communications Satellite Group, with Deputy Attorney General Nicholas Katzenbach and Jerome Weisner (now White House science adviser) as co-chairmen. The State

Department, Justice Department and the Federal Communications Commission were members of a subcommittee that monitored the Comsat Corporation's plans for inviting foreign governments to participate in the global network.

West European governments were the prime targets for this effort. The technical and economic viability of the proposed satellite network depended heavily on European-American cooperation. About two thirds of all international telecommunications traffic took place in the North Atlantic region. The Europeans had closely tracked American progress in communications satellite technology and were clearly interested in joining a global network. They were also wary of U.S., and particularly Comsat, intentions to keep tight control of the network. Despite these concerns, the Europeans were ready to cooperate in supporting plans for an interim comsat network while details for a permanent system were being worked out.

European governments were acutely aware of their weak bargaining position in negotiating such arrangements, given the American lead in satellite technology. Only five years before, in the 1958 Treaty of Rome, they had taken the first steps towards regional economic planning, creating the European Economic Community organization. The community took steps, tentatively at first, to reduce barriers to an integrated West European economy. American industry was a particular beneficiary of these moves. Hundreds of U.S. corporations opened production and marketing facilities inside the community's borders, anticipating a free-trade area consisting of a quarter billion customers that promised to rival the U.S. market.[20] The swift evolution of communications satellite technology in the early 1960s forced the Europeans to consider a united front against American economic and technological power. They challenged the Comsat Corporation's plans for bilateral agreements with West European governments. The first group to see the threat was the small but politically well connected European space industry. Its leaders recognized that, unchallenged, American companies would dominate the potentially lucrative space equipment business, including communications satellites. They reacted by forming Eurospace, a coalition of 146 aerospace companies (including eight American firms as associate members) to support Western European industrial interests in space. It was the first attempt to deal with one of the critical issues in developing a global system, namely, assurances that non-American companies could compete for space equipment contracts.

Eurospace was a critical step towards a regional approach in negotiations with the Americans on political and economic issues. In a move encouraged by European Community officials, a European Conference on Satellite Communications (ECSC) was formed in July 1963. Its stated purpose was "to provide, to the extent possible, a counterpart to the U.S.

Communications Satellite Corporation."[21] In the following year, the Europeans strengthened their satellite credentials by creating a multilateral European Space Research Organization (ESRO) and a European Space Vehicle Launcher Development Organization (ELDO).[22]

These developments were followed closely by the White House and the State Department. The Europeans' moves reinforced the Kennedy administration's belief that the global network had to be organized in ways that gave foreign governments some measure of ownership and control over its operations. The long-term danger was that the Europeans would develop a competing network which would reduce the economic and technological advantages of an integrated global system.[23]

Comsat Corporation officials, backed by AT&T and the other carriers, which owned half the firm's stock, continued to insist on a Comsat-owned venture. Their rigid position began to soften in the face of the political realities involved in getting European support for an interim satellite network. The turning point occurred three months after the Comsat Act was approved. The occasion was an ITU conference in Geneva, called to set frequency standards for space communications networks. (Up to that time, all space frequencies had been allotted for research uses only.) These allotments were critical to any U.S. plans to move ahead on a global satellite system. With support from the Europeans and, grudgingly, the Soviet Union, most of the American proposals needed to implement the Communications Satellite Act's mandate for a global system were adopted.[24]

The ITU space frequency conference also provided an opportunity for informal discussions between American and European officials on plans for organizing the communications satellite network. The Europeans presented a united front as members of the European Conference on Satellite Communications. They made it clear that they wanted to cooperate in forming the new network but that they were unwilling to negotiate with Comsat on a bilateral basis. Their bluntness convinced Comsat officials to back down on their plans for a system owned and managed by the corporation.[25]

Their decision opened the way for substantive negotiations on a network in which foreign governments would have a financial and managerial stake. The negotiations took place primarily among the industrialized North Atlantic democracies, plus Australia and Japan.[26] The agenda did however include a discussion of the potential role of satellite communications in Asia, Africa and Latin America, the home of three quarters of the world's population. In October 1962, the British government had invited its Commonwealth partners to a Commonwealth Conference on Satellite Communications in London. It was a first small move in recognizing what was later to become a major factor in satellite communications—its role in stepping up the pace of economic development in the world's poorer regions.

Meanwhile, the Americans and Europeans agreed on the need for quick action in setting up interim arrangements for a network that would initially serve their needs in the North Atlantic region. They also recognized that, given the complex technical and economic issues involved, an interim organization should be formed to manage the network before considering permanent arrangements.

In Washington, the Comsat Corporation accepted the White House's plan for a strategy that would govern American negotiators in the upcoming interim arrangement negotiations. The strategy proposed joint ownership of the network by governments who agreed to join the interim organization. It was a significant reversal of Comsat's original position. Comsat also agreed that the U.S. negotiating team would be jointly headed by Leo Welch, the company's chairman, and a State Department official, Abraham Chayes, the State Department's legal adviser.

For their part, the Europeans accepted the American position that the proposed network should be planned as a global venture, for both economic and technological reasons. They also accepted the reality that the network would be, at least in its early phases, basically an American operation. Their strategy was to position themselves for the longer term, particularly in assuring themselves an adequate measure of ownership and operational control in any agreement setting up a permanent organization. In understanding that Comsat was the only organization capable of building and operating the network, the Europeans did not want to give the corporation a completely free hand, setting precedents that would be hard to change later on.

This view was expressed succinctly by a British telecommunications official in a House of Commons debate in February 1964. He declared that "the only way of preventing an American monopoly in this sphere is to join in a partnership with the United States and other countries and so secure the right to influence the course of events."[27] The European position in the interim arrangements negotiations emphasized five points:

- Comsat management of the system would eventually be phased out, to be replaced by an international management arrangement.
- The system's terrestrial facilities (e.g., earth stations) would be owned and managed by local telecom authorities, with Comsat restricted to managing the space portion.
- Voting procedures and ownership allocations in the interim system would allow fair representation for Europeans and other users.
- European industry would be given a fair share of the equipment contracts involved in building the project.

• There would be a time limit for the interim arrangements, with firm provisions for planning a permanent organization to operate the network.[28]

The Europeans got most of what they wanted in the negotiations, which began in February 1964 and lasted for five months. The Comsat Corporation was designated manager of the interim organization, operating under general guidelines set by an Interim Communications Satellite Committee (ICSC). The committee was made up of investors in the system, all of them government organizations with the exception of the Comsat Corporation, the U.S. government's chosen-instrument representative.

ICSC voting was weighted according to shares held by each member. Agreement on substantive issues would, however, require a total vote of 12.5 percent above the ownership weight of any one member. This was a relatively minor restraint on Comsat, which owned 61 percent of the shares. The West Europeans had a 30.5 percent share, while Canada, Japan and Australia together had 8.5 percent. Other countries joining the ICSC would be limited to a total of 17 percent of the vote. This formula assured that Comsat had an effective veto over ICSC decisions.[29]

In the negotiations on dividing up equipment contracts for the venture, the Europeans called for parity with the United States. This was opposed by the American delegation as unrealistic from both a management and technical viewpoint. Comsat, in particular, took a hard line on the issue. Commenting on the European proposal, Comsat president Leo Welch declared: "We say to them, we don't believe any of you are far enough advanced today. However, when you are ready, we'll be glad to ask for proposals."[30]

The Europeans were successful in putting a five-year time limit on the interim agreements, overriding American objections that this would not be long enough to work out the details of a permanent organization. The Europeans' resistance was based on their calculation that any longer period would solidify American, and specifically, Comsat, domination of the network.

In balance, the 1964 interim agreement was a pragmatic response to the challenge of matching technology strength with political and economic realities. Many hard decisions were postponed or ignored during the negotiations in the interests of moving ahead on a basic framework for building and managing the system. Beyond the rhetoric of international cooperation, the interim system (which became known as Intelsat) was a cartel of government-owned or regulated telecommunications organizations.

Intelsat was, in effect, a creature of an old-boy's cartel of the industrialized countries which controlled over 90 percent of global communications resources. The interim agreement's major accomplishment was that it set out a framework for an open-ended system, one that was flexible enough to allow for the eventual participation of all countries.

For the time being, however, Intelsat belonged to the industrialized democracies. As noted above, none of the so-called developing countries, representing over half the earth's population, participated in the interim negotiations. Nevertheless, the interim agreement made provision for their eventual entry into the system, albeit as minority partners, by setting aside a 17 percent share of ownership shares for their participation.

The Soviet Union and the People's Republic of China were also excluded from the early Intelsat negotiations. The Chinese routinely criticized plans for the proposed network, taking propaganda sideswipes at its allegedly imperialist aims. During early congressional debates on the subject, the Kennedy administration held to its position that the network would be open to all countries. In answer to a congressman's statement opposing "equal time for Red China, financed at the United States taxpayer's expense," USIA director Edward R. Murrow replied: "This would be a two-way street. If the Chinese were prepared to say we could get words and pictures from the satellites to their sets, and they could get words and pictures from the satellites to our sets, I would have no doubt where the advantage would lie at the end of the day."[31]

The Soviet government took a wary approach to the Intelsat negotiations. Unlike the Chinese, the USSR was a member of the ITU and therefore technically eligible to join the network. As noted earlier, Moscow also had the potential capability to build its own global network and to invite foreign participation in it, undercutting American efforts. This led to a White House decision to try to co-opt the Soviet government by encouraging it to participate in the interim Intelsat arrangements. In February 1963, the U.S. Embassy in Moscow was authorized to suggest exploratory talks with the Soviet government on the prospects of joining the proposed satellite system. The offer was initially rebuffed, but the Soviet government left the door open for future meetings.[32]

This reluctance to cooperate reflected Moscow's general confrontational cold war stance. Soviet membership would be an implicit acknowledgement of an American space achievement. The USSR did not launch a comsat with intercontinental capabilities for a decade after AT&T's Telstar. Moreover, Moscow knew that it would be a distinctly minority partner in the Intelsat organization, since ownership shares would be based on a formula tied to a country's international traffic. The Soviet share in Intelsat management and profits in the 1960s would have been about 1 percent—a demeaning situation for a self-proclaimed superpower. Soviet officials argued that "a truly global system could only be created through the ITU and the U.N. Committee on the Peaceful Uses of Outer Space."[33] Meanwhile, the Soviet government built a domestic satellite system ("Orbita"), which was used primarily for relaying Moscow television programming to provincial stations. In 1968, the USSR announced plans for its own global satellite system, Intersputnik, offering each country that joined an equal vote, as distinguished from Intelsat's weighted voting formula. There were other provisions in the Soviet proposal, however, which made it clear that Moscow intended to maintain strict control over the network.

Intersputnik's charter members included the Soviet client states in Eastern Europe, plus Cuba and Mongolia. Subsequently only Algeria and North Vietnam joined the system. Intersputnik did not become operational until 1972. By that time, Intelsat member countries represented over 95 percent of global communications traffic.

Once agreement was reached on an Intelsat interim organization, Comsat, the State Department and other government agencies focussed on transforming a satellite system from a paper blueprint into a global reality. The ICSC agreement contained many ambiguities as part of a strategy of accommodating the disparate interests of the countries that signed it. As a result, a number of details about the ICSC organization were left unresolved as planning for its operations began.

A more subtle problem was changing the mindset of officials of national telecommunications monopolies abroad, whose cooperation was critical to making the new network a success. Many of them saw a global satellite system as a potential threat to their monopolies. They wanted to be assured that Intelsat operated primarily as an international network under their control. As a result, the interim Intelsat agreement contained provisions that limited the prospects for a unitary global system. Intelsat members were allowed to develop alternate comsat networks that would compete with Intelsat for traffic revenue. As noted above, the West Europeans had already set up arrangements which included plans for a regional network. In 1969, France announced plans for a national satellite system that would also provide links to North America and to Africa.[34]

Faced with these prospects, American officials emphasized the urgency of building a global system as quickly as possible. They were aided by a technological stroke of good luck. For two and a half years after the original Telstar launch in 1962, the Comsat Corporation had to rely on Telstar technology in its planning. Telstar was a low-orbit system that required as many as 18 satellites to provide worldwide coverage, along with earth stations that cost up to $10 million each.

This limitation ended in April 1965 with the successful launching of "Early Bird," a Hughes Aircraft satellite for which Comsat had contracted as a possible alternative to Telstar. Early Bird dramatically speeded up the prospects for a global system. It was a geosynchronous satellite floating in orbit 22,000 miles above the Equator, well above the 300 miles of Telstar's orbit. This gave Early Bird a terrestrial "footprint" wide enough to require only three satellites to cover the earth. Moreover, the Hughes satellite had far greater circuit capacity, capable of transmitting 1,500 phone calls simultaneously (compared to Telstar's 240-circuit capacity) as well as four video channels.

Early Bird and its successors allowed Comsat to step up its plans for a fully global network. This breakthrough was summed up by Bert Edelson, a pioneer in satellite technology: "Prior to Early Bird, satellites were an experiment. Early Bird made money."[35] The economic and technical advantages of the geostationary satellites had a major impact on American planning for the 1969 conference on a permanent Intelsat organization, mandated under the ICSC interim agreement.

As Comsat proceeded to build out its satellite network in the late 1960s, the Johnson administration set up an inter-agency task force to plan for the 1969 conference that would negotiate a permanent Intelsat organization. The effort was coordinated by the White House director of telecommunications management (DTM), a post created by the Kennedy administration in February 1962.[36] The major agencies involved in the satellite planning group were NASA, the FCC and the Departments of State, Justice and Defense.

The State Department role in the policy process was strengthened by a 1965 Johnson administration executive order that spelled out more clearly the department's responsibilities under the Communications Satellite Act. The order specified that the secretary of state "shall have direction of the foreign relations of the United States with respect to the Act, including all negotiations by the United States with foreign governments or with international bodies in connection with the Act."[37]

By clarifying the State Department's foreign policy responsibilities, the order challenged Comsat Corporation claims that, as manager and builder of the system, it had the authority to deal directly with foreign governments. Armed with this White House mandate, the department stepped up its effort to assure a strong U.S. policy posture in the upcoming negotiations on permanent Intelsat arrangements. This effort involved negotiations with foreign countries as well as with many federal agencies and industry groups at home. The Comsat Corporation proved to be an unwilling cooperator. In accordance with State's congressionally mandated role as adviser to Comsat, corporation officials grudgingly informed the department on its dealings with foreign governments.[38]

Meanwhile, Comsat sought to influence the shaping of the American position at the 1969 conference, with a view to maintaining the corporation's dominant position as builder and manager of the network. It objected to a government proposal to divide Intelsat's managerial functions into two parts—administrative and operational. Under the plan, Comsat would keep the latter functions, while the former would be internationalized. Comsat officials mounted a strong lobbying campaign in Congress against the proposal, arguing that the company had to control all of the network's functions for efficiency's sake. Their position was weakened however when AT&T and other U.S. international carriers supported the government on the issue.[39]

On another front, the State Department rejected a Defense Department proposal recommending a joint Defense-Comsat satellite network. The department informed the White House that "many countries would find it impossible politically to participate in a commercial system one component of which was reserved exclusively for the U.S. National Communications System."[40] The proposal was dropped, and Defense officials proceeded to develop a separate military satellite network.

During the interim arrangements period, the State Department played a strong role in garnering support for Intelsat among developing nations. As noted earlier, these countries had not participated in the negotiations that created the interim Intelsat organization. As the 1969 deadline for negotiating a permanent agreement approached, American policy planners realized that Third World involvement with Intelsat would strengthen the organization's credentials as an integrated global system. Moreover, Third World membership would weaken the Soviet Union's chances for getting developing countries' support for its proposed comsat network.

The State Department coordinated an aggressive campaign to induce Asian, African and Latin American governments to join the Intelsat interim arrangements. Department officials emphasized the satellite system's potential advantages in speeding up economic development programs as well as in improving educational resources. This latter point was pressed by Leonard Marks, director of the U.S. Information Agency and the former private attorney for President Lyndon Johnson's radio and television holdings. One result of Marks' close relations with the president was a Johnson offer of American help to fund educational broadcasting by satellite in Latin America. Johnson made the offer in an April 1967 speech at an Organization of American States conference in Uruguay.

In another initiative, the White House sought to remove a major stumbling block to developing country participation in Intelsat. This was the high cost of earth station equipment needed to link national telephone systems to the space network. An elaborate plan to finance this equipment was developed, including the use of Export-Import Bank guarantees, USAID technical assistance and Ford Foundation grants.[41] These arrangements proved largely unnecessary as American equipment manufacturers moved into the market, offering attractive concessional terms.

The State Department's effort to bring developing countries into Intelsat was an overall success. By the time the conference on permanent arrangements opened in February 1969, Intelsat has added more than 30 Asian, African and Latin American countries to its list of owners.

The conference opened in Washington under auspicious circumstances for American negotiators. A global Intelsat network was in place, operating on all continents. The threat of a preemptive Soviet move to set up a rival system had receded. Although many issues about Intelsat's permanent form remained, the technical and economic viability of the network was secure.

The conference included delegations from the 66 countries that were Intelsat investors, plus observers from 30 nations. Among the observer delegations was the Soviet Union, headed by a deputy minister of communications, N. V. Talyzin.[42] None of the Soviet client states in Eastern Europe attended, having been warned by Moscow earlier that they were not to consider joining Intelsat. The partial exception was Yugoslavia, which became an Intelsat member in February 1970 as part of Marshal Tito's campaign of defiance of Soviet hegemony in the region.[43]

The American delegation was headed by Leonard Marks, who had resigned as USIA director to take the assignment. Marks was a partner in Cohn & Marks, one of the largest Washington law firms dealing with communications policy. He had also been one of the incorporators of the Comsat Corporation seven years earlier. Marks was accordingly recognized as a good choice to deal with the complex skein of U.S. private sector interests involved in the negotiation.

The American delegation had its first crisis three weeks before the conference began. The newly installed Nixon administration began a sweeping review of all major foreign policy areas, including the Intelsat negotiations. Suspicious of a conference that, according to Comsat lobbyists, was about to surrender U.S. control of the satellite network to an international organization, the White House ordered that the conference be postponed.

The idea of putting off the conference after five years of preparation panicked top State Department officials, many of them newly appointed Republicans. They pointed out to their White House colleagues that the United States had a treaty obligation to other Intelsat countries to convene the conference by March 30. A crisis was averted when White House officials backed down, after stipulating that all major proposals by the American delegation be cleared with them—a provision that was normal procedure in any event.

The Intelsat negotiation was the largest international conference ever held in Washington. It was also the longest. It took two and a half years, and three sessions, to reach final agreement on a treaty setting up a permanent space communications organization. Delays in reaching an agreement were caused largely by disputes over Comsat's role in the new organization.

The corporation mounted a strong lobbying campaign, aimed primarily at Congress and the White House, to support its contention that Intelsat's growth and efficiency depended on long-term Comsat management. The company had a strong ally in Senator John Pastore, a Rhode Island Democrat and the powerful chairman of the Senate Commerce Committee. Speaking of the White House strategy in the Intelsat negotiations, he announced: "I certainly would hope that this won't develop into a foreign aid program and that we again give away the birth right of Americans."[44]

Comsat officials argued that a shift to international management would take Intelsat down what they called "the U.N. path," with jobs filled by national quotas and decisions made by committees. At one point early in the negotiations, Comsat chairman James McCormack, informed the U.S. delegation that any other arrangement "would render us unable to sign the operating agreement" for a permanent Intelsat.[45]

This threat evaporated in the face of demands by most other conference delegations, led by the Europeans, that a time limit be put on Comsat's managerial role. As it became clear that no agreement would be reached without such a provision, a compromise plan calling for a six-year phase-out of Comsat's contract was crafted.[46] This provision became the centerpiece of a major restructuring of Intelsat operations. A board of governors, dominated through weighted voting by the major Intelsat nations, would set ongoing Intelsat policy. An assembly of parties, representing all member governments, would meet every two years to discuss general policy. An international executive staff, headed by a director general, would carry out general management functions.[47]

By May 1971, the final texts of two agreements—one between governments and the other between their telecommunications organizations—were completed. The treaty was approved by the necessary two-thirds of Intelsat members on August 20—seven years after the interim Intelsat arrangements had been approved. Among the guests present at the treaty signing ceremony was science writer Arthur C. Clarke, who first outlined the prospects for satellite communications 26 years earlier in an obscure British scientific journal. Speaking to the assembled delegates, Clarke described the permanent Intelsat agreements as "the first draft of the federation of the United States of Earth."[48]

At the time of the treaty signing Intelsat had 92 member nations which accounted for over 95 percent of global communications. As the negotiations concluded, the first of the Intelsat IV geostationary satellites was launched, with a capacity of 4,000 phone circuits and separate TV channels—a 10-fold increase over the original Early Bird. Although most of the network's traffic was bunched in the North Atlantic region, it was expanding in Asia, Africa and Latin America.

Intelsat was also beginning to have a significant public impact as vast audiences around the world watched televised news and sports events "live by satellite." However, television transmissions were a small part of Intelsat's traffic. Its economic health depended largely on commercial telephone and data traffic which increased exponentially as earth stations linked to Intelsat "birds" expanded around the globe.

Moreover, Intelsat was an entirely new kind of global organization. It was a pragmatic example of modifying sovereignty claims in ways that matched modern technological and economic realities. For the first time, a part of traditional national control over communications facilities was handed over to a transnational organization. It was a formula brokered by diplomats, engineers and businessmen, and fitted into an old-fashioned treaty format.[49]

The United States made the biggest compromise in reaching this agreement. American willingness to modify its technical, economic and political control of the system was based on a calculation that a jointly owned network would better serve long-term national interests. The short-term price it paid was the phasing out of Comsat's role as manager of the network, as well as a reduction in the corporation's stake in Intelsat ownership from over 60 percent in 1964 to 38 percent by 1972.

The compensating benefit was to confirm American preeminence in building a global communications and information infrastructure. One of the lasting achievements of the Intelsat treaty, as we shall see, was its resilience in dealing with changing circumstances over the years.

This flexibility was important because the technological and economic assumptions on which the treaty was based began to erode almost immediately after the agreement went into effect. In particular, Intelsat soon faced a formidable challenge from alternate technologies, notably high-capacity fiber-optic cables. Fiber cables steadily reduced Intelsat's share of international communications traffic beginning in the mid-1980s. Nevertheless, Intelsat was still the most important single segment of the global communications infrastructure at the beginning of the twenty-first century.

In terms of our survey, the 1972 Intelsat treaty was the beginning of the end of insularity and ad hoc policies in international communications within the federal government in general and in the State Department in particular. For the first time, the department was continuously involved with other Washington agencies and with the private sector on major communications issues, a role that has expanded steadily ever since. Moreover, Intelsat's promise of an integrated world network opened up a new set of digital diplomacy issues for American policymakers.

NOTES

1. Nina G. Seavey, "Creating a satellite system: Comsat's early years," in *The great international celebration of satellites in space* (Washington, DC: Society of Satellite Professionals, October 1987).

2. For the early history of communications satellites, see: Wilson P. Dizard, *Television: A world view* (Syracuse, NY: Syracuse University Press, 1966), pp. 253–282.

3. "An investigation on the possibility of establishing a space ship in an orbit above the surface of the earth," A.D.R. Report R-48, Department of the Navy, November 1945. The Air Force also became heavily involved in similar research, beginning with a 1946 report, "The preliminary design of an experimental world-circling spaceship," prepared by the Rand Corporation. For an account of the Defense Department's early involvement in communications satellites, see: Jonathan Galloway, *The politics and technology of satellite communications* (Lexington, MA: D. C. Heath & Co., 1972), pp. 105–120.

4. "Laying the great cable in space," *Fortune*, July 1961, p. 255.

5. Ibid., p. 256.

6. "Policy planning for space telecommunications," Staff Report, Committee on Aeronautical and Space Sciences, U.S. Senate, 86th Congress, 2nd session, December 1960, p. 3.

7. "Laying the great cable in space," op cit., pp. 259–260.

8. Galloway, op cit., pp. 22–23.

9. "Report to the President-elect of the ad-hoc committee on space," reprinted in "Defense space interests," House Committee on Science and Astronautics, 87th Congress, 1st session, 1961, pp. 17–18.

10. The message to Congress is in *Public papers of the presidents of the United States, John F. Kennedy, 1961*, Vol. 1, p. 404. The July policy statement is in the same volume, pp. 529–531.

11. Galloway, op cit., p. 26.

12. The department's attitude was reflected in its response to a Senate committee's query about its telecommunications policy arrangements. "Policy planning for space communications," op cit., pp. 146–149.

13. Interview with Richard Parlow, a member of the inter-agency planning group at the time, 22 January 1998.

14. Galloway, op cit., p. 69.

15. "Communications satellite hearings," Senate Committee on Aeronautical and Space Sciences, 87th Congress, 2nd session, 1962, p. 165.

16. Communications Satellite Act of 1962, Public Law 87–624, 87th Congress, 2nd session, August 31, 1962.

17. Ibid., Section 305, p. 7.

18. The outcome of this decision is described in Robert Burkhardt, "Comsat: Speculation in the space age," *New Republic*, 27 June 1964, pp. 11–13.

19. Galloway, op cit., p. 81.

20. For a survey of EEC policy in the communications sector, see: Wilson P. Dizard, "Europe calling Europe: Creating an integrated telecommunications network," in Alan W. Cafruny and Glenda M. Rosenthal (eds.), *The State of the European Community*, Vol. 2 (Boulder, CO: Lynne Rienner Publishers, 1993), pp. 321–336.

21. The ECSC's activities at the time are described in a State Department report, "Summary of European regional organization in the communications satellite field," reprinted in *U.S. Congressional Record*, 88th Congress, 2nd session, 9 January 1964, p. 175.

22. European efforts to develop regional space capabilities are described in

"International cooperation and organization for outer space," Staff Report No. 56, Senate Committee on Aeronautical and Space Sciences, 89th Congress, 1st session, pp. 105–117, 123–128.

23. The department's views were outlined by Richard N. Gardner, deputy assistant secretary for international organization affairs, in "Space meteorology and communications: A challenge to science and diplomacy," *Department of State Bulletin*, 13 May 1963, p. 774.

24. "Report of the chairman of the U.S. delegation," reprinted in *U.S. Congressional Record*, 88th Congress, 2nd session, 9 January 1964, pp. 166–174.

25. Galloway, op cit., p. 87.

26. Both the State Department and Comsat agreed that including the developing countries in the initial negotiations for an interim satellite organization would unduly complicate the discussions. See the testimony of department official, William G. Carter, in *Hearings on satellite communications 1964*, Part 2, House Committee on Government Operations, Military Operations Subcommittee, 88th Congress, 2nd session, p. 663.

27. Parliamentary Debates (Commons), 690 (1964), p. 421. The speaker was the Postmaster General, who had overall supervision of the British telephone network.

28. The European positions are analyzed in "Tensions at Intelsat," *The Economist* (London), 27 July 1968, p. 46.

29. Galloway, op cit., pp. 98–99.

30. Quoted in "Taking a flyer in outer space," *Newsweek*, 16 March 1964, p. 87.

31. "Congress debates satellite arrangements," *New York Times*, 15 July 1961, p. 12.

32. Galloway, op cit., pp. 122–135.

33. I. Chepov, "Global or American space communications?" *International Affairs* (Moscow), No. 12, p. 70.

34. "French plan commercial satellite system," *Aviation Week and Space Technology*, 24 November 1969, p. 22.

35. Quoted in "Four decades of progress," *Via Satellite*, October 1997, p. 13.

36. "Assigning telecommunications management functions," Executive Order 10995, Office of the President, 16 February 1962.

37. "Providing for the carrying out of certain provisions of the Communications Satellite Act of 1962." Executive Order 11191, Office of the President, 4 January 1965.

38. "The Comsat compromise starts a revolution," *Fortune*, October 1965, p. 128.

39. "Comsat, State Department split on negotiations," *Aviation Week and Space Technology*, 31 March 1969, p. 22.

40. Letter from Llewellyn E. Thompson, acting deputy undersecretary of state, to General James D. O'Connell, White House director of telecommunications management, 10 July 1964, reprinted in "Hearings on satellite communications—1964," Part 1, House Committee on Government Operations, 88th Congress, 2nd session, p. 747.

41. The project was authorized in two National Security Council action memoranda: NSAM 338, 15 September 1965 and NSAM 342, 1 July 1966. The author

was the executive director of the White House working group which was set up to implement the two directives.

42. "Soviets to join U.S. parley on space communications," *New York Times*, 23 January 1969, p. 7.

43. "Yugoslavia becomes first East European member to join Intelsat," *New York Times*, 2 March 1970, p. 7.

44. Senator Pastore's remarks, and those of other congressional supporters of Comsat's position, were widely circulated by the company. See: "Congressional comments on the Intelsat Conference," Comsat Corp. memorandum, 11 March 1969.

45. "Business negotiations involved in the present conference." Memorandum sent to members of the U.S. delegation to the conference by Comsat chairman James McCormack, 11 March 1969.

46. "Comsat dethroned," *The Economist* (London), 29 May 1971, p. 72.

47. For a useful summary of the Intelsat treaty negotiations, see: Brenda Maddox, *Beyond Babel* (New York: Simon & Schuster, 1972), pp. 105–114.

48. "Intelsat agreement signed by delegates of 54 lands," *New York Times*, 21 August 1971, p. 16. The treaty's provisions are summarized in "The permanent charter for Intelsat," *Department of State Bulletin*, Vol. 65, No. 1686, 18 October 1971, pp. 414–418.

49. For a summary of how the organization was restructured in the early years after the treaty was approved, see: "Intelsat moves towards permanent form," *Aviation Week and Space Technology*, 10 January 1977, pp. 90–91.

Chapter 4

The Spectrum Wars

Intelsat was a turning point in world communications. It broke the mold of incremental network expansion by offering a means of connecting any two points on earth in ways that supplied services directly or by linking into ground networks. Its satellites released the global system from its primary reliance on earthbound wire technology.

In the process, satellites changed the content and direction of American digital diplomacy. For the first time, it dealt with a communications policy issue that had to be negotiated on a global scale. Satellites do not recognize national boundaries. Their terrestrial footprints, to use the engineer's term, cover regions and continents. The barriers to a universal system were, in fact, no longer technical. Instead they involved political and economic obstacles that hampered effective use of a powerful new force in human communications.

As we have seen, the United States was strongly positioned technologically and economically to build a space comsat network. It also had the national will to undertake the enterprise and to see it through to completion. Cold war considerations played a critical role in this decision. Even before the first Telstar satellite was launched, Washington policymakers feared that the USSR would be the first to build a similar network using its own technology. Such a turn of events would have been a major political as well as psychological triumph for the Soviet government, equal to if not greater than its 1957 Sputnik success.[1]

This did not happen. Moscow's formidable space program never caught up with the American effort in comsat technology. The Intelsat network was up and running for almost a decade before Soviet engineers launched a geostationary satellite capable of providing international services.[2] Moreover, Intelsat was a solid economic and political success from the start. The organization was commercially viable, paying its member-nation stockholders a steady 14 percent dividend every year. By 1974, the network's membership had increased to 89 countries that were collectively responsible for over 95 percent of all global communications.

Intelsat's managers had anticipated a slow steady buildup of global traffic on their network. In fact, the demand for network services consistently outstripped their estimates. Circuit space on each new satellite was filled, often before the satellite became operational.[3] This technological bottleneck was eventually eased by the introduction of more sophisticated machines. During its first decade of global operations, Intelsat benefited from four generations of technological upgrading in its satellites. The most important of the new satellites was Hughes Aircraft's Intelsat-IV-A, with a capacity of 6,000 circuits—about six times greater than the first Early Bird machines. The Hughes' "bird" became the network's standard technology throughout the 1980s.

Intelsat's initial success seemed to justify the early high promise of comsat technology—a world in which every place, down to the most remote village, would be linked electronically. These hopes were soon dampened by stubborn realities. By 1980, after 15 years of operations, Intelsat traffic represented less than 1 percent of all global communications. Moreover, 80 percent of the network's traffic was concentrated in the North Atlantic and North Pacific regions, where its circuits were used primarily for commercial voice and data traffic. The network was a particular boon to multinational corporations, strengthening links with their overseas operations and expanding their market reach, particularly in Western Europe and East Asia.

Intelsat's impact on other regions was considerably less dramatic. The network became a potentially important asset for Asian, African and Latin American nations, opening up communications links with their neighbors and with other continents. With U.S. encouragement, Intelsat priced its services on a global basis, a move that had the effect of providing a subsidy for less-developed countries. (In normal telecommunications practice, big users get preferential rate treatment.) Despite this advantage, Intelsat operations in developing regions were limited to what were known as "thin route communications," involving less than 10 percent of the system's total traffic.[4]

A major deterrent for most developing countries in Intelsat's early years was the high cost of satellite earth terminals. Ninety-foot "dishes" costing up to $25 million were needed to pick up the weak signals from the early generations of satellites. Although prices (and the size of the terminals) dropped steadily, few countries could afford more than one dish, resulting in a traffic bottleneck. It was a major factor in delaying the vision of millions of small earth terminals linked to a global network.

Small affordable terminals, some no bigger than a pie plate, emerged as a practical reality only in the late 1990s. Dealing with such rapid technical change became a critical part of American digital diplomacy's agenda for expanding global communications through satellites and other advanced systems.

Comsat technology was the first big test of digital diplomacy's ability to keep up these changes. Washington policy planners also had to cope with a range of other new technologies such as fiber-optic cables and advanced microwave circuitry. Undersea fiber networks in particular presented a direct threat to Intelsat's intercontinental traffic because of their high circuit capacities. By the 1990s, a fiber cable linking Europe and East Asia contained 120,000 circuits capable of carrying 600,000 phone conversations simultaneously.[5] Despite continuing improvements in its satellites, Intelsat could not match the economic advantages of such cables, particularly in high-traffic international routes. One result was that the share of U.S. overseas traffic carried on Intelsat satellites dropped from 80 percent to 20 percent in the decade after 1988.

Satellites, fiber cables and the other new technologies share a common attribute: they are based on a digital standard. This is not new: the Morse telegraph was a primitive form of a digital system, the digits being represented by dots and dashes. Before 1970, however, almost all telecommunications (including the early comsats) were tied to slow-paced analog technology, whose efficiency is constrained by continuously fluctuating current or voltage.

The early breakthroughs in modern digital communications took place in the 1940s, mostly at AT&T's Bell Laboratories and other U.S. research installations. Their experiments were grounded in a new theory of measuring a unit of information by reducing it to its lowest common denominator—a choice that resolves uncertainty (e.g., up or down, left or right, in or out). The symbolic electronic equivalent of these choices became one or zero. These were the binary digits that quickly became known as bits, the invisible building blocks of the information age.[6]

It took two decades to turn the new information theory into practical ways of storing and transmitting electronic bits. The first breakthrough came with the development of transistor technology. Transistors had a limited capacity however. They worked well in small radios but not in computers where the heat they generated was a problem. This barrier was resolved with the development of silicon-based semiconductor chips that could store many transistors. The result was an astonishing series of technological leaps. The first 1971 Intel commercial chip contained 2,700 transistors. By the mid-1990's Intel's Pentium Pro series included 5.5 million transistors.

The impact of these technical leaps on U.S. society are well known. Our focus here is on how this impact has affected the content and style of U.S. diplomacy. The changes brought about by the introduction of advanced digital resources were global in scope. By the turn of the century, North America, Western Europe and Japan had made the transition to digitally based economies. Most of the rest of the world is just beginning to catch up.

The impact of this shift now permeates all aspects of American foreign policy—trade, national security, human rights, energy resources and the environment, among other subjects. We will take a closer look at these specific impacts in later chapters. Here we will examine a basic issue—the need to negotiate a new set of technical rules so that digitally driven communications would operate effectively across national borders. In particular, digital standards were required to supplement (and eventually replace) those that governed analog communications. Analog technology involved separate sets of regulations for transmitting telephone, television, computer data and other services. Digital technology erased this distinction by allowing these services to be sent down a single high-capacity wire or wireless "information pipe" in mix-and-match fashion.

As digital services expanded after 1970, the need for new technical standards became urgent. Because of the economic stake the United States had in promoting digital technology, developing these standards became a major concern of American policymakers. Their agenda covered a wide variety of new rules which would determine how (or even whether) digital technologies would be efficiently deployed globally in the information age.

The most critical decisions involved the radio spectrum. The spectrum is the essential natural resource for the fastest growing technology in the digital age—wireless communications. Digital wireless circuits have opened the way to a wide range of new services, from cellular telephones to projects for making contact with extraterrestrial life.

Created in the first few seconds after the Big Bang 10 billion years ago, the radio spectrum is a figurative thing: it does not exist until it is used. Its raw material is electromagnetic radiation, invisible waves moving through space and matter. The spectrum's existence was unknown until the end of the nineteenth century. In 1888, Heinrich Hertz, a German physicist, produced the first man-made electromagnetic radiation by sending a strong electrical charge across a spark gap, causing a smaller spark—evidence of the presence of an electrical field—to jump across a second gap some distance away.

The Hertzian spark opened up a new era in global communications. A dozen years later Guglielmo Marconi sent the first shortwave wireless signal—the letter S—from England to Massachusetts. For decades, the practical uses of wireless communications were limited to the shortwave bands, located in the lowest 1 percent of the radio spectrum. Wireless spectrum use has since expanded dramatically, providing circuits for radar, space satellites and mobile phones, among other new services. Billions of dollars of investment in these services ride on changes in spectrum rules, a function managed by the Geneva-based International Telecommunications Union.[7]

The United States became politically involved in spectrum issues for the first time in 1903, when it sent a delegation to a Berlin conference of the International Telegraph Union, the predecessor of today's ITU. The union had been created in 1865 to establish technical rules for coordinating wire telegraphy in Europe. The Berlin meeting was the first to deal with the implications of Marconi's wireless breakthrough a few years earlier.

The American government had previously ignored the Telegraph Union, seeing it as an organization dominated by the Europeans who might try to regulate U.S. domestic communications.[8] The American presence at the conference was largely the result of another threat—the anticompetitive attempts of the Marconi Company, based in London, to establish a British monopoly in global wireless communications. The United States collaborated with the union's European members to turn back the threat.

The Berlin conference was the beginning of a long, and often contentious, U.S. relationship with the ITU and its activities. American involvement with the union deepened with the growth of radio broadcasting in the 1920s. Radio stations in the United States could claim a frequency simply by sending a postcard to the Department of Commerce in Washington. The result was signal interference among local stations that had claimed the same frequency. The problem had international implications since U.S. stations often interfered with Canadian and Mexican stations.

The federal government took two steps to deal with the problem in the 1920s. A Federal Radio Commission was created to regulate the domestic broadcasting industry, including the assignment of frequencies to individual stations. The second step was to host a 1927 conference in Washington of the International Telecommunications Union, the successor to the Telegraph Union. It was the first such meeting to consider all telecommunications services that depended on spectrum resources. The conference established a system, still in use, of frequency planning by services on a global basis. The plan included the high-frequency bands used for shortwave radio broadcasting, a service that became more politically contentious in later years when these bands were used for international propaganda purposes. A 1938 conference in Cairo set the first spectrum regulations for the new technology of television broadcasting.

World War II underscored the national security importance of spectrum regulation, particularly for radar and other new microwave services. In 1947, the United States took the lead in expanding the rules for global spectrum management by hosting three consecutive ITU conferences, all held in Atlantic City. At the same time, the union became part of the new United Nations organization as one of its specialized agencies. The Atlantic City meetings authorized a new spectrum allocation table, as well as a specialized ITU unit, the International Frequency Registration Board, to register and monitor spectrum uses worldwide.[9]

The other major change in the postwar ITU was its political makeup. For over 100 years, the organization had been run primarily for the benefit of the Western industrial powers that controlled, directly or indirectly, most global communications facilities. The needs of other countries where most of the world's population lived were largely ignored, except as they served the colonial interests of Great Britain and other European powers.

This pattern began to erode in the early postwar years for several reasons. One was that the interests of the leading ITU members in the industrialized West began to diverge. Spectrum policy was no longer a simple matter of providing protection for radio broadcasting and a few other services. Emerging new technologies required more sophisticated spectrum decisions that were increasingly driven by strategic political and economic interests.

The situation was further complicated by the new communications dominance of the United States. One consequence was that the other industrial powers feared that American communications strategy, including spectrum planning, was aimed at reducing their influence in global communications. It was a theme that was usually implied rather than expressed publicly. Nevertheless, it increasingly dominated the policies and actions of America's democratic partners in Western Europe and in Japan.

Meanwhile, the ITU was undergoing major changes in its membership. As decolonization swept the postwar world, the balance of power in the organization shifted. The ITU had 76 members in 1947; by 1965 this figure had risen to 129, with most of the increase accounted for by new Asian and African nations. At the turn of the century, ITU membership stood at 190. The industrial nations, who were the biggest spectrum users, were now outnumbered in a one-vote, one-country organization.[10] The ITU's new members initially played a passive role in the organization, in part because they lacked the technical expertise to deal with complex spectrum issues. By the 1970s, however, they had become a more active force in the union's deliberations as they gained a better understanding of the political and economic importance of spectrum resources.

These changes have set the tone and pace of international spectrum politics ever since. The United States necessarily took on a leadership role, as the largest and most technologically advanced user of spectrum resources. The American response was complex, but it focussed on one principle. This was the need for flexibility in assuring efficient use of the finite spectrum, particularly in accommodating to technological advances. This represented sound engineering practice. It also reflected U.S. economic interests as the leading producer and user of high-technology communications products and services.[11]

This emphasis on a flexible approach has shaped American spectrum politics in recent decades. It has also tended to isolate the United States in international negotiations. Its industrialized partners fully understood the technical logic behind spectrum flexibility. However, they were often less supportive of American proposals in this area for political and economic reasons. Their suspicions were motivated, in part, by the fact that their own communications industries were less competitive than the U.S. telecommunications sector, both in technological resources and in marketing.

The bigger threat to U.S. spectrum flexibility proposals came from the ITU's new Third World members, suspicious of "Northern" domination of the spectrum. Their position was summed up by a Sudanese official in 1979: "The developed nations have 90 per cent of the spectrum and 10 per cent of the population. We have 90 per cent of the population and 10 per cent of the spectrum. We want our share."[12]

Spectrum issues became part of a larger ideological offensive by Third World countries in the 1970s. Proclaiming a "new world information order" (NWIO), these countries saw the then-current ITU spectrum rules as supporting economic colonialism. The United States and other industrialized countries were, they argued, attempting to dominate global information and communications resources by controlling ITU allocation of spectrum frequencies. Their campaign to revise the rules became an important element in U.S. spectrum strategy.

In Washington, this led to changes in the way spectrum policy was organized. The subject had been dominated in the early postwar years by the Defense Department's interest in protecting the technical integrity of its worldwide communications network. In 1951, President Harry Truman appointed a commission to look at broader spectrum needs, but the inquiry had little effect on day-to-day policy. Spectrum policy decisions were made by an Interagency Radio Advisory Committee (IRAC), an engineering group primarily concerned with protecting federal government spectrum needs. IRAC's recommendations were usually accepted without change by non-technical officials in the State Department and other agencies.

This arrangement was increasingly inadequate as the political and economic issues surrounding spectrum use became more complex. Domestically, new microwave services (satellites, radar, etc.) were competing with older technologies for spectrum space. Spectrum congestion was becoming a significant problem for the first time as these older services expanded and newer ones interfered with their transmissions. Overseas, similar problems arose as communication networks expanded. Meanwhile, as noted above, the ITU's new Asian and African members were lobbying for fundamental changes in global spectrum management.

By 1970, these factors combined to increase the pressure for a sweeping revision of spectrum management in ways that would accommodate the new digital services. In 1973, ITU members approved a plan for a 1979 world conference that would review the union's management of the spectrum from top (275 gigahertz) to bottom (10 kilohertz).

Inevitably, the United States played a central role at the 1979 meeting, known as a World Administrative Radio Conference. As the leading user of spectrum resources, it had the biggest stake in assuring that advanced electronic technologies, many of which were still on the drawing boards, could be accommodated in any spectrum reform. There were also important national security issues to consider, given the cold war environment in which the negotiations would take place. Overall, American interests called for an integrated approach to spectrum management, balancing the needs of old and new technologies, with enough regulatory flexibility to anticipate future technical advances.

However reasonable this approach seemed to U.S. policymakers, it met stubborn opposition in ITU spectrum negotiations. A key element in American proposals was the retention of a long-standing ITU regulation that frequencies would be allocated to the union's member countries on a first-come, first-served basis. Simply put, the country that initially applied to the ITU for a spectrum slot would have priority in using it, unless it negotiated a different arrangement with later claimants. The procedure had several advantages. It assured that the initiating country would have clearly defined access to spectrum needed for a particular service. Furthermore, it encouraged only such spectrum requests for telecommunications projects (e.g., a new satellite network) that would actually be implemented.

This approach clashed with political realities that governed ITU decision making from the 1970s on. Developing countries, the union's new voting majority, wanted a system that would pre-allocate spectrum resources (known as a priori planning) that would assure them the frequencies they might need when they were in a position to expand their communications resources. They contended that the most desirable frequencies were already assigned to the industrialized countries under the first-come, first-served formula. The United States and its industrial allies were, in fact, the primary beneficiaries of the first-come, first served system. Nevertheless, the Europeans were somewhat sympathetic to a priori planning, in part because they anticipated that the United States would lay first claim to desirable parts of the spectrum for advanced services being planned by American telecommunications companies, an area where the Europeans and Japanese generally lagged.

The politics of a priori planning became a frustrating issue for U.S. digital diplomacy for two decades after 1970. It surfaced first as a negotiating issue in a 1977 specialized ITU conference, called to determine spectrum allocations for the new technology that made possible transmission of television signals from satellites to small earth stations. (The technology became known as DBS—direct broadcasting satellites.) It was a particularly touchy subject for Third World countries. Foreign DBS programming, they argued, would be an extension of the already heavy influence of Western media, particularly American television programming and advertising, on their cultures. Seeing a chance to embarrass the Americans, Soviet spokesmen called for a ban on space broadcasting, suggesting that a country had the right to shoot down DBS satellites.[13]

America and its democratic allies in the ITU were soon caught up in the electronic imperialism debate. European intellectuals in particular sounded the alarm against the "CocaColasation" of European culture by American media. At another level, European television officials worried about the potential inroads on their audience base of DBS broadcasting channels which, they correctly foresaw, would be dominated by popular American programs.

The focus of the ITU's 1977 space conference was on frequencies in the 12 gigahertz band, which had only recently been opened for practical use for a variety of services, including DBS broadcasts. The American proposals at the conference stressed an evolutionary approach to planning and utilizing the band. It pointedly rejected the a priori assignment of both frequency resources and the geostationary "slots" in space where DBS satellites would be located.[14]

A priori planning of the 12 gigahertz band became the dominant focus of the conference's work. U.S. delegates argued that such rigid planning would tie up spectrum resources that might never be used. Moreover, they pointed out, DBS technology was still in its infancy. No such satellites existed at the time, so there was no need to adopt a plan that would have to be revised later.[15]

These arguments failed to persuade supporters of a strong a priori plan. The conference approved the permanent allocation of over 900 satellite broadcasting channels divided among all ITU member countries, including such tiny states as Andorra, Liechtenstein and the Vatican. The only concession the United States could get was an agreement to defer any DBS decisions in the Western Hemisphere for a future regional conference on the subject.

The 1977 direct broadcast conference's endorsement of a priori spectrum planning was seen by American policymakers as part of a larger pattern to restrict global information flow. At the time of the ITU conference, the United Nations Economic, Scientific and Cultural Organization (UNESCO) was debating proposals to limit Western media operations in Third World countries. Meanwhile, another U.N. group, the Committee on Peaceful Uses of Outer Space, was considering restrictions on direct satellite broadcasting from space without permission from the receiving country.[16] We will take a closer look at these developments in the next chapter as part of the overall effort U.S. digital diplomacy faced (and still faces) in dealing with information barriers abroad.

Meanwhile, the 1977 ITU decision on rigid planning of satellite frequencies pointed up the difficulties the United States faced in planning for the 1979 World Administrative Radio Conference (WARC), which would review all spectrum frequencies. As one State Department official noted at the time: "The Third World now has the votes and the ability to set the agenda in ITU meetings from here on in."[17] Meanwhile, U.S. communications industry leaders expressed fears that the ITU spectrum planning process had become too politicized to represent American interests in maintaining open information channels worldwide.[18]

Another set of pressures came from Congress, reacting to these industry concerns. For the first time, an ITU conference attracted major congressional attention, two and a half years before the conference began.[19] On the Senate side, the banking and commerce committee became the focus of criticism directed at State Department preparations for the conference. The committee had two Republican members, Barry Goldwater of Arizona and Harrison Schmidt of New Mexico, each particularly knowledgeable about spectrum matters. (Schmidt was a former astronaut, and Goldwater was a longtime radio ham operator.) Prodded by the two senators, the committee commissioned a study by Arthur D. Little Inc., a Boston consulting firm, which claimed that the State Department's preparations for the 1979 WARC conference were inadequate.[20]

The department met strong criticism from another congressional group, the House subcommittee on international operations, whose chairman was Dante Fascell, a Florida Democrat. The subcommittee found fault with what it regarded as the department's weak administrative structure for dealing with telecommunication issues, including the preparations for the 1979 WARC. The committee's criticism set in motion changes that led to a major reorganization of digital diplomacy issues in the State Department and other federal agencies several years later, as we will see in Chapter 7.

In addition to congressional criticism, the State Department had to cope with inter-agency squabbles over WARC issues. Jurisdiction over telecommunications policy overlapped a dozen other federal agencies. Unlike the State Department, each of these agencies had a strong domestic constituency. The FCC was protective of the interests of the private telecommunications and broadcasting sectors. The Commerce Department strenuously opposed proposals that it felt would limit the trade interests of its corporate supporters. The Defense Department raised the banner of national security. At one point, it suggested that its 25 percent allotment of spectrum slots assigned to the United States under ITU rules be increased to 40 percent.

Meanwhile, the State Department lobbied its WARC proposals among other ITU members. By and large, the Europeans, Canadians and Japanese agreed to most American positions, but support from the hundred or more Third World countries was more problematical. In the mid-1970s, a Broadcasting Organizations of the Non-Aligned Countries was formed to deal with spectrum issues. An "Arusha Declaration," issued after a 1978 meeting in Tanzania, declared the "the non-aligned countries should form a common and single point at the 1979 WARC."[21]

These Third World efforts were supported financially and ideologically by a varied group of public and private organizations. These included UNESCO, the U.N. Economic Commission for Africa, West Germany's Konrad Adenauer Foundation and the International Institute of Communications, a public policy group in London. Another interested group was the Brandt Commission, headed by former West German chancellor Willy Brandt, which had been formed to study Third World economic needs. The commission advanced the idea of an international tax on radio spectrum use that would fund communications expansion in developing countries. Since an outsized proportion of the tax would be paid by American companies, the State Department dismissed the proposal out of hand.[22]

The 1979 WARC opened in early September at the ITU conference center in Geneva. It attracted little public attention, although it was, by many measures, the most complex international conference ever attended by the United States up to that time. With more than 1,000 delegates from 153 nations, the conference agenda dealt with over 15,000 proposals over a period of three months.[23] The ITU budgeted for 27 million pages of documents in the three conference languages—English, French and Spanish. The American delegation, with University of Virginia law professor Glen O. Robinson as its chairman, was the largest presence at the meeting, with over 100 delegates and support staff. (By contrast, the average delegation had fewer than five members.) This meant that American delegates could be represented in each of the dozens of committee meetings which simultaneously debated spectrum issues.

The United States had another advantage: daily computer tracking of all of the conference proposals. It was the first time that any country made extensive use of computers at a major international conference. A Hewlett-Packard desktop computer in the U.S. delegation's offices stored the 15,000 conference proposals. Decisions made in each day's proceedings were fed into the computer overnight. As a result the American delegation had the only accurate record of what had happened at the dozens of conference committee and working group sessions each day.

From a political standpoint, the conference itself was a welcome anticlimax for the U.S. delegation. The prospect of a North-South confrontation, which could have forced the meeting into gridlock, was largely defused in the first few days. Third World countries were united on only one point: they wanted one of their own as conference chairman, a post that in past years had been filled by an official from a neutral country, often Scandinavian. The issue was resolved by the election of an Argentine official who met the Third World litmus test without being an ideologue. An even more sensitive election involved the chairmanship of the committee on frequency allocations, where most of the significant decisions would be made. The conference elected Mohamed Harbi, an Algerian delegate, who proved to be both technically competent and politically evenhanded in dealing with contending forces within the committee.

These decisions tended to modify the influence of the more ideologically zealous Third World delegations. They never managed to organize an effective caucus to press their demands. On the other hand, the Europeans, with Canadian support, presented a generally united front in defending their regional positions, some of which ran against American interests. The Soviet delegation played an anomalous role, siding with Third World interests when it could, while letting U.S. negotiators take the ideological heat from Third World delegates in defending unpopular positions that were often identical with Soviet spectrum policy.

The conference produced an 1,100-page final document that revised most ITU spectrum regulations without serious harm to American interests. In a few instances where its strategic interests were threatened, the United States took the unusual step of refusing to pledge compliance, particularly in the area of military communications. "We didn't do this lightly," said Ronald Stowe, an industry representative on the delegation, "but it was critically important in convincing other countries to take our positions seriously."[24]

American negotiators lobbied successfully to have a number of contentious issues postponed to future conferences. This set the stage for making spectrum negotiations a continuing concern for U.S. digital diplomacy ever since. WARC conferences are now held roughly every two years.

Confrontation within the ITU over spectrum issues has been reduced substantially in recent years. This is partly the result of steady improvements in spectrum technology that allows greater capacity to be squeezed into finite frequencies. Third World spectrum claims have become less strident, in part because many of their demands have been accommodated under new ITU rules. Equally important are the changes that have taken place in the global communications environment as a whole in recent decades. The American decision to end the AT&T monopoly in 1984 was the first step towards what would become a worldwide trend to end national telecommunications monopolies, replacing them in whole or in part by privatized competitive businesses.

This has introduced a note of pragmatic realism into recent negotiations over global spectrum issues. Ideological confrontation is generally a thing of the past. The ITU has reorganized its spectrum management procedures to accommodate the new competitive environment. In particular, as noted above, it has put the negotiation of spectrum issues on a regular schedule, with each conference dealing with a few limited issues. This has allowed a more structured approach to working out political accommodations to technological and economic changes affecting spectrum use.

The agreements reached at the ITU conferences in the 1980s, and in smaller conferences since then, represent an overall success for American digital diplomacy. As we shall see in the next chapter, the same claim cannot be made with regard to other politically charged digital issues, particularly those dealing with cross-border information flows.

NOTES

1. "An analysis of the Socialist states' proposal for Intersputnik," *Villanova Law Review*, Vol. 15, No. 1, Fall 1969, pp. 83–88.

2. Joseph N. Pelton, *Intelsat: Politics and functionalism* (Mt. Airy, MD: Lomond Books, 1974), p. 49.

3. Jonathan F. Galloway, *The politics and technology of satellite communications* (Lexington, MA: D. C. Heath & Co., 1972), pp. 147–154.

4. Intelsat's early impact on developing countries is discussed in Richard R. Colino, "International satellite telecommunications and developing countries," *Journal of Law and Economic Development*, Vol. 3, No. 1, Spring 1968, pp. 8–41.

5. "Seventy nations agree to lay longest undersea cable," *Financial Times* (London), 16 January 1997, p. 2.

6. For a survey of the development of digital technology, see: Wilson P. Dizard, *The coming information age*, 3rd ed. (New York: Longman Publishers, 1989), ch. 3.

7. The politics and economics of ITU regulatory policies are described in James G. Savage, *The politics of international telecommunications regulation* (Boulder, CO: Westview Press, 1989).

8. Daniel R. Headrick, *The invisible weapon: Telecommunications and international politics 1851–1945* (New York: Oxford University Press, 1991), pp. 120–121.

9. George A. Codding, Jr. and Anthony M. Rutkowsky, *The International Telecommunications Union in a changing world* (Dedham, MA: Artech House, 1982), pp. 121–126.

10. Ibid., pp. 39–44.

11. The growth of U.S. telecommunications in the 1970s is documented in Gerald W. Brock, *The telecommunications industry: The dynamics of market structure* (Cambridge, MA: Harvard University Press, 1981).

12. "Conferees to divide airwaves and orbits," *Washington Post*, 17 June 1979, p. G-1.

13. "Soviets ask UN to bar intrusions by satellite TV," *New York Times*, 11 August 1972, p. 14.

14. "U.S. to oppose broadcast satellite plan," *Aviation Week and Space Technology*, 10 January 1977, pp. 85–86.

15. For useful background on international satellite regulation, including the 1977 conference, see: Martin A. Rothblatt, "ITU regulation of satellite communications," *Stanford Journal of International Law*, Vol. 18, No. 1, 1982, pp. 214–226.

16. "U.S. is worried by world efforts to curtail flow of information," *New York Times*, 26 February 1978, p. 1.

17. "WARC 79: The haves vs. the have-nots," *Broadcasting*, special report on the state of the fifth estate, 1 January 1979, p. 32.

18. "Stanton fears that ideology may curb WARC technology," *Broadcasting*, 17 September 1979, p. 73.

19. "OTP briefing kicks off Capitol Hill participation in WARC '79 planning," *Telecommunications Reports*, 23 May 1977, p. 30.

20. "Gloomy WARC assessment," *Satellite Week*, 10 September 1979, p. 1.

21. "Document of the third meeting of the committee for cooperation," Committee for Cooperation of Broadcasting Organizations of the Non-Aligned Countries, Arusha, Tanzania, October 1978, p. 51. For a useful survey of the non-aligned countries' preparations for the 1979 WARC, see: "WARC '79: The haves vs. the have-nots," *Broadcasting*, op cit.

22. "International tax?" *Broadcasting*, 23 July 1979, p. 7.

23. The U.S. proposals, 900 pages long, are summarized in "World Administrative Radio Conference," Special Report No. 57, Bureau of Public Affairs, Department of State, August 1979.

24. "The Third World lays a claim on the airways," *Business Week*, 28 January 1980, p. 32. For a description of the 1979 WARC results and their impact on American policy, see: Glen O. Robinson, "Regulating international airwaves: The 1979 WARC," *Virginia Journal of International Law*, Vol. 21, No. 1, Fall 1980, pp. 1–54.

Chapter 5

The Threat to Global Information Flows

Removing barriers to global information flows has been the most complex issue American digital diplomacy has dealt with in recent decades. The United States played a unique role in bringing the subject to international attention in the 1940s. It has actively pursued the issue ever since, with policies and actions that at times have met with resistance from almost every other country on earth.

The issue involves the right to send and receive information in any form across borders. Limited largely to printed materials in the past, the subject has been expanded in recent decades to include a wide range of electronic channels, from television to the Internet.

American advocacy of open information flow challenges long-standing claims of national sovereignty, in particular a government's right to control communications channels and the information they transmit. This U.S. stance is often seen by foreign governments as interference in their internal affairs, a high-handed attempt to extend First Amendment principles and practices to the rest of the world.

U.S. free-flow policy has a strong ideological base. But it also includes more mundane interests. One of these is the reduction of communications and information barriers to U.S. international trade. This factor has become more important in recent decades for two reasons. The first is to support the growth in the export of American communications goods and services, collectively the biggest item in the country's overseas trade package. The second reason is to assure efficient communications access for U.S. enterprises operating abroad, either as traders or as offshore producers of goods and services. Both these economic needs have been increasingly threatened in recent decades by foreign laws and practices designed to protect local political, economic and cultural interests.

On balance, American efforts to lower global information barriers have been successful. Open information flow is now routinely accepted, both as a concept and as a pragmatic benefit by most industrial democracies and by a growing number of Third World economies. Many barriers remain but the trend is powerfully towards reducing them, largely because of pressures to make national economies more competitive in an information-driven world marketplace. Another pressure, less measurable but equally important, comes from ordinary men and women who want to be linked to the new networks, whether it involves an ordinary telephone call or access to a high-technology database.

One result has been the dramatic expansion of the U.S. information sector at home and abroad. It has also opened up the domestic economy to overseas competitors, particularly those involved in digital goods and services. Foreign firms such as Sony, Siemens, Nortel, Reuters, Bertlesmann and Nokia, largely unknown to American consumers 20 years ago, are now major players in the U.S. information economy.[1]

These changes have taken place largely since 1970. Before that time, global electronic communications resources were primitive, scarce and expensive to use. International telephone calls usually involved unreliable shortwave circuits. Telegraph and telex traffic moved over low-capacity cables. It was not until the introduction of satellites and high-capacity submarine cables that transborder electronic traffic became significant. In 1960, there were less than 1,000 North Atlantic cable circuits linking Europe and the United States, primarily for telegraph and telex traffic. At the turn of the century, there are more than 50 million cable and satellite circuits in the region, providing a full range of high-speed voice, video and data services. A similar expansion has taken place in the Pacific and East Asian region.

Establishing workable rules-of-the-road for this change has dominated the American digital diplomacy agenda in recent decades. We have seen in the two last chapters its effects in two critical areas—the organization of the Intelsat network and the restructuring of the radio frequency spectrum to accommodate satellites and other advanced technologies. These negotiations were part of a larger diplomatic effort to adjust old practices to new electronic realities. By and large, this has involved the removal of political and economic barriers that protected national communications monopolies abroad.

In 1982, the United States dismantled its own version of a national monopoly—the AT&T phone network. The result was to open the domestic telecommunications market to competition. It took another 14 years for Congress to pass a law, the Telecommunications Act of 1996, which set the ground rules for full competition in all communications and information services.[2]

In addition to hastening the shift to an American information economy, these changes have had strong repercussions overseas. Beginning with Western Europe, other countries began to accept the need for restructuring their own communications systems. This has led to U.S. diplomatic negotiations—bilaterally and in international forums—with over 150 countries, each in a different stage of information age development. Control over communications resources in these countries was, until recently, a hallowed sovereign right, handed down from an age when kings and priests dominated the production and distribution of information. Maintaining these controls in modern times has become more difficult, given the ability of advanced electronic technologies to bypass official controls—through the Internet or by direct television broadcasting from satellites, for instance.

By the 1980s, American digital diplomacy became increasingly focussed on ending political and economic barriers to open communications flows throughout the world. Initially, this effort was strongly resisted by many governments abroad. The sharpest opposition came from totalitarian nations. The Soviet Union and China railed against U.S. open-flow policies as an attempt to impose American political, economic and cultural hegemony over the rest of the world. This theme was picked up by many critics in the newly decolonized nations of Asia and Africa. Opposition was also strong in Europe, fueled by the opposition of cultural elites to what they saw as the Americanization of their cultures. A French cultural minister, Jack Lang, famously echoed this theme in 1984 when he described the impact of U.S. information exports as "a real crusade—let's call things by their names—this financial and cultural imperialism that no longer grabs territory, or rarely, but grabs consciousness, ways of thinking, ways of living."[3]

Despite these criticisms, U.S. information flow diplomacy has had a long-range impact. It introduced a subject that had never been given sustained international attention. Moreover, it did more than simply increase the visibility of an important human right. It also laid the groundwork for profound changes in attitudes and actions on the subject. In many ways, these efforts are the most lasting legacy of U.S. digital diplomacy in the past half-century.

American strategy for reducing global communications and information barriers divides roughly into two periods since the late 1940s. Initially the effort was focussed on resisting ideological efforts to expand restrictions on communications flow, with an emphasis on the mass media. Since then, it has concentrated more directly on trade-related barriers—the complex web of tariff and non-tariff regulations that continue to limit global commerce in information goods and services. In this chapter, we will look at the ideologically oriented issues dealt with by American diplomacy in the decades after 1945. The newer trade-related issues will be dealt with in Chapter 8.

As noted in earlier chapters, communications and information issues were a peripheral concern for U.S. diplomacy until the middle of the last century. The events of World War II changed this. For the first time, a global U.S. military presence highlighted the need for dependable overseas communications. American troops built a worldwide communications system and in the process displaced the prewar dominance of British and French networks.[4] After the war, American mass media came into its own as an international force, as Hollywood filmmakers, radio and television broadcasters and print publishers expanded abroad. As cultural critic Emily Rosenberg notes:

The nation's rise to world power was inextricably linked with the dissemination of images of affluence, consumerism, middle-class status, individual freedom, and technological progress. The appeal of American mass culture facilitated overseas expansion and identified the United States with progress. Not only in Western Europe but throughout the world cultural transmissions facilitated the emergence of what Gertrude Stein and later Henry Luce called the the American Century.[5]

In many ways, this impact has set the tone and pace of U.S. digital diplomacy in recent decades. It has involved a complex pattern of mass acceptance of U.S. information products worldwide, coupled with strong elite resistance to the powerful effects these products have had on local cultural patterns.

Americans generally react to this change with a somewhat guileless belief that exporting their information products, from the mass media to World Wide Web pages, is a good thing. Many governments and their citizens do not see it that way, for a variety of political, economic and cultural reasons. In one celebrated instance in 1972, 100 countries voted in the U.N. General Assembly in favor of a proposal to restrict transborder information flows by satellite, clearly aimed at what they regarded as undue American media influence. The U.S. delegation cast the only negative vote.[6]

On most information flow issues, American negotiators have dealt in recent decades with three separate groups of countries, each with a different agenda on the subject. The first of these groups were the Communist states, primarily the Soviet Union and its East European clients. At the time, the Chinese Communist regime played a minor role, restricting itself largely to ritualistic attacks on American information imperialism. Mainland China was effectively cut off from global information flow until the mid-1970s. AT&T reported that before it was allowed to resume limited phone service to China in 1971, it had handled only about 20 calls a year. Moreover, the service was available only for an hour and a half each day.[7]

Information issues became an increasingly important element in cold war strategy as positions on both sides hardened. After its largely unsuccessful attempts at psychological warfare operations (described in Chapter 2), the United States settled down to a dual strategy of information operations against Communist regimes. The first part involved economic warfare, denying access to Western technology and information resources that would give the Soviets an edge in the East-West military confrontation. This was done largely through the Paris-based Coordinating Committee for Multilateral Export Controls (COCOM), whose membership was largely made up of NATO countries.[8]

At the same time, American policy sought to open information channels to citizens in Communist countries through cultural agreements and limited USIA operations within the Soviet bloc. Its most important channel, however, was radio—the Voice of America, Radio Liberty and Radio Free Europe—the latter two funded and managed by the Central Intelligence Agency until the 1970s.[9]

The second group of countries involved in information flow negotiations were the industrial democracies, particularly those in West Europe. Overall, they have been sympathetic to American free-flow initiatives. But they were also suspicious that the United States was using the issue to promote its trade interests. By the 1980s, the West Europeans had fallen behind in developing advanced information and communications resources. This was, in part, a result of the fractionalization of these resources in more than a dozen separate national industries serving local markets and protected by their governments. They were no match for the American companies that moved into the European Community (EC) to take advantage of the largest communications market outside the United States. By the 1980s, IBM had become the largest computer supplier in every EC country except Great Britain. One result was that EC companies at the time had only a 15 percent share of the global market in information goods and services. The rest was split almost evenly between American and Japanese firms.[10] Warnings that Europe would fall even further behind in information resources became a common theme. French journalist Jacques Servan-Schreiber was the first to raise the specter of a Europe in economic decline due to the dominance of IBM and other U.S. multinationals.[11] A 1978 French government study emphasized the need to protect European economic and social institutions while accommodating to American-dominated information technologies.[12] It was not until the late 1980s that the European Community (now the European Union) took effective steps to restructure its regional telecommunications and information sectors to make them more competitive in world markets.

The third and largest group of countries involved in U.S. free-flow diplomacy were the newly independent nations in Asia and Africa. Their colonial rulers had left few communications resources when they departed in the decades after World War II. Most of the new governments were authoritarian, with leaders who had little interest in building up communications systems that they might not be able to control. These countries were also small but occasionally important players in the larger field of Soviet-American cold war confrontation. Although most publicly professed non-alignment, they showed an ideological tilt towards Soviet claims about their alleged exploitation ("economic imperialism") by the West in general and by the United States in particular.[13]

As in other areas of American policy towards the new nations, these attitudes affected digital diplomacy. It was a new situation, involving regions where the United States had few communications interests and even fewer precedents on how to deal with the subject. There was, however, an imperative to act, given the cold war factors involved. What was missing were guidelines for dealing with the problem.

American academics came to the rescue with a doctrine for dealing with the role of communications in the new nations. The doctrine's shorthand name was modernization, a strategy for hastening the transition from traditional tribal and ethnic patterns to centralized and, hopefully, democratic governments. "Nation building" became the rubric for this new approach, which was developed largely by social scientists at MIT and other Boston-area schools. Its success depended heavily on the use of modern communications techniques. As MIT professor Daniel Lerner, one of the key players in the project, noted, the task was to create "a forced march to modernity" in the new countries, with a strong emphasis on the mass media and other information resources to guide the marchers.[14]

Modernization was an appealing doctrine, fitting easily into America's latent missionary impulses. It also served as an ideological counterweight to Marxist-Leninist theories about imperialist attempts to exploit former colonies, substituting political rule with economic and cultural domination. It was a theme that Soviet propaganda exploited with drumbeat regularity throughout the cold war. Modernization doctrine drove U.S. strategy in Asia, Africa and Latin America in the early decades of the cold war era, with the dual purpose of containing Soviet and Chinese influence and of creating more stable political conditions. It was the ideological basis for, among other initiatives, the Kennedy administration's Alliance for Progress in Latin America and for the Peace Corps. Information resources were given a prominent role in these programs, along with military and economic support, as part of the effort (in the then-current phrase) to win the hearts and minds of men.

The doctrine soon sagged under the weight of the complexities involved in turning around traditional societies. It proved to be an inadequate guide to any quick-fix resolution of political and economic problems. Mass media projects, begun with high hopes of winning converts to modernization, stressed the role of radio and television as carriers of the message. Their failure was documented in, among other studies, a Ford Foundation–sponsored survey of broadcasting in over 30 developing countries. The study showed that radio and TV broadcasting was being used largely to glorify local political regimes and to supply lightweight entertainment, much of it American imports.[15]

Modernization strategy was also undercut by larger political developments in the 1960s. The most important of these was aggressive Soviet and Chinese advocacy of "wars of national liberation" against alleged American political and economic domination in Asia, Africa and Latin America. This threat was backed up by large-scale aid from Moscow and Beijing to dissident groups in these regions. Modernization programs seemed to be a pallid response to these moves. By 1962, American policy had shifted to a more muscular doctrine—counterinsurgency—emphasizing military operations. Economic and social modernization was relegated to secondary status, displaced by a new emphasis on using force to deal with local insurgencies. Vietnam became the most prominent example of the risks and penalties of this approach.

In summary, U.S. digital diplomacy in the early postwar decades dealt with three separate groups in pressing its strategy of open information flow—totalitarian regimes, the industrial democracies and the new nations of Asia and Africa. This was complex enough in itself, and it was made more so by the dispersal of responsibility for information policy—both domestic and foreign—among Washington agencies. It is useful to review the evolution of U.S. international information flow policy in the postwar decades. Its foundations were formed during the war as the United States moved into a commanding role as a global communications power. Its doctrinal tone was originally set in President Franklin Roosevelt's January 1941 speech to Congress on the "four freedoms," including freedom of speech, as human rights goals for the postwar era. For the first time in history, information freedoms were given equal status with political and economic issues in an international context.

In the initial flush of postwar optimism, the United States pressed for recognition of information rights in the new United Nations organization. A general declaration expanding on the Four Freedoms information theme was passed at the first meeting of the General Assembly in 1946. It was quintessential American free-flow doctrine, stating that "all states should proclaim policies under which free flow of information, within countries and across frontiers, will be protected. The right to seek and transmit information should be insured to enable the public to ascertain facts and appraise events."[16]

A U.N. commission, chaired by Eleanor Roosevelt, was created in 1946 to draft a Universal Declaration of Human Rights. The draft, which was approved by the General Assembly two years later, expanded on the assembly's earlier declaration, affirming the right "to hold opinions without interference and to seek, receive and impart information and ideas through any media regardless of frontiers."[17] It was a sweeping extension of human rights, approved by 48 countries with no negative votes. (There were eight abstentions.) As Fred Cate, a University of Indiana communications specialist, points out, the declaration proposed the extension of the First Amendment rights of American citizens to everyone everywhere.[18]

Despite strong rhetorical support for the Universal Declaration, reservations about its broad inclusiveness surfaced during the U.N. debates leading up to its adoption. Many delegations were not prepared to surrender traditional sovereign controls over information flows, particularly those involving the mass media. They proposed amendments designed to water down the declaration's sweeping defense of individual information rights. Under Mrs. Roosevelt's leadership, the United States managed to defeat these proposals. Nevertheless, the stage was set for a confrontation between the American version of information freedoms and that of most other countries. It was a dispute that was to dominate the free-flow debate in the United Nations and other international fora over the next three decades.[19]

The Universal Declaration's weakness was that it was only a statement of principles. An American proposal to include provisions for investigating information rights violations was turned down. In part, this reflected the fact that human rights, including information access, had become a cold war weapon as attitudes and policies hardened on both sides of the ideological divide. By the early 1950s, the Soviet Union began pressing for revisions in the Universal Declaration that would support the right of governments to regulate the mass media and other information channels. In one formulation, the Soviets proposed a code of ethics for journalists which included a pledge to expose warmongers and fascist ideas and stating that their "primary duty" was to promote friendly relations among nations.[20]

These changes were unacceptable to the United States and most other Western countries. However, they found a receptive audience among the growing number of former colonies that now formed the largest bloc within the United Nations. For the first time, the United States found itself on the defensive on freedom-of-information issues in the world organization.

The first major confrontation on information sovereignty issues took place in an unlikely forum—the U.N. Committee on the Peaceful Uses of Outer Space (COPUOS). Created in 1959, the committee was assigned the task of drafting an international treaty governing the new science of space exploration. A treaty was eventually approved in 1967 that defined, among other subjects, limits to national sovereignty claims in space. This opened the door to a debate on the use of satellites that could broadcast directly into television and radio receivers on earth.

Direct broadcast satellite (DBS) technology was in its early research-and-development stages at the time. Nevertheless, its technical prospects were good. This was given formal recognition by the International Tele-communications Union in 1963 when it expanded its spectrum regulations to include DBS experiments. By 1971, the regulations were amended to include spectrum that could be used for regular broadcasting from space.

The political implications of DBS technology were recognized early on by the two space powers—the United States and the Soviet Union. The weak beeps from Sputnik, the first orbiting space machine, signaled a Soviet triumph in October 1957. A year later, an American satellite, Score, broadcast a Christmas message from President Dwight Eisenhower. The idea of receiving television signals from space became one of the more popular promised benefits of space exploration.[21] At the same time, there were dire warnings in the American media that the Soviet Union might develop its own DBS capability for broadcasting Communist propaganda across the globe.[22]

Although both the Americans and Soviets focussed primarily on building conventional communications satellite networks during the 1960s, each began to explore direct broadcasting prospects. NASA invited industry proposals for a DBS feasibility study in November 1965.[23] A detailed description of American DBS plans was presented to an international space symposium in Paris by a NASA official several weeks later.[24] Meanwhile, the specific political impacts of direct broadcasting were being considered for the first time. NASA outlined the issues involved in a November 1965 document:

A direct broadcast system could be used unilaterally, bilaterally or in conjunction with existing or new international organizations; in every case, the issues of sovereignty, program material control, satellite ownership, and broadcast schedules would be raised. The effect of a centralized unified broadcasting service on political and social developments would have to be considered.[25]

These factors became grist for an extended United Nations debate on broadcasting satellites, centered in the outer space committee. At issue was the right of a country to broadcast from space into another country without the latter's prior permission. In effect, it was an extension of information sovereignty into outer space. The technical difficulties involved in developing space broadcasting, or of blocking it once it began, were largely ignored in the discussion. The emphasis was the need to regulate this new technology's capability for distributing mass media in a way that bypassed national information controls.

The debate was directed almost exclusively against the United States, the only country that had publicly announced its intention to exploit DBS technology. It was a ready-made issue for the Soviet Union, which took the lead in encouraging developing countries to back DBS restrictions.

As the debate droned on in the outer space committee, the State Department set up an inter-agency committee to monitor the subject. Its public position was that DBS could eventually speed up economic development in the Third World. It proposed a set of "voluntary principles" as a substitute for international regulations that would require satellite broadcasters to obtain the prior consent of countries they intended to serve. The American delegation in the outer space committee argued that DBS was a new technology that should not be hampered by regulation before its full potential had been explored.[26]

This strategy was reinforced by the swift progress made in American direct broadcast capabilities in the early 1970s. Hughes, RCA, General Electric and other space equipment firms had each made important technical breakthroughs in both DBS satellites and in earth stations, looking primarily at a potential domestic market.[27] By 1973, NASA had launched the first of a series of experimental satellites to demonstrate broadcasting satellite uses within the United States. The agency's Advanced Technology Satellite (ATS) project was a success, providing educational and training links to remote schools, health clinics and other facilities in the Rocky Mountains, Appalachia and Alaska, using an advanced ATS-6 satellite. The next step was to carry out similar demonstrations in overseas locations, in part to undercut political objections to broadcasting satellite transmissions.[28]

The first international experiments had begun in 1971, involving simple two-way voice messaging. The satellite, named Peacesat, linked over a dozen South Pacific island-nations from a base terminal at the University of Hawaii, giving them a regional communications network for the first time. Although Peacesat had a predicted design life of five years, it continued to operate for over 15 years.[29]

Three years later, the ATS-6 satellite was moved along its equatorial path 22,500 miles in space, using short jet bursts to push it around the globe. At its various stops, it demonstrated its potential educational and economic development uses for government officials and professional groups in Asia, Africa and Latin America. The most elaborate demonstration took place in India where, for almost two years, ATS-6 broadcast

educational and health programs into simple chicken-wire earth terminals located in 2,000 villages. All of the programs were produced by
Indian groups.[30]

The ATS project had mixed political effects on the direct broadcasting
satellite debate in the United Nations. At one level, it confirmed America's technological lead and its willingness to share DBS technology with
the rest of the world. But it also fueled demands for prior-consent restrictions on broadcasting satellites. Satellites that could deliver educational resources to remote villages could also broadcast American
gangster movies and Coca-Cola advertising, according to critics of the
project. This, they claimed, was the sinister purpose of the ATS demonstrations.

The DBS debate dragged on for another half-dozen years in the U.N.
outer space committee. The Soviet Union introduced a draft treaty in
1972 that included a prior-consent provision, together with one restricting DBS transmissions to broadcasting organizations under the direct
control of governments.[31] It also authorized governments to use "the
means at its disposal to counteract illegal television broadcasting of
which it is the object." This was widely interpreted as a Soviet threat to
destroy offending satellites.[32]

The United States found itself largely isolated in opposing the Soviet
draft treaty. This was made clear when it cast the only negative vote in
the General Assembly political committee debate on a proposal to water
down the more controversial parts of the Soviet proposal to a set of
principles, including a voluntary prior-consent clause.[33] A later attempt
at a compromise, developed by Canada and Sweden, preserved the
prior-consent concept, while suggesting that any disputes should be settled in bilateral or regional negotiations between the countries
involved.[34] The effort failed, and eventually the direct broadcasting issue
was reduced to ritualistic charges and countercharges in obscure meetings.

Ironically, the DBS issue eventually became moot largely because of
the success satellite operators had in promoting direct broadcasting networks around the globe. The first such network, Astra, was developed
by Luxembourg interests in the 1980s to supply direct-to-home news and
entertainment programs in Western Europe. Other networks, sponsored
by American firms, were built to provide similar services in Asia, Africa
and Latin America. The Star network, controlled by media magnate Rupert Murdoch, provided an eclectic menu of American and local programs, to a vast audience in 30 countries across Asia, from the
Philippines to the Persian Gulf. The major direct broadcasting issue in
recent years has not been objections about cultural imperialism by Third
World nations, but complaints by American program providers about

their revenue losses from the extensive piracy of their programs via illegal satellite dishes in these countries.

As the debate over DBS faded, other free-flow issues took its place.
The United Nations set up a commission on transnational corporations,
with a mandate that included a study of the alleged control of global
data flows by multinational firms. Meanwhile, the United States introduced proposals for including information and telecommunications services under the General Agreement on Trade and Tariffs (GATT). The
result, as we shall see in Chapter 8, was a 1994 treaty setting up a new
World Trade Organization, including liberalized regulations for the information goods and services.

The more immediate problem for U.S. policymakers in the 1970s, however, was the new prominence of UNESCO in the free-flow debate. The
DBS issue in the U.N. outer space committee was limited to regulating
a single technology, one that in fact was still in the future. UNESCO
shifted the debate to the larger issues of mandating global restrictions
over information flows through a wide range of channels, including
broadcasting satellites.

Over and above their implications for information freedoms, the
UNESCO proposals were a clear threat to U.S. information exports. In
the years after World War II, this trade had expanded dramatically, particularly in the mass media sector. American films (and, later, television)
became a staple entertainment source for foreign audiences. Book and
magazine publishers moved into overseas markets for the first time.
Reader's Digest led the way, marketing over a dozen separate language
editions in more than 100 countries by 1980. Overseas editions of *Time*
and *Newsweek* attracted a smaller but influential elite readership on all
continents.[35] However, American media companies were faced with a
serious challenge to their overseas sales. They had dealt previously with
occasional attempts by national authorities to censor their products. The
UNESCO proposals were different, calling for blanket restrictions on a
worldwide basis. Faced with this prospect, the industry turned to the
State Department for help.

Ironically, the United States had played a major role in UNESCO's
creation in 1946. It was the first time that the American government had
supported an international organization that sponsored educational and
cultural programs. The decision triggered domestic criticism from the
start, particularly from conservative groups. An early indication, as we
saw in Chapter 2, was congressional grumbling about an American modern art show in 1946 at UNESCO's inaugural meeting in Paris. Despite
such criticism, the United States was the largest contributor to
UNESCO's budget. From the start, the American focus was on practical
programs such as literacy campaigns, teacher training and (the most visible sign of UNESCO activities) the preservation of cultural treasures

such as the temples at Angkor Wat and ancient monuments in Egypt which were threatened by dam construction on the Nile.

UNESCO policy was supposed to be guided by the recommendations of cultural commissions in each member country. The American commission had 100 members and was managed by an ineffective secretariat.[36] Other national commissions were equally unorganized, or nonexistent. It was an unwieldy arrangement, and power soon shifted to bureaucrats at UNESCO headquarters in Paris. With a few exceptions, they were, in the words of one observer, a collection of erstwhile Scandinavians, second-rate academics and Third World careerists. It also included a large contingent of employees from the Soviet Union and its client states, many of them espionage agents using UNESCO as a convenient cover for their activities.

By the 1960s, UNESCO had lost all semblance of being guided by its national commissions. Its bureaucrats had increasingly free rein to develop their own programs. One of these was an "Ideas Bureau" whose purpose was to hatch big projects. One of the bureau's recommendations was a "Waxwork Museum of Culture Heroes of all Civilizations." Another was a prototype tent for Arab storytellers with simultaneous translation facilities.[37] Most of the Bureau's ideas never saw the light of day, but others did, each involving large conferences, which produced reports written in a unique form of UNESCO corkscrew prose. By the early 1970s, UNESCO was managing over 300 projects on a budget of over a quarter billion dollars.

Most of these projects were of little interest to the American government or to domestic private sector groups. The U.S. National Commission was increasingly ineffective. Its difficulties were compounded by the fact that, in its early years, it was the responsibility of two separate State Department offices—the bureaus of public affairs and international affairs.[38] Meanwhile, UNESCO's Paris bureaucrats increasingly took positions that tilted towards the anti-American biases of cultural elites around the world.

The U.S. list of grievances against UNESCO was a long one, but it was dominated by a digital diplomacy issue. This was the organization's role in attempting to impose restrictions on international media flows. The effort was focussed from the start on curbing American media. One target was the news agencies, particularly the Associated Press and United Press International. Not only did they dominate global news flow, critics charged, they also presented a consistently unfair image of events in Asia, Africa and Latin America.[39]

The main thrust of the UNESCO-inspired grievances, however, was against American film and television products. Exports of both were booming in the postwar decades. Television production companies in New York and Hollywood took advantage of the opportunities offered by hundreds of new stations abroad, each with program needs that could not be met with locally produced products. Cheap and attractive American shows filled the gap. The industry set up a Television Program Export Association in 1960 to promote its wares abroad. Exports jumped from $30 million to $120 million in the next four years.[40]

With its long experience in overseas sales, Hollywood fared even better in the new markets. Export promotion was a major goal of its trade association, the Washington-based Motion Picture Association of America (MPAA). The film industry's export success was based primarily on its ability to produce what came to be called international films. Its stars, from Shirley Temple to John Wayne, were as familiar in New Delhi and Paris as they were in Boston and Des Moines. Unlike their overseas competitors, the Hollywood studios hired foreign directors, actors and writers and then proceeded to make films in all parts of the world. The French writer Andre Malraux once summed up Hollywood's genius as the ability to produce a film in which a Swedish actress playing a Russian heroine working for an American director could draw tears from the Chinese.

All of this added up to American cultural imperialism for UNESCO bureaucrats and their supporters around the world. The Soviet Union had long exploited this theme in its propaganda. The issue gained further visibility by the late 1960s as dozens of former Asian and African colonies organized themselves as a caucus of non-aligned nations, with an extensive agenda of political and economic grievances aimed at the West in general and the United States in particular. The media issue was prominent on the list. It was eventually codified as a demand for a New World Information and Communications Order (NWICO) to end the imbalances between "northern" and "southern" information resources.[41]

The debate over global media flows was a continuing concern for American digital diplomacy for over 20 years, with UNESCO as the main international forum for the controversy. The organization's first initiative took place in 1970 when its members authorized a program to help member states develop mass communications policies. The issue was expanded two years later at a UNESCO general conference when the Soviet Union submitted a draft of a mass media declaration. Its thrust was that governments should use media to further social and political goals, with the added proviso that states were responsible for the foreign activities of all mass media under their jurisdiction.

The media restriction debate was now joined, pitting a minority led by the United States against most of UNESCO's membership. Since the organization's conference rules required a consensus on all proposals, action on the Soviet draft was postponed to allow time to work out a compromise draft. However, radical voices dominated the political maneuvering. The chief strategist was Amadou-Mahter M'Bow, a Senegalese official who was elected UNESCO's director general in 1974.[42] A drafting group, meeting in December 1975, failed to come up with a suitable compromise. Most of the provisions in the Soviet mass media draft were approved. The new draft also included a clause that equated Zionism with racism, an addition designed to solidify Arab support for the draft.

Thirteen delegations, including the Americans, walked out of the meeting in protest. The incident led to a warning by Secretary of State Henry Kissinger that the United States was prepared to quit UNESCO. Congress reacted initially by withholding the American share of the organization's budget. It finally voted a partial payment of $3.5 million, the minimum that would permit the American delegation to vote at the next general conference.

Meanwhile, the Non-Aligned Movement, now expanded to over a hundred countries, became more militant on communications issues. At a 1974 meeting, the group adopted an "action program" for developing mass media and other communications resources within and between their countries. Its aim was to end what its drafters called cultural dependency on Western resources. One result was the formation of a Non-Aligned News Agency pool, run by Tanjug, the Yugoslav press agency.[43]

The 1976 UNESCO general conference, held in Nairobi, was a major turning point in the mass media debate. An amended Soviet draft provoked a bitter discussion. The Zionism/racism reference had been dropped but the provisions calling for government controls over media operations remained. Since the required consensus was clearly unobtainable, the draft was tabled by a 78–15 vote.[44] The Nairobi conference avoided a showdown on the mass media issue by approving two projects designed to defuse the subject for the time being. Both were reluctantly supported by the United States. The first was an "international program for the development of communications" (IPDC), run by an independent commission, which would provide financial aid for Third World communications and information projects. The second project was a study of "the totality of communications problems in modern societies," to be carried out by a group that came to be known as the MacBride Commission, after its chairman, former Irish foreign minister Sean MacBride.

These concessions gave the United States and its free-flow allies time to negotiate changes in the mass media declaration. A watered-down version of the original Soviet draft was approved at a 1978 UNESCO general conference. It supported the general principle of more open global communications flow but eliminated the Soviet draft's provisions mandating government responsibility for the activities of mass media organizations.[45]

Although the United States had promised support for the IPDC and for the MacBride Commission, both projects were treated warily in

Washington. Congress was increasingly disenchanted with UNESCO, and particularly with any plans for increasing American financial contributions to its activities.[46] This attitude was reinforced by the continued skepticism of U.S. media organizations about reforming UNESCO.[47] Newspaper publishers took the lead in funding a Washington-based World Press Freedom Committee that aggressively monitored attempts to restrict media flow abroad, including the UNESCO proposals.[48]

The MacBride Commission presented a special problem for State Department officials. Sean MacBride was a respected figure who had won a Nobel peace prize for his work on behalf of international human rights. The commission was originally split between two apparently irreconcilable views of the media's role—as an instrument for promoting social goals or one which was free to gather and report on events as it chose. Among the ideas initially supported by commission members were the licensing of journalists and a requirement that there should be an immediate correction of any errors made by them.

Another proposal called for the protection of reporters working in foreign countries—a provision strongly opposed by the American media as an excuse for governments to keep their correspondents on a leash. Sean MacBride's own formula for assuring more open flow was to create press councils which would meet yearly under UNESCO's auspices to review cases of alleged violations of constructive news reporting. What was at stake, the London *Economist* editorialized,

is no mere harmless Unspeak. If this version of MacBride should survive through the final report of the press commission, two things could happen. More governments could feel free, as Malta's did last year, to ban journalists who come from certain outside countries. And a kind of international closed shop could come about. Without a journalist's card or license, historians, novelists and politicians might be prevented from travelling the world and reporting what they saw.[49]

State Department officials pointed out to MacBride that in the long run these media restrictions would harm both human rights and economic development. After long, often testy negotiations with MacBride and other members of the commission, a report was issued in 1980, four years after it was authorized.[50] Most of the restrictive recommendations in earlier drafts had been removed or modified through semantic waffling designed to satisfy all sides in the debate.

The department's approach to the MacBride Commission reflected, in part, U.S. trade concerns, in particular the then-current belief that the American lead in communications exports was slipping. James Buckley, the undersecretary of state who handled technology matters, saw support of free information flow as a key element in American strategic interests. In a 1982 statement to a congressional committee, he declared: "For the United States, communications and information technologies represent a leading edge of U.S. strength. Policy and practice in international communications and information activities must actively enhance the overall well-being of the United States, the lives of its people, and its system of government."[51]

Buckley's statement was one of the first public acknowledgements by a high department official that information issues were an integral part of U.S. strategic planning. It was a theme, as we shall see, that would be repeated with many variations as digital policies took on a larger role in the foreign policy community, not only as issues in themselves but as a factor in most other policy areas.

Meanwhile, international interest in restricting the mass media began to wane, although there were rear-guard attempts to keep it alive in UNESCO and other forums. These efforts were strengthened by a Non-Aligned Movement initiative to expand the issue beyond media controls to the general problem of the North-South gap in overall communications resources, from telephones to advertising agencies. The "new world information order" theme was later made part of another non-aligned campaign—the New World Economic Order (NWEO).

Meanwhile, criticism of UNESCO mounted in the United States. Congress balked at providing even minimal funding for IPDC, the program for assisting Third World communications development. Responding to criticisms that IPDC funds were being wasted, the State Department announced that it would fund only projects of which it approved.[52] American disenchantment with UNESCO was later reinforced by a critical General Accounting Office survey of the organization's operations, describing a bloated bureaucracy and poor financial management among other faults.

The chief American complaint about UNESCO was, however, the organization's determination to push free-flow restrictions. In 1983, the Reagan administration decided to withdraw from the organization. Following the formal withdrawal in December 1984, the State Department set up a monitoring committee, headed by Washington lawyer Leonard Marks, to assess UNESCO promises to reform its operations. Although a number of reforms were made, attempts to persuade the Americans to rejoin the organization were unsuccessful.[53] U.S. relations with UNESCO have since been limited to small cooperative projects involving professional organizations.

While the debate over media restrictions was taking place in UNESCO, American policymakers were presented with an opportunity to lift information barriers within a cold war context. Its origin was the Nixon administration's decision in the early 1970s to encourage detente with the Soviet Union. Opening up information channels to the Soviet people was a critical part of the plan.

One result of the Nixon initiatives was the Helsinki Accords—more officially, the final acts of the Conference on Security and Cooperation in Europe. The accords were signed in August 1975 after three years of negotiations involving the United States, the Soviet Union and 31 other countries. The agreements included an important concession sought by the Soviet government—recognition of the territorial changes it had imposed on Central and Eastern Europe after World War II. In exchange, the Soviets agreed to limited cooperation with the West on a series of military, economic and information issues.

During the negotiations, these issues were bundled into three "baskets." The first two covered political and economic matters. The third basket dealt with information issues, broadly defined as cultural, educational and person-to-person contacts. These issues emerged as the most sensitive part of the negotiations, as the Soviets and their East European client-states attempted to limit such contacts. The Western countries, in turn, made third-basket issues the key to their acceptance of the provisions in the other two baskets. As one British diplomat summed up the Western position at the time: "If we don't lay eggs in the third basket, there will be none in the other ones either."

Given the prospect of losing important political concessions, the Soviet government agreed to increases in East-West information and cultural exchanges. It also accepted the idea of follow-on meetings to monitor progress in implementing all three basket agreements. Compliance with the Helsinki Accords came slowly from the Soviet side, particularly in carrying out the Basket Three provisions. Nevertheless, the Helsinki agreements played a special role in preparing the way for the eventual collapse of communist rule in eastern Europe and the Soviet Union. In part, this resulted from the increase in East-West contacts grudgingly allowed by Communist authorities. One example was the increase in exchanges of large exhibits by the Soviet and American governments. The exchanges provided tens of millions of Soviet bloc citizens with a tantalizing view of life beyond their borders.

Equally important, the Helsinki agreements emboldened dissident groups within the Soviet sphere. A Helsinki Monitoring Group was founded in Moscow shortly after the accords were signed. It became a leading dissident center, despite the fact that some of its leaders, including Anatoly Scharansky and Aleksandr Ginzburg, were given long prison sentences for their activities. Similar initiatives were taken in eastern Europe, notably Prague's Charter 77, whose organizers included Vaclav Havel, later the first president of post-Communist Czechoslovakia.

Digital diplomacy played a special role in the Helsinki agreements, particularly in the effort to end jamming Western radio stations. The

Soviets balked at a specific promise to end jamming at Helsinki. Their practice had been to suspend jamming of individual Western broadcasts for limited times, using the tactic as a barometer of cold war relations. After Helsinki, there was a slow but steady cutback in jamming by Moscow and its client states. The result was a dramatic rise in audience access to Western broadcasts within the Soviet bloc.

Together with other areas covered by the Helsinki agreements, the limited agreements on information flow had a powerful cumulative effect. As historian Richard Davy has noted:

The Final Act as it emerged was almost the opposite of what the Soviet Union had wanted. Instead of endorsing the status quo it was a charter for change. Instead of legitimizing the Soviet sphere of influence it legitimized Western intrusion into it. Instead of making frontiers immutable it specifically affirmed the principle of peaceful change. Instead of putting contacts under official control it emphasized the role of individuals.[54]

The specific impact of opening up Western broadcasting channels was later described by Lech Walesa, the founder of Poland's Solidarity movement: "If it were not for independent broadcasting, the world would look quite different today. Without Western broadcasting, totalitarian regimes would have survived much longer. The struggle for freedom would have been more arduous, and the road to democracy much longer."[55]

China posed the other major information barrier for American digital diplomacy. As noted earlier, its citizens were even more isolated from the outside world than those of the Soviet Union and its client states. The Chinese leadership had effective control over all information outlets, including a nationwide network of wired loudspeakers that supplied only official programs. Foreign stations were jammed; punishment was harsh and swift for clandestine listening. These information barriers began to erode very slowly after 1970. The catalyst was the Nixon Administration's "opening to China" initiative, resulting in the restoration of diplomatic relations after a quarter century.

This was followed by a series of carefully choreographed steps in which exchanges of ping pong players initially played an outsized role. Richard Nixon's 1972 visit to Beijing advanced the process as hundreds of foreign journalists covered the event. Communist authorities decided to allow satellite dishes to be brought into the country for the first time on a temporary basis. The result was global television coverage of the visit that tended to show China and its people in a favorable light. After the visit, the Beijing government bought the satellite dishes as the first equipment for what became an extensive domestic satellite network.

It was a small first step in the Chinese decision to modernize the country's ramshackle communications system. The decision was based on a realistic appraisal of the need for modern telecommunications to make the Chinese economy operate more efficiently. The corollary was that the government could continue to keep tight control over the system, and particularly the information flowing through it. Its determination was tested harshly during the 1989 Tienanman Square events, with its crackdown on students who used telephones, fax machines and the Internet to organize their protests.

Since that time, Chinese authorities have continued the expansion of their network, while attempting to control its use. American digital diplomacy has made only limited progress in influencing Chinese leaders to loosen these restrictions as part of an overall agenda of human rights issues between the two countries. Nevertheless, there have been strong indications since the late 1990s that Chinese government controls over information flows are being steadily eroded.

Internet access is widespread, despite attempts to restrict it to officially sanctioned users. Illegal satellite dishes pick up foreign television and radio channels. For the first time, a significant group of Chinese citizens have alternative information sources. If history is any measure, this change could have a critical role in the future of Communist rule in the world's largest country.[56]

The overall effort to reduce global barriers to information flow has been a singular achievement of American digital diplomacy. The United States succeeded in raising the subject as an international issue for the first time, giving it an ideological base in the 1948 U.N. Declaration of Human Rights. It then began the more difficult task of translating the declaration's sweeping statements into workable rules and practices. Many information barriers remain, but open information flow is now firmly rooted as a principle as well as a day-to-day reality in most parts of the globe.

In part, this is the result of recent advances in communications technologies. The new digital networks have the general effect of neutralizing political attempts to restrict information flows. A visible example of this is direct broadcasting by satellite. Once seen as a threat to be controlled, DBS is now a ubiquitous (and highly popular) presence in all parts of the world. Another example is the Internet. Attempts by national governments to control its use have largely failed.

Nevertheless, the global expansion of the Internet has created a new agenda of digital diplomacy issues. One of the issues involves privacy protection on the Internet. American policy emphasizes voluntary guidelines, monitored by Internet data suppliers. Many other countries have strict laws to assure adherence to privacy standards. Another issue is protection against "cybercrime" on the Internet, in particular the introduction of digital viruses that invade databases and destroy their content. The first global conference on the subject in May 2000 concluded that such virus attacks are virtually unpreventable.[57]

In the early years of the new century, economic issues dominate the U.S. free-flow agenda. Information barriers remain a major threat to exports of information goods and services—the fastest-growing area of U.S. overseas trade. Moreover, American companies control a large part of the global flow of electronic data. The steady increase in this so-called "invisible trade" brought greater attention to the parallel growth of overseas tariff and non-tariff barriers which threaten further expansion of American data exports.[58]

The growing debate on commercial data flows has had important political implications for U.S. policymakers. The dispute was centered primarily around relations with America's major overseas allies, the industrial democracies. Unlike the vague ideological arguments that governed most of the mass media controversy, data-flow issues involved hard questions about national sovereignty and economic independence in the newly emerging information age.

The stakes were outlined in extremis by a Canadian economist:

The USA may soon own all our secrets—unless we start insisting that computerized information stay on this side of the border. Super-computers and international communications lines—a pair of blinking, beeping modern marvels that are supposed to help everyone find the good life—may be combining instead to sap Canada's secrets, its chances for progress, and even its ability to make what industry we have behave, according to worried computer experts in the business world and civil service.[59]

We will take a closer look at this aspect of digital diplomacy in Chapter 8, when we examine its role over the past two decades in reducing barriers to commercial data flows. It is no accident that those countries which have lowered such barriers are those who lead the world's economies. Trade considerations have proven to be the most powerful pressure on other countries to take similar steps.

In advancing its free-flow initiatives, American diplomacy has also strengthened its overall digital policy agenda. Information factors are now built into almost every major issue, from national security and trade promotion to environmental regulations. It has also transformed the ways in which negotiations on these issues are carried out. In a digital era, the prospects of secretive, closed-door diplomacy are fading. The new diplomacy is increasingly a public affair, guided and often led by information resources in the hands of non-government organizations. How do the State Department and other foreign affairs agencies deal organizationally with these new responsibilities? We will take a closer look at this subject in the next chapter.

NOTES

1. The global implications of this shift are described in Daniel Yergin and Joseph Stanislaw, *The commanding heights* (New York: Simon & Schuster, 1998), pp. 346–348. See also: Fred H. Cate, "The First Amendment and international "free flow" of information," *Virginia Journal of International Law*, Vol. 40, No. 2, Winter 1990, pp. 372–420.

2. The impact of the AT&T divestiture is described in Robert W. Crandall, *After the breakup: U.S. telecommunications in a more competitive era* (Washington, DC: The Brookings Institution, 1991). For the political and economic forces involved in the 1996 telecommunications legislation, see: Wilson P. Dizard, *Meganet: How the global communications network will connect everyone on earth* (Boulder, CO: Westview Press, 1997), pp. 122–144.

3. "French minister cites U.S. cultural influence," *New York Times*, 16 November 1984, p. C-26.

4. The politics of this development is described in Daniel R. Headrick, *The invisible weapon: Telecommunications and international politics 1851–1945* (New York: Oxford University Press, 1991), chaps. 12–14.

5. Emily S. Rosenberg, "Cultural interactions," in Stanley Kutler (ed.), *Encyclopaedia of the United States in the twentieth century* (New York: Scribners, 1996), p. 695.

6. "U.N. votes to take up satellite telecasts," *New York Times*, 10 November 1972, p. 9.

7. "AT&T resuming calls to mainland China on a regular basis," *Wall Street Journal*, 3 September 1971, p. 1.

8. For a useful summary of the information technology embargo, see: "Technology transfer," in *Enclopaedia of U.S. foreign relations*, Vol. 4 (New York: Oxford University Press, 1997), pp. 179–182.

9. These radio operations and their impact on listeners are described in Michael Nelson, *War of the black heavens: The battle of Western broadcasting in the cold war* (Syracuse, NY: Syracuse University Press, 1997).

10. Wilson Dizard, "Europe calling Europe: Creating an integrated telecommunications network," in Alan W. Cafruny and Glenda M. Rosenthal (eds.), *The state of the European Community: The Maastricht debates and beyond* (Boulder, CO: Lynne Rienner Publishers, 1993), p. 321.

11. Jacques Servan-Schreiber, *The American challenge* (New York: Simon & Schuster, 1967).

12. Simon Nora and Alain Minc, *The computerization of society: A report to the president of France* (Cambridge, MA: MIT Press, 1981).

13. Philip C. Horton (ed.), *The Third World and press freedom* (New York: Praeger Publishers, 1978).

14. Daniel Lerner, *The passing of tradtional society: Modernizing the Middle East* (Glencoe, IL: The Free Press, 1958). The subject of communications in the modernization process spawned a wide variety of academic studies. Among the more important were: Max F. Millikan and Donald L. M. Blackmer (eds.), *The emerging nations: Their growth and United States policy* (Boston: Little, Brown & Co., 1961); Lucian W. Pye, *Communications and political development* (Princeton, NJ: Princeton

University Press, 1962; and Wilbur Schramm, *Mass media and national development* (Stanford, CA: Stanford University Press, 1964).

15. Elihu Katz and George Wedell, *Broadcasting in the Third World* (Cambridge, MA: Harvard University Press, 1977). For a later study, which includes the print media, see: Robert L. Stevenson, *Communications, development and the Third World: The global politics of information* (New York: Longman Publishers, 1988).

16. U.N. General Assembly resolution 59 (1), 1946.

17. U.N. General Assembly resolution 217 (III), 1948.

18. Cate, op cit., p. 374.

19. Leonard R. Sussman, "Many rulers still fear full freedom," in *Everyone has the right* (Washington, DC: World Press Freedom Committee, 1998), pp. 7–20.

20. "UN efforts are revived on information codes," *Editor & Publisher*, 14 November 1953, p. 12.

21. "TV direct from satellite to your home—It could be soon," *U.S News and World Report*, 26 June 1967, p. 32.

22. See, for instance, a fanciful scenario about Soviet DBS domination of global television in Edward Diamond, "Whose eye in the sky?" *Show*, February 1963, p. 59.

23. "NASA issues request for proposals on direct broadcast satellites," Press release 65-363, National Aeronautics and Space Administration, 24 November 1965.

24. Leonard Jaffe, "Broadcast satellite possibilities," paper submitted to the Meeting of Experts on the Use of Space Communications by the Mass Media, UNESCO House, Paris, 6–10 December 1965.

25. Letter from NASA associate administrator Robert Seamons, Jr. to Leonard H. Marks, director of the U.S. Information Agency, 23 November 1965.

26. This position was outlined in the section on international broadcasting in "U.S. Positions at 29th General Assembly," Special Report no. 13, Bureau of Public Affairs, Department of State, February 1975, p. 21. For a general survey of American DBS policy, see: Wilson P. Dizard, "The U.S. position: Direct broadcast satellites and free flow," *Journal of Communication*, Vol. 30, No. 2, Spring 1980, pp. 157–168.

27. While U.S. television broadcasters supported State Department efforts to resist prior-consent restrictions abroad, they opposed domestic DBS applications, seeing them as "the seeds of destruction" for terrestrial commercial television. "Broadcasters see ruin of local service by satellite-to-home," *Broadcasting*, 8 November 1975, p. 42.

28. "AID sets space program for underdeveloped areas," *Aviation Week and Space Technology*, 17 May 1976, p. 12.

29. The early organization and technical capabilities of the project are described in "Peacesat Project Networks," a background paper issued by the Peacesat project office, University of Hawaii, November 1975.

30. There is an extensive literature on the results of the ATS-6 international experiments. For a review of the most important demonstration, see: Dr. Clifford Block, "A case study of India's satellite instructional television project," Agency for International Development, Washington, DC, January 1977.

31. "Soviet asks U.N. to bar intrusion by satellite TV," *New York Times*, 11 August 1972, p. 4.

32. "Right to destroy satellites sought by Soviet in UN," *Aviation Week and Space Technology*, 22 October 1972, p. 9.

33. "U.N. votes to take up satellite telecasts," *New York Times*, 10 November 1972, p. 4.

34. A watered-down version of the Canadian-Swedish plan was adopted by the General Assembly in 1982: "International cooperation in the peaceful uses of outer space," General Assembly resolution 37/92, 10 December 1982.

35. The impact of *Time, Newsweek* and similar publications on elite foreign audiences is documented in Ralph L. Lowenstein, "The progression of media development," in John C. Merrill and Ralph L. Lowenstein, *Media, messages and men* (Philadelphia: McKay, 1971), pp. 98–123. See also: Jeremy Tunstall, *The media are American* (London: Constable, 1977).

36. For a description of the U.S. National Commission's activities at the time, see: *UNESCO and the U.S. National Commission for UNESCO*, Department of State Publication 7491, International Organization and Conference Series 37, September 1977.

37. The history of the Ideas Bureau, which was eventually closed down, is told in "Onward and upward with UNESCO," *The Reporter*, 5 March 1958, pp. 41–43.

38. Ibid., p. 43

39. For a description of the overseas role of American news agencies at the time, see: Oliver Boyd-Barrett, *The international news agencies* (Beverly Hills, CA: Sage Publications, 1980).

40. Wilson P. Dizard, *Television: a world view* (Syracuse, NY: Syracuse University Press, 1966), pp. 159–160. See also: Alan Wells, *Picture tube imperialism* (Maryknoll, NY: Orbis Publications, 1972).

41. The NWICO was largely the creation of a Tunisian communications official, Mustapha Masmoudi, who represented his country at UNESCO. His views are outlined in Mustapha Masmoudi, "The New World Information Order," *Journal of Communication*, Vol. 29, No. 2, Spring 1979, pp. 172–185. See also: Robert L. Stevenson, *Communication, development and the Third World* (New York: Longman Publishers, 1988), pp. 75–95; Jonathan Gunter (ed.), *The United States and the debate on the World Information Order* (Washington, DC: Academy for Educational Development, June 1979).

42. M'Bow's role in the mass media debate is described in "The bad news from UNESCO," *Columbia Journalism Review*, April 1976, pp. 57–59.

43. For a survey of this and other non-aligned media projects, see: A. W. Singham, *The non-aligned movement in world politics* (Westport, CT: Lawrence Hill Publishers, 1977). On the cultural dependency issue, see: "Forms of cultural dependency: A symposium," *Journal of Communication*, Vol. 25, No. 2, Spring 1975, pp. 120–193.

44. The text of the amended draft is contained in Document 19/c, Nineteenth UNESCO General Conference, Nairobi, Kenya, 7 July 1976.

45. "Declaration on fundamental principles concerning the contribution of the mass media to strengthening peace and international understanding, to the promotion of human rights and to countering racialism, apartheid and incitement to war." Draft declaration 20C/20, adopted at the Twentieth UNESCO General Conference, 22 November 1978.

46. *UNESCO challenges and opportunities for the United States*, hearing before the

Subcommittee on International Organizations, Committee on International Relations, House of Representatives, 94th Congress, 2nd session, 14 June 1976.

47. "Third world vs. fourth estate," *Time*, 20 November 1978, p. 64.

48. The committee produced, among other publications, a useful summary of the UNESCO mass media controversy: *The Media Crisis* (Washington, DC: World Press Freedom Committee, 1980).

49. "When UNESCO protects journalists," *The Economist* (London), 31 March 1979, p. 11.

50. *Many voices, one world*, Final report of the International Commission for the Study of Communications Problems (London: Kegan Paul, 1980).

51. James Buckley, "International communications and information objectives," *Department of State Bulletin*, 4 March 1982, p. 22. The policy genesis of Buckley's statement can be found in a document issued 15 months earlier: "The foundations of United States information policy: A U.S. government submission to the high-level conference on information, computer and communications policy, Organization for Economic Cooperation and Development, October 6–8 1980," NTIA-SP-80-8, National Telecommunications and Information Administration, Department of Commerce, October 1980.

52. "UNESCO shifts its tactics on press in Third World," *New York Times*, 30 November 1981, p. 12.

53. "UNESCO woos Washington to no avail," *New York Times*, 12 February 1995, p. 8.

54. Richard Davy (ed.), *European détente: A reappraisal* (London: Royal Institute of International Affairs, 1992), p. 19.

55. Quoted in Nelson, op. cit., p. xi.

56. For background on the decision to expand Chinese telecommunications resources, see: Milton Mueller and Zixiang Tan, *China in the information age: Telecommunications and the dilemma of reform* (Westport, CT: Praeger Publishers, 1996).

57. "Multination conference confronts cybercrime," *Washington Post*, 17 May 2000, p. A-18.

58. "American 'invisible' trade hampered by invisible barriers," *National Journal*, 15 September 1979, pp. 1547–1549; "A new threat to multinationals," *Computer Decisions*, August 1978, pp. 34–38.

59. Quoted in Russell Pipe, "Transnational data flows," *Intermedia* (London), November 1979, p. 12.

Chapter 6

Restructuring Diplomatic Communications

Digital diplomacy issues and techniques have had to be shoehorned into a policymaking system run by officials who were initially uninterested in and often suspicious of the subject. They were, moreover, usually poorly informed about the technological and economic trends that have made electronic resources newly important factors in U.S. global strategy.

By and large, these difficulties are being overcome. An older diplomatic generation has come to accept, and a newer one to embrace, the changes. Increasingly, they share the new pop culture of information age attitudes and activities, including those that touch on foreign policy. Here we will examine how the administration of American foreign policy has adjusted to this shift in recent decades.

In general, the State Department has been more reluctant than most Washington agencies to recognize the value of the new information technologies in its operations. There are various explanations for this (budgetary restrictions, for instance) but the overriding one involves the mindset of diplomats themselves. One of its characteristics has been general resistance by department officials to the idea that technology (in this case, information machines) was a critical part of their arcane trade. Until recently, they shared a belief that theirs was an elite profession and that its practitioners could rely primarily on their personal skills in dealing with its agenda. To their credit, most American diplomats never lost sight of the populist roots of U.S. foreign policy. Nevertheless, elitism played a role, given the tradition of a small group of men set apart, with special instincts for understanding the esoteric art of dealing with other cultures.[1]

Their view of their trade was misplaced. Diplomacy is an exercise in what political scientist Yaacov Y. I. Vertzberger calls "the grand architecture of coping." Its foundation stone is processing the imperfect information that can be gathered about other societies, interpreting it, and assessing its relevance to the problems at hand. It is, at best, a risky, accident-prone exercise that often introduces more uncertainty than it resolves.[2] The significant difference between traditional diplomacy and today's version is the accelerating pace, volume and breadth of information which diplomats need to make informed decisions. It is a long way, chronologically and otherwise, from the era when President Thomas Jefferson famously wrote to his secretary of state, James Madison: "We have not heard from our ambassador in Paris for two years. If we do not hear from him by the end of this year, let us write him a letter."[3]

Piecemeal approaches to information management in foreign affairs are no longer possible. A torrent of data flows in and out of the State Department and other foreign affairs agencies in Washington every day, increasingly in digitized formats. By the turn of the century, State's communications division was electronically processing over 140,000 official records and 90,000 data messages each day, supporting more than 250 diplomatic posts. Over 20 million e-messages were being posted annually by the department's employees.[4]

Although gathering and analyzing data has always been one of its primary duties, the State Department generally has not accorded high priority to information management. It did not get around to setting up its own telegraph facilities for almost a quarter century after the invention of the Morse telegraph.[5] Until very recently, the department relied primarily on paper documents, filed away in steel cabinets. The content of cable traffic to and from overseas posts was limited largely to important policy subjects. By 1939, the department's daily cable traffic had increased to only 500 incoming and outgoing messages. Cordell Hull was probably the last Secretary of State who personally approved all outgoing messages.[6] Most diplomatic messages were still sent to and from overseas missions in pouches, usually by ship. With the beginnings of international airline services after World War II, "air pouches" were introduced. Pouches containing classified documents were accompanied by diplomatic couriers whose numbers reached 70 in the postwar years.

Although the volume of message traffic accelerated in recent decades, there was little change in the way the State Department dealt with its worldwide communications. Telephone contact with overseas missions was rare because of the unreliability of shortwave radio circuits. This began to change after 1955 with the introduction of submarine coaxial cables capable of providing reliable phone services. In general, however, State's communications pattern in the early postwar years relied primarily on slow-moving telegraphic messaging between Washington and overseas posts.

The event that forced changes in this pattern was the 1962 Cuban missile crisis, the first major confrontation in nuclear age diplomacy. It was a hair-trigger situation whose resolution depended on the availability of direct, quick and reliable communications between Washington and Moscow. The lack of such facilities was responsible for misunderstandings that could have led to nuclear exchanges between the two contending powers. The crisis took place in the half-shadows of missed or delayed communications for which both sides shared the blame.

Twenty-five years after the crisis, communications failures on the Soviet side were described by Anatoly Dobrynin, who had been his country's ambassador in Washington at the time. Speaking at a conference at Georgetown University, Dobrynin revealed that his embassy did not have direct telephone or radio communications with Moscow during the Cuban crisis. Many of his messages on the negotiations were entrusted to Western Union bicycle messengers who, as he put it, may have stopped for snacks or to chat with friends, oblivious of the world-shaking implications of the telegrams they were carrying. "There is a reason," he said, "why in the decisive phase of the conflict, a couple of messages from (Soviet leader) Khrushchev addressed to President Kennedy were conveyed simultaneously through me and announced over Radio Moscow, to make sure they reached the White House as fast as possible."[7]

American communications resources during the crisis were not as primitive, but they had their own set of troubles. The State Department's cable network was thrown into virtual gridlock as a result of the dramatic increase in messages dealing with the Cuban crisis. A global LIMDIS ("limited distribution") restriction on most routine traffic was ordered. Despite this precaution, at one point President Kennedy received a critical Khrushchev statement from Tass, the Soviet news agency, before he got the State Department's official cable version.[8]

Once the confrontation over the Cuban missiles was settled, the Kennedy administration moved quickly to improve the nation's crisis communications resources. A National Communications System, managed by the Defense Department, was set up to oversee all military communications and to assure better coordination with other Federal systems and with AT&T and other commercial networks.[9] Meanwhile, Congress passed legislation giving the president authority to negotiate radio rights with foreign countries, particularly to permit wireless facilities at American missions. This would allow direct communications with Washington, ending the then-current practice of using circuits controlled by local governments.[10] By the end of the 1960s, most overseas posts had such direct communications access to department facilities in Washington.

Within the State Department, an operations center, opened in 1961, was rapidly expanded to coordinate communications in crisis situations. In addition to the department's regular cable networks, the center established single-sideband shortwave radio links as an emergency channel to overseas posts. This addition proved its worth a few years later when it provided the only link available in coordinating a NATO military exercise to rescue American missionaries and others under siege by a mob at the U.S. consulate in the African city of Stanleyville.

The Kennedy administration also addressed a critical hazard exposed by the Cuban crisis—the lack of immediate means of reaching Soviet leaders during a crisis. The result was the Washington-Moscow "hot line," later described by Secretary of State Dean Rusk as "a child of the Cuban missile crisis." Contrary to myths created by Hollywood films at the time (notably in Stanley Kubrick's classic *Dr. Strangelove*), the hotline was not a telephone link between the president and his Kremlin counterpart. It was a clunky teleprinter that transmitted messages between the two capitals by a cable link that zigzagged through London, Copenhagen, Stockholm and Helsinki before reaching Moscow. The facility was opened in April 1963, with a message from Washington informing the Russians that the quick brown fox jumped over the lazy dog. In reply, the Russians asked why the fox was jumping over the dog. When it was explained to them that it was a test of the teleprinter keys, the Russians responded with a lyrical description of the Moscow sunset.

The hot line's technology was upgraded in 1971 when two satellite circuits were installed, which provided primary and backup connections between the two capitals. The arrangement was one of the first agreements reached in the Strategic Arms Limitation Talks (SALT) negotiations that emerged from the Nixon administration's limited détente initiative in the early 1970s. The hot line was seldom used during the cold war period. Although information about its role as a back-channel diplomatic link remains largely classified, Henry Kissinger, among others, has described its role in several crises, including the 1973 Arab–Israeli war. Nevertheless, the hot line served a purpose, one that President Kennedy called a "limited but practical step forward in arms control and disarmament."[11]

The State Department's communications network facilities were also upgraded in the wake of the Cuban missile crisis. The improvements were, however, piecemeal. There was no overarching plan for an advanced information facility linking the department with its overseas missions, much less interconnections with the dozen or more major Washington agencies involved in foreign policy decision making.[12]

In particular, there was little consideration given by State officials to the rapidly developing capabilities of computers. In June 1966, the Johnson White House issued a directive to all federal agencies to "explore and apply all possible means to use the electronic computer to do a better job." Computerization had begun to take hold in the government with about 2,600 of the machines already installed in various agencies. Within the foreign policy establishment, the CIA and other intelligence agencies led the way in computer use.

A modest step towards advancing computerization in the foreign affairs community had been taken in 1965 when the Bureau of the Budget authorized a study of the subject. Known as FAIMS (Foreign Affairs Information Management System), the study focussed on computer uses for routine administrative chores in State, USIA, AID and the Arms Control and Disarmament Agency (ACDA). It was a limited but practical approach: the big wall-sized machines available at the time were primarily an improved way to store and access greater amounts of information. Their potential as heuristic resources in defining and analyzing complex policy problems was three technical generations down the road. The FAIMS report referred to these prospects in a general way, but it focussed on computerization of administrative chores—payrolls, personnel records and other routine chores.[13]

The State Department moved cautiously in implementing the FAIMS recommendations. Budgetary constraints were a chronic problem. So was the reluctance of the department's administrators to give up slow but time-tested practices. However, they were under pressure to change them, particularly after October 1965 when the Johnson White House mandated that all federal agencies introduce a new management technique known as the programming-planning-budgeting system (PPBS) in all their operations. PPBS called for the kind of detailed administrative information that only computers could process. In the absence of adequate computer resources, PPBS quickly became a management burden rather than an effective aid in policy planning. As a result, the system was quietly dropped a few years later.

By the end of 1966, the State Department had installed its first computers, all designed to handle routine administrative tasks. At the same time, the first nodes in a network of regional data processing centers were set up in Paris and Bangkok.[14] A year later, an automated terminal for processing, storing and distributing incoming and outgoing telegrams was installed.

Meanwhile, the prospect of using computers for broader foreign policy tasks was being examined for the first time. An advisory group was set up by Secretary Dean Rusk in 1966 to examine, among other issues, the role of computers in diplomatic negotiations. One of the group's members was John Diebold, a business consultant and a pioneer in advocating the computer's potential as a strategic management tool. Diebold brought a new perspective to the State Department's operations at a time when computer technology was beginning to break away from its origins as simply a better way to store and retrieve routine data.

Computers did not offer quick-fix solutions to stubborn diplomatic problems, Diebold noted, but they could vastly improve the quality of information available to policy planners and negotiators. In an article that appeared in the department's newsletter, he wrote: "It is my judgment that as the new technology becomes applied to foreign affairs, reliance on personal judgment and personal and national moral standards will increase—not decrease. As the horizons of factual ignorance and misinformation fade, the decision-maker will be presented with vast new areas of choice."[15]

Diebold suggested that negotiating treaties across a table might become anachronistic when diplomats would be able to sit at their own desks, sometimes oceans apart, and draw upon an agreed-upon database whose information would define the agenda and the options open to the negotiators. Such a database could provide accurate information on the probable impact on both sides of their competing proposals. Diebold predicted that "leaders of nations" would eventually confer face to face on closed-circuit television. Ambassadors, he noted, might be relegated to the role of "note-gatherer, pulse-taker and holder-of-hands."

The idea of using computers for substantive diplomatic operations was given a further boost in a department document published in November 1966. It was an 88-page pamphlet entitled *The computer and foreign affairs: Some first thoughts.* Its author was Fisher Howe, a senior Foreign Service officer who had recently been assigned by the department to the University of Utah as a diplomat-in-residence. Howe used his sabbatical year to explore the relationship between computers and the work he had been doing in the foreign service.[16]

Howe's study was the first that related computers to the realities of diplomatic work in terms that his fellow officers could understand. Despite the then-current technical limitations of computers, he picked up on suggestions by John Diebold and other management experts that computers could be used not only to better organize information for diplomatic negotiations but also to clarify policy options. Among other subjects, Howe discussed the idea of computer-based gaming as a resource for examining intricate problems. He also reviewed the then-emerging research in artificial intelligence and described the early experience in building computer models of the information processes underlying human thought.[17]

Howe's pamphlet became a primer on the subject for a small group of computer buffs in the State Department and the Foreign Service. However, the report's recommendation that the role of the computer in substantive policy work be further explored left most department officials unmoved. Their general attitude was that computers were alright for managing payrolls, but had little value for the high art of diplomacy. They were part of an establishment still dominated, as one observer noted, by "a wistful yearning for good old days that really never were, a diplomatic Walter Mittyland in which an elite group of professional diplomats, all looking and acting like George Kennan, have the President's ear."[18]

Overall, the Department reacted to the prospects described in the Howe report with modest steps, citing budgetary problems and the general difficulties of introducing a new technology to an operation scattered across the four corners of the earth. Nevertheless, the concept of computers as a foreign policy tool gradually took hold beginning in the early 1970s, in part as a response to new policy challenges and organizational growth. The department was coping with the needs of 50 new embassies in Asia and Africa. Communications traffic was increasing exponentially. Despite these pressures, computerization still had a relatively low priority on the department's agenda. As a result, it fell behind other agencies in the foreign policy community in installing the new machines. The CIA and other intelligence agencies, in particular, reorganized large parts of their operations around computers.

The State Department also lagged in matching the speed with which computerization was being adopted by the private sector in its global operations. International trade, in particular, was affected by the change. An early example was the 1973 oil crisis in which the global economy was threatened with a sudden steep rise in crude oil prices by Arab producers. MIT political scientist Ithiel de Sola Pool has described it as the first global economic crisis, primarily because new computer and satellite network technology allowed all the players—buyers and sellers alike—to share the same information almost instantaneously. The State Department, meanwhile, continued to rely on slow-speed telegrams and on file cabinet documents to track the crisis.

During the 1970s, computerization proceeded in fits and starts within the department. The process was slowed down by an ill-considered decision to standardize the process in Washington and overseas missions with desktop machines produced by the Wang Corporation, a Massachusetts computer firm. The Wang computers were technologically state-of-the-art at the time, but they were quickly outmoded by a new generation of more powerful small computers developed by IBM and Apple.

Meanwhile, the pressure for more computerization in the department continued with partisans and doubters drawing up sides. One of the more vociferous partisans was President Carter's national security adviser, Zbigniew Brzezinski. Traditional diplomacy in the age of computers was a boondoggle, he told a *New York Times* reporter in 1983: "Governments should conduct business the way international corporations do, with special representatives in modest offices utilizing telecommunications. The whole diplomatic system needs to be modernized so that it can operate with more rapidity instead of maintaining extraordinarily costly establishments and entertainments."[19]

This and similar comments set off what became a continuing debate on the role of overseas missions in an increasingly high-tech information environment. The subject also included television's new ability to provide satellite images of fast-breaking events abroad, in effect scooping diplomatic reporting. Television's impact on foreign policy had its roots in the Vietnam conflict. Public support for American involvement waned in part because of the nightly video images of death and destruction transmitted by satellite to the New York networks. The so-called "living room war" was a powerful lesson for policymakers on the power of television to set the political agenda.

In recent decades, television's impact on the foreign policy process has become increasingly sophisticated. The oft-cited example is the role played by the Cable News Network (CNN) in reporting crisis situations overseas as they unfolded. The network's coverage of these events is now routinely monitored in foreign affairs offices around the world, including the State Department. Journalist Johanna Neuman described one such instance:

Strobe Talbot (Deputy Secretary of State) was watching the Russian White House burn in the tumultuous events of September 1993, talking to a counterpart at the Russian Foreign Ministry, both of them watching CNN. Helicopters appeared on the screen. . . . For several minutes, as events unfolded on Black Monday, these two top diplomats, who were charged with working out the crisis, instead watched television while they sat on a secure line saying absolutely nothing. This freeze-frame picture of their conversation makes starkly clear the intrusion of instant, global TV pictures into diplomacy.[20]

By 1980, the State Department had begun to take seriously the need to adapt to rapid changes in information technology. In particular, the storage and transmittal of information was being transformed by semiconductor technology ("chips"). For the first time, mass computerization became a possibility as the new chips opened the prospect of replacing room-sized computers with advanced desktop models that were both cheaper and potentially capable of sophisticated operations far beyond the limited number-crunching capabilities of the older machines. The first of these machines (known as cathode-ray terminals) began to appear in State Department offices in the late 1970s. A centralized computer facility was set up to manage an automated document system. For the first time, paper files were being displaced by an electronic system that identified the content of individual messages so that they could be stored, routed and accessed efficiently throughout the department.[21]

These new facilities initially allowed the department to handle administrative tasks more efficiently. But they were soon being deployed on a limited basis as a resource in diplomatic negotiations. The first such use was in the long-running Law of the Sea treaty negotiations, which began in 1958 and continued for 24 years. In the last decade of the negotiations, the American delegation made increasing use of computer facilities to track the treaty's myriad issues, from the location of undersea minerals to the mating habits of lobsters.

An even more dramatic breakthrough in computerized negotiating took place in 1979 at the ITU World Administrative Radio Conference in Geneva, dealing with radio spectrum allocations (the conference is described in Chapter 4). Among the 150 delegations, the Americans alone had an advantage of knowing the status of each of the conference's 15,000 agenda proposals each day. As each item was negotiated, changes were recorded in a Hewlett-Packard desktop computer at the delegation's offices. Having a timely and accurate record of the conference's progress gave the U.S. delegates a critical advantage in planning their negotiating strategy.

This early use of computers in negotiations involved a better way to sort and access raw information. The next step was to pick up on the prospects outlined by John Diebold and others—namely, using computers as an analytic tool. A small cottage industry had developed by the 1980s among information technology specialists looking at the prospect for so-called smart computers as a foreign policy resource. They focussed on what came to be called crisis forecasting, building on the theories of John von Neumann and other information theory pioneers that computers could be programmed to make inferences and suggest remedies in real-life situations through crisis gaming and other simulation approaches. These techniques have since earned a small but respectable niche in foreign policy planning.[22]

In the 1980s, however, this prospect had low priority in State Department planning. The department's focus was on improving its communications facilities, with particular attention to making them user-friendly for technology-shy Foreign Service officers and other employees. The project had two major objectives. The first was to install personal computers on a large scale in Washington and at overseas posts. The second was to upgrade the worldwide network that would link these computers with one another.

Both projects quickly ran into trouble. The goal of a personal computer on every employee's desk was thwarted by the earlier decision to select Wang computers as the standard for the entire department. Wang technology had been overtaken by the more nimble desktop products developed by other computer firms. Nevertheless, the Wang machines remained the department's standard even after the company filed for bankruptcy in the 1990s.[23] By that time the department had fallen seriously behind in its plan to expand computerization to all its employees.

Meanwhile, the department moved ahead with plans to upgrade its global telecommunications network—an unwieldy system that had been allowed to grow Topsy-like over the years. It was split into a half-dozen incompatible circuits, none of which could "talk" to the others. The department's proposal was to replace them with a digitally integrated network—DOSTN, the Department of State telecommunications network.[24] DOSTN was designed as a high-speed secure network linking 273 locations at home and abroad. Unlike the department's existing system, it would be completely independent of networks run by private companies or by other governments. Moreover, DOSTN would be available to all Washington agencies involved in foreign operations, from USIA to the Foreign Agricultural Service. Within the State Department, it would provide desktop computer connections linking most of its employees into an advanced information facility.

The DOSTN project ran into trouble from the start. It involved technologies that were untested on such a global scale. Meanwhile, Congress balked at its high cost, estimated at a half billion dollars. Work on implementing both DOSTN and FAIMS was slowed down for years as funding and technical problems were worked out. The delays caused a slippage that seriously affected the department's ability to acquire state-of-the-art technology. By 1992, 80 percent of the agency's classified networks and an even higher percentage of unclassified circuits were obsolete.[25]

The lagging effort to modernize the department's information capabilities had been given a lift in 1989 with the appointment of Ivan Selin as undersecretary for management, a post traditionally held by a Foreign Service officer. Selin was the first "outsider" in the position. He brought strong credentials to the assignment as the founder and chief executive officer of American Management Systems, a pioneer in helping private firms install advanced information resources. Selin reorganized the department's plans for managing its information systems, putting stronger emphasis on building a single facility within Washington and at overseas posts.[26] The result was the first integrated plan, known as the Foreign Affairs Information System (FAIS), for upgrading all of State's information and communications facilities.[27]

Despite the new energy and ideas that Ivan Selin and his colleagues brought to the effort, their modernization program continued to meet obstacles. Building the network they envisioned involved technologies that had never before been tested on a global scale. Politically, Congress continued to balk at providing full funding for the project. Concerns were raised about security safeguards in the new network, particularly in handling classified information.

After Selin's departure in 1991, the information modernization program proceeded at a slower pace.[28] By the late 1990s, however, the department had stepped up its efforts to complete a high-tech integrated global system, incorporating Internet facilities and other advanced technologies.[29] This initiative led to a major reorganization of the department's information technology operations in March 1998. Until that time, responsibility for these operations was divided among several units. The 1998 reorganization brought them together in a single office, the Bureau of Information Resources Management (IRM). Equally important, the bureau was headed by an undersecretary of state. It was the first time that information operations were given equal status with political and economic concerns at the department's highest levels.[30]

The new bureau, headed by a political appointee, Bonnie Cohen, was given sweeping authority over all of the department's information and communications facilities, from payrolls to Web site operations. Its duties included management of the Nuclear Risk Reduction Center's computer system that oversees U.S. relations with the nuclear states of the former Soviet Union. The bureau's major effort at the turn of the century was to install an unclassified information infrastructure that would provide each overseas post with access to all parts of the department's integrated network. By 2000, these capabilities had been put in place in Washington and at over 130 overseas posts.

The new facility also improved access to advanced digital technologies such as global positioning satellite facilities and geographic information systems. The latter capability has special relevance to diplomatic negotiations. A prototype system, developed by the Defense Department, was deployed during the 1995 Bosnian peace negotiations in Dayton, Ohio. The system provided access to detailed map displays, including three-dimensional terrain imagery, in ways that facilitated the task of establishing boundary lines between the contending parties, a key factor in arriving at a final agreement.

These changes in State Department information operations have markedly improved the agency's ability to deal with events in the fast-moving, highly interdependent world of digital diplomacy. Commenting on the new resources in 1998, Secretary of State Madeleine Albright noted: "This will make us all wiser, quicker to understand each other and better able to work together on the world's problems."[31]

NOTES

1. This factor is discussed in *Reinventing diplomacy in the information age*, report of the CSIS advisory panel on diplomacy in the information age, Center for Strategic and International Studies, Washington, DC, December 1988, pp. 52–77.

2. Yaacov Y. I. Vertzberger, *The world in their minds: Information processing,*

cognition and perception in foreign-policy decisionmaking (Stanford, CA: Stanford University Press, 1990).

3. For a survey of the early history of the State Department's information resources, see: "Franklin sent messages in triplicate—or even quintuplicate," *State Magazine*, April 1987, pp. 15–16.

4. "At Beltsville, they get the message," *State Magazine*, October 1998, pp. 36–38.

5. Daniel R. Headrick, *The invisible weapon: Telecommunications and international politics 1851–1945* (New York: Oxford University Press, 1991), p. 74.

6. "How Cordell Hull handled the press when he was 'at home'," *State Magazine*, May 1987, p. 28.

7. " '62 missile crisis, via Western Union," *Washington Post*, 18 November 1989, p. 6.

8. "Cuban missile crisis was a communications 'watershed'," *State Magazine*, June 1987, p. 25.

9. Paul Polishuk, "Telecommunications policy making and institutions of the U.S. government," *Telecommunications Policy*, December 1976, p. 35.

10. "Cuban missile crisis was a 'communications watershed'," op cit., p. 24.

11. "U.S. hot line to Soviets: little use for 20 years," *New York Times*, 4 April 1983, p. 16.

12. "State's tangled web," *Foreign Service Journal*, May 1984, p. 32.

13. "A development program for a foreign affairs information management system (FAIMS)," prepared for the Bureau of the Budget, Report 551-2, Systems Science Division, Dunlop and Associates, Washington, DC, 7 June 1965.

14. "Financial management improvement in the Department of State," *State Department News Letter*, October 1966, p. 42.

15. "John Diebold on computers and foreign affairs," *State Department News Letter*, October 1966, p. 20.

16. Fisher Howe, *The computer and foreign affairs: Some first thoughts*, Occasional Paper No. 1 (Washington, DC: Center for International Systems Research, Department of State, November 1966).

17. Ibid., p. 48.

18. "Fantasies from the fudge factory," *Washington Post*, 19 August 1971, p. D-1.

19. "Has diplomacy become out of date?" *New York Times*, 6 January 1983, p. 16.

20. "Ambassadors: Relics of the sailing ships?", Annenberg Washington Program on Communications, Washington, DC, 1995, p. 2. See also: Johanna Neuman, *Lights, camera, war: Is media technology driving international politics?* (New York: St. Martin's Press, 1996).

21. The Department's early experience with automated document storage and retrieval is described in "The information manager," *Information Manager*, May/June 1979, pp. 20–25; "A new way to look at files," *Department of State News Letter*, August–September 1976, p. 31.

22. For a useful survey of early "smart computer" developments in the foreign policy field, see: Alan Kotok, "Information, please," *Foreign Service Journal*, March 1987, pp. 21–31.

23. "State Dep't contract gives Wang a boost," *New York Times*, 22 August 1990, p. B-5.

24. "Uncle Sam wants vendor for integrated network system," *Communications Week*, 19 October 1987, p. 6.

25. Warren E. Littrel, deputy assistant secretary for information management, quoted in "Major programs to 'migrate' to more modern computers is launched," *State Magazine*, March 1993, p. 15. See also: "The State Department: A snail in the age of e-mail," *New York Times*, 6 March 1995, p. A-6.

26. "Selin, Perkins inform Congress about their plans," *State Magazine*, November 1989, p. 7.

27. Details of the FAIS plan are given in "Foreign Affairs Information System quick reference guide," Office of User Services, Bureau of Information Management, Department of State, 1991. See also: "Introducing the DOSTN: State prepared to rebuild its information network," *Foreign Service Journal*, June 1990, p. 23.

28. "An 'interchange' at Foggy Bottom: State to get an information superhighway," *State Magazine*, June 1994, pp. 18–19.

29. The department's plan for an advanced system is outlined in "Diplomacy for the 21st century: Justification and summary of the information resource management modernization initiatives," Office of the Undersecretary for Management, Department of State, 11 September 1996.

30. "Information resource management: A new bureau for a new era," *State Magazine*, October 1998, pp. 36–38.

31. Ibid., p. 36.

Chapter 7

Organizing Digital Diplomacy

In the previous chapter, we looked at the State Department's problems in integrating advanced electronic technologies in its operations. Here we will examine the difficulties it has encountered in reshaping its policy structure to deal with the digital realities that are driving so much of American foreign policy these days.

Communications issues were an occasional foreign policy concern for most of the 150 years after the invention of the Morse telegraph. They were dealt with in episodic fashion, usually involving the need to react to technological developments in the field. A prime example, as we have seen, was the policy challenge presented by communications satellite technology in the early 1960s.

Bureaucratic foot-dragging was only part of the State Department's reluctance to becoming involved in communications issues. It also reflected deep-seated ambiguities about government's role in this area. Unlike other countries, the American communications and information sectors have historically been controlled by private firms, not by public agencies. U.S. companies routinely invoke First Amendment principles in resisting government controls over their activities. It took almost a century after Samuel Morse's invention to pass a national law, the Communications Act of 1934, which mandated mild regulatory restraints on the telecommunications industry.

This arms-length relationship between government and industry carried over into the global activities of U.S. communications firms. For many decades, AT&T operated what was, for all intents and purposes, its own foreign office, which negotiated agreements on telephone links directly with government agencies abroad. AT&T and other companies seldom called upon the State Department or other Washington agencies for support in carrying out their overseas network operations.

This situation began to change after 1970 as U.S. communications and information technology firms moved out aggressively into world markets. Their activities reflected the shift in the U.S. domestic economy away from industrial activities to the production of information goods and services.[1] The classic case was IBM, which by 1980 dominated the global computer sector. Its experience was replicated, with variations, by other U.S. firms armed with advanced technologies and the managerial nimbleness to market them.[2] Foreign sales of communications goods and services increased to the point where they are now collectively the largest U.S. export sector.

This shift to information-related global trade now dominates the U.S. digital diplomacy agenda. The transition has not been a smooth one. Bureaucratic turfs have been trampled on as the State Department and other federal agencies have adjusted to the new trade realities. It is useful to review how this has changed both the style and operations of digital diplomacy in recent decades.

The need for a more structured policy approach to digital trade issues arose first in the early 1960s. The occasion was the emergence of communications satellite technology, as we saw in Chapter 3. It was an event that called for American leadership in dealing with a completely new kind of global communications system. The policy mechanisms for dealing with this opportunity did not exist in Washington. The State Department's resources consisted of a small office buried in the third level of its economic bureau. Other agencies had even fewer capabilities.

Faced with the need to act quickly in dealing with comsat technology, the Kennedy administration managed policy responsibilities for the project directly from the White House. The Department of Justice was given the leadership role, primarily because the president's brother, Attorney General Robert Kennedy, was seized with the strategic importance of exploiting the new technology. In the 10 years leading up to the creation of a permanent Intelsat network, comsat policy was dealt with in a series of ad hoc inter-agency committees and working groups. Little attention was given to the need for a more permanent structure to handle the issues created by communications satellites and other advanced technologies.[3]

In the late 1960s, the Johnson administration took the first step towards creating a unified structure for U.S. communications policy, including its international dimensions. A White House task force on the subject was authorized in August 1967. The group's membership, drawn from government agencies, was headed by Eugene Rostow, the undersecretary of state for political affairs. It had a large staff, together with a mandate to produce a report within a year.[4]

The Rostow task force focussed primarily on domestic issues, responding to industry pressures on the federal government to reduce AT&T's domination of the telecommunications sector. Economists on the staff were sympathetic with this position, arguing that market forces should be allowed to operate in the sector. Although their position was validated in the long run, they lost the day. The group's final report generally affirmed AT&T's position that domestic telecommunications had to be managed as a natural monopoly. The Rostow task force also considered, and rejected, staff proposals to set up an executive branch Department of Communications.[5] Instead, the group's report recommended "a new Federal capability" for managing the government's diverse communications responsibilities. This vaguely worded proposal was never acted upon.

The task force was more forthright in its recommendations on international policy. It proposed combining the overseas operations of AT&T, the Communications Satellite Corporation and several smaller firms into "a single entity for U.S. international transmissions"—in effect, a government-sponsored cartel. The report's rationale was that such an organization would be more technically efficient and would give the United States greater negotiating clout in dealing with other countries, all of whom relied on centralized organizations to handle their international traffic.[6]

Reactions to the task force report were mixed. The sharpest comments came from the telecommunications industry, which objected particularly to the idea of a single international carrier.[7] Overall the report drew little public comment, in part because it dealt with an arcane subject in largely legalistic terms. Moreover, the report was completed in the lame-duck last weeks of the Johnson administration.

The incoming Nixon administration ignored the Rostow report, as part of its general suspicions about policies inherited from eight years of Democratic control of the White House. The new president assigned communications policy responsibilities to New York investment banker Peter Flanigan, who had joined the administration as a White House aide. Flanigan soon found himself involved in bureaucratic infighting, centered around a proposal by the new secretary of commerce, Maurice Stans, that the government's telecommunications policy responsibilities be consolidated within his agency.[8]

After long negotiations, the Stans proposal was dropped in favor of a September 1970 decision to create an Office of Telecommunications Policy (OTP) in the White House. The mission of the new agency, headed by Clay (Tom) Whitehead, was to advise the president on policy issues and to coordinate the policy and operational activities of all federal agencies, including the State Department.[9]

The OTP had a checkered career from the start. Most of its concerns involved domestic developments, particularly the rapid growth of cable TV systems. Its international activities were relatively limited. One of its initiatives was a proposal to allow the Comsat Corporation to compete commercially with AT&T and other U.S. firms for international traffic, a longtime lobbying goal of Comsat's management.[10] The proposal would have modified Comsat's congressionally mandated role as a "carrier's carrier," doing business as the chosen government instrument for handling all Intelsat traffic to and from the United States. The proposal was withdrawn in the face of strong opposition from AT&T and other communications carriers. It would be another 25 years before Comsat's control over Intelsat traffic was modified.

The OTP's effectiveness as a policy group ended when it became involved in a White House–inspired project to punish the New York television networks for alleged anti-Nixon bias in their news reporting. The White House eventually backed down, but the OTP's influence withered. Tom Whitehead resigned as head of the office in 1974, to be replaced by a series of short-term appointees. At one time, the OTP was without a permanent director for 21 months.[11]

As a result, OTP was one of the Nixon-era agencies slated for oblivion when Jimmy Carter moved into the White House in January 1977.[12] The office had not only lost public credibility. It also lagged in addressing the policy implications of the rapid changes taking place in the communications sector. Technologies such as fiber optics and semiconductor chips were moving out of the laboratories and on to production lines, speeding up the pace and complexity of operations within the communications industries.

The global trade implications of this shift were becoming more evident in the early 1970s as American data networking firms began to move into overseas markets. International networking had previously been limited by the lack of technologies that could handle computer-to-computer transactions. Data networking usually involved slow-moving telex circuits.

This changed with the introduction of a technique known as packet switching, which increased both the speed and quality of information transfers. Installed first in domestic networks, packet switching expanded internationally in 1977 when the FCC authorized Western Union International to offer computer-to-computer service to Europe. Packet-data networking became the norm for global data traffic, leading in recent years to the explosive growth of the Internet.[13]

Using packet-switching technology, U.S. companies soon dominated global trade in data networking. This raised warning flags among other industrial democracies, particularly in Europe, as they began to recognize the implications of an American-dominated information industry in their own countries. Their response was to raise tariff and other barriers against U.S. data exports, creating a major digital diplomacy issue for Washington policymakers after 1980.[14]

The new prominence of information exports led to pressures on Congress by industry firms to take a closer look at international communications policy. They found a particularly sympathetic ear in Senator Ernest Hollings, a South Carolina Democrat, who was chairman of the Senate communications subcommittee. "No single agency of the U.S. government has comprehensive authority over international communications," he declared in 1977, "nor has the distribution of functions among the several agencies been the result of planned allocation. Rather, it grew like Topsy, responding to technical or industrial problems as they arose."[15]

One outcome of these pressures was the first congressional study of barriers to American data exports. Among other recommendations, the report proposed that a high-level office for communications policy be set up in the State Department. Although legislation based on this proposal was not acted upon at the time, the report had a direct influence on the reorganization of the department's communications policy structure a few years later.[16]

This congressional interest, fueled by industry lobbying, led the new Carter administration to look at different approaches to organizing telecommunications and information policy. The OTP experience had shown that top-down attempts to deal with the problem from the White House were ineffective. During its five year tenure, the OTP was never able to carry out its charter requirement to coordinate the communications policy activities of federal agencies, including those in the foreign policy community, each with separate and often conflicting mandates in this area.

In drawing up proposals for a new organizational approach, the Carter administration focussed primarily on domestic communications policy.[17] However, White House planners soon found themselves involved in the international dimensions of the subject. In part, this was a response to a General Accounting Office report that was critical of past White House policy in dealing with changes in global communications.[18]

The new administration also had advice on the subject from a congressionally funded blue ribbon panel, which had recently submitted a plan for reorganizing the Washington foreign policy agencies.[19] Known as the Murphy Commission, after its chairman, retired diplomat Robert D. Murphy, the group quickly became enmeshed in competing proposals from hundreds of witnesses, ranging from the Secretary of State to representatives of the Gay Liberation movement.

The Murphy Commission's final report was, however, an exercise in bureaucratic shuffling. Of relevance to this survey, it dismissed in one sentence the role of communications and information as emerging foreign policy issues. Its suggestion was to give the subject slightly more prominence in the State Department's policy hierarchy, recommending that responsibility for these issues be moved from the third level of the economics bureau to the second level of a new bureau headed by an undersecretary for economic and scientific affairs.[20]

Despite this weak recommendation, the Murphy Commission report was one of the earliest acknowledgments by any group looking at the State Department that global communications policy needed greater visibility. The commission's recommendation was a small step towards a decision, a decade later, to create a full-fledged bureau at State to deal with the subject.

Meanwhile, the Carter White House proceeded with plans to replace the Nixon OTP with a more effective communications policy structure. The result, after months of negotiating with congressional leaders, was a decision to create a National Telecommunications and Information Administration (NTIA) in the Department of Commerce. The new unit merged the functions of the OTP and an existing Commerce bureau, the Office of Telecommunications, together with several smaller offices dealing with technical research. A well-known Washington communications lawyer, Henry Geller, was named to head the new unit.[21]

Although NTIA's responsibilities were focussed primarily on domestic policy, they also affected the evolution of digital diplomacy. The executive order creating the agency defined, for the first time, executive branch responsibilities for international communications policy. It is useful to quote the relevant passage, since it attempted to draw bureaucratic lines of responsibility in an area where domestic and foreign issues overlap:

The Secretary of Commerce shall develop and set forth, in coordination with the Secretary of State and other interested agencies, policies and programs which relate to international telecommunications issues, conferences and negotiations. The Secretary of Commerce shall coordinate economic, technical, operational and related preparations for United States participation in international telecommunications conferences and negotiations. The Secretary shall provide advice and assistance to the Secretary of State on international telecommunications policies to strengthen the position and serve the best interests of the United States in support of the Secretary of State's responsibility for the conduct of foreign affairs.[22]

There were enough ambiguities in this formula to assure that the issue of responsibility for international communications policy remained unsettled. In particular, another part of the executive order identified NTIA as adviser to the White House in all national communications and information matters, without differentiating between domestic and international issues. The implication was that the State Department had a secondary role. The stage was set for a series of inter-agency disputes over the ways in which overseas communications policy was organized for the rest of the century.[23]

Meanwhile, a White House unit, the National Security Council, began to play an active role in global communications policy for the first time. The impetus for change came from Zbigniew Brzezinski, the Carter administration's national security adviser. He was the first official at the White House level to fully comprehend the implications of advanced communications and information resources in U.S. strategic planning.

Brzezinski came to this understanding while a rising young star in foreign policy studies at Columbia University. His views were outlined in a seminal book, *Between two ages: America's role in the technotronic era*, published in 1970, six years before he joined the Carter White House.[24] A generation later, the book is a remarkably prescient account of the U.S. role as, in his words, "the principal global disseminator" of advanced technologies in a new computer-driven era. Although the book identified a wide range of scientific developments, it gave special attention to communications and information technologies.

Since Brzezinski's academic expertise at the time was in Communist studies, the book focussed heavily on cold war issues. However, he also cast a wider policy net, stressing the potential long-term effect of U.S. information resources on the global power balance. His analysis of the international impact of computer resources was one of first to point out the significance of the growing gap between American and Soviet capabilities in this area.

His conclusion was that changes in the structure and style of U.S. foreign relations were overdue, including a better understanding of the role of information technologies:

Wider diplomatic use of computers and direct sound-and-sight electronic communications should permit the reduction in the size and number of United States foreign missions, making them operationally similar to the more efficient international corporations. Washington's policymaking process needs to be similarly streamlined and freed from its tangle of bureaucratic red tape.[25]

At the White House, Brzezinski took steps to get the NSC more involved in communications issues. Given the council staff's longtime inattention to the subject, mistakes had been made. One 1980 example was a proposal to cut off all communications circuits to Iran in retaliation for the seizure of the American embassy in Tehran following the overthrow of the Shah by Islamic militants. The proposal was ill advised for several reasons. One was that the United States was party to treaties (including the 1972 Intelsat agreements) which made it impossible to get the necessary support of other governments in carrying out the threat. More-over, there were too many technical alternatives that would allow the Iranians to get around the boycott. The proposal was quickly dropped.[26]

Brzezinski's most important contribution to digital diplomacy was to encourage an integrated policy approach to the many issues involved in communications policy. An NSC working group was set up to review strategic policy on communications and information. In March 1979, the group issued a presidential review memorandum, PRM-35, which laid out a series of policy guidelines on all aspects of the subject.[27] It was the first time that policy planners identified the problems involved in each issue and also examined their relationship to each other in crafting a larger U.S. strategy.

NSC-35 was an important step towards providing an integrated frame-work for handling digital diplomacy issues. What it neglected to do was to assign firm bureaucratic responsibilities for dealing with these issues among the half-dozen federal agencies directly involved in the subject.[28] Moreover, the document generally underestimated the quickened pace of changes taking place in the evolving domestic information economy and its effect on foreign policy.

The most important of these domestic developments was the process leading up to the 1982 Department of Justice consent decree ending AT&T's near-monopoly in domestic telecommunications. It was an un-precedented event in U.S. industrial history as the largest corporation in the country gave up 60 percent of its assets—the 22 local Bell telephone companies. AT&T had for years fought a rear-guard action to maintain its dominant status, using platoons of lawyers and its formidable lob-bying resources at the federal, state and local levels. However, its mo-nopoly had lost its reason for being. No one company could keep up with the size and pace of developments taking place in the new infor-mation economy.

Behind the dry legalisms of the consent decree lay a stunning fact: the United States became the first industrial democracy to begin to adapt its economy to information age realities.[29] It opened an era of vigorous growth in the communications sector. Thousands of new companies en-tered the field, competing among themselves and against AT&T. Many industry analysts saw the loss of AT&T's prime assets, its local phone companies, as confirmation that its glory days were over. They were wrong. After a series of false starts, AT&T reinvented itself to the point that, at the end of the century, it was still a major presence in the U.S. communications sector.

In the aftermath of the AT&T breakup, the newly competitive industry focussed primarily on the domestic market. However, it soon began to look abroad for trade opportunities. Communications and information goods and services were a small but growing part of U.S. exports. After the AT&T breakup, overseas markets were a tempting target. We will take a closer look in the next chapter at how digitally based trade evolved as the largest single item in American exports since 1980. Here we will examine how digital diplomacy was restructured to deal with this development.

As noted above, the Justice Department consent decree had the immediate effect of making the domestic communications market more competitive. But it had other impacts more directly relevant to digital diplomacy. One of these was to encourage foreign communications companies to set up shop in the United States. The American market had always been open to them, but they found it difficult to compete against AT&T's dominant role.

With this barrier lowered, overseas firms seized the opportunity to sell their wares in the world's largest market. Sony, Mitsubishi and other Japanese electronics giants moved in with production and marketing organizations. Within a few years, a hitherto obscure Canadian company, Northern Telecom, threatened AT&T's lead in advanced network equipment. Siemens, the German electronics giant, opened up 50 factories and other facilities. Britain's Cable & Wireless became the fifth-largest telephone company in the country.[30]

This trade invasion highlighted what has become the most persistently troubling issue in U.S. digital diplomacy, namely open access to foreign markets for U.S. business. In the pristine world of economic theory, American communications firms should have had an equal chance to compete abroad. In fact, these markets were largely closed to them, the result of protectionist rules that limited the importing of foreign communications equipment and services.

A major obstacle to removing these barriers was the ways in which communications services were organized in other countries. In almost every instance, these services were controlled by government monopolies, known as PTTs—post, telephone and telegraph organizations. The PTTs were cautious bureaucracies with no incentive to encourage competition. Moreover, they were firmly entrenched politically. In larger countries, their equipment needs were met by local firms that were single-source providers, protected against foreign competitors by high tariff walls, subsidies and other government practices. These restrictions fell most heavily on a resurgent U.S. communications sector.

Dismantling these barriers became the chief task of U.S. digital diplomacy in the past two decades. It has also been the most successful. The PTT-monopoly system is rapidly being phased out abroad. American policies played a significant role in bringing this about through negotiations at the global, regional and bilateral levels. Competitive telecommunications networks are now the norm in countries supplying 95 percent of all communications traffic worldwide. The laggards are small developing countries, mostly in Africa.

This shift to a competitive communications sector did not come easily for most overseas governments. Strong rear-guard actions by supporters of the local PTT system delayed reforms. These efforts were opposed by even stronger pressures, particularly from local industries, to upgrade communications facilities. The PTT monopolies looked more and more like industrial age dinosaurs, unable to adapt to new technical and economic realities. The U.S. experience in deregulating telecommunications, including the AT&T breakup, became a rough benchmark for local reformers in developing their own versions of a competitive market.

Britain was the first country to close down its PTT, which was a subdivision of the British post office. A private corporation, British Telecom (BT), took over the post office's functions in 1981. A second company, Mercury Communications, was created to provide limited competition to BT. Somewhat reluctantly, other West European countries succumbed to the inevitability of developing their own versions of competitive markets. The defining event was a series of decisions by the European Community (now the European Union) mandating the opening of its members' telephone networks to competition by 1992.[31] Within a few years, Japan, Canada and Australia made similar decisions, followed by the newly emerging Asian economies.

Telecommunications deregulation created a new policy environment for American digital diplomacy. For over a century, its business had been conducted largely through negotiations with a single monopoly authority in each country—a relatively simple task handled by a small office in the State Department's economic bureau. The phasing out of the PTTs and the rise of private sector competitors introduced a different set of players and a more complex pattern of issues. Workload requirements increased dramatically. By 1980, the State Department was committed to negotiations in two dozen major telecommunications-related conferences in the following decade. It was a dramatic change in what had been, only a few years before, a leisurely schedule of widely spaced meetings. A 1980 report by the National Committee on Library and Information Sciences identified 97 international groups with which the United States carried out negotiations on information matters.[32]

The State Department bureaucracy was slow to respond to proposals for dealing with these changes. The old-line bureaus were resistant, fearing a loss of status in any new arrangements. There were rumblings from other federal agencies, led by the Department of Commerce's NTIA, with its loose mandate to coordinate all national communications policy. The Federal Communications Commission became more insistent in claiming a role in international policy, having set up a bureau to deal with the subject in the 1980s.[33]

Meanwhile, pressures grew for strengthening the State Department's communications policy apparatus. Industry groups pressed the department for help in resolving trade barrier disputes. The subject became grist for the congressional legislative mill. Bills proposing an overhaul of overseas communications policy were introduced into both houses in the early 1980s. Congressional committee hearings on the proposed legislation were dominated by dark warnings that foreigners, notably the Europeans and Japanese, were organizing against American high-technology trade, particularly in information services.[34]

Although they differed in details, most of the proposed bills were critical of the State Department's handling of communications issues. "The reason for this legislation," Rep. Glenn English, an Oklahoma Democrat, declared, "is that the State Department has the authority to coordinate efforts but hasn't been doing it, has given no indication that it wants to do it or is going to do it."[35] Several bills called for a White House–level council on international communications and information to coordinate policy in the field. The Senate version proposed that the Secretary of Commerce would be chairman of the council. A House version assigned the chairmanship to the U.S. Trade Representative.

The State Department took a dim view of both proposals as undercutting its policy authority. At the same time, it dismissed suggestions for setting up a bureau for communications and information policy within the department. James Buckley, the undersecretary for science and technology, described the idea as "superficially appealing" but unnecessary. "Given the very diversity of the geographic and substantive issues involved," he told a congressional committee in 1981, "establishment of a new bureau would not, in the final analysis, replace the requirement for effective internal coordination."[36]

Amidst this bureaucratic foot-dragging, the pressures for change intensified. A major challenge came from the Commerce Department's NTIA. It took the form of a 244-page report on U.S. communications goals, submitted to Congress in March 1983. In a section titled "disturbing trends," the report called for a new framework for coordinating international communications policy at a single point. The result, the report stated, would be "a single Executive Branch position . . . which individual agencies are not free to contradict, ignore or undermine."[37]

The NTIA report stopped short of recommending where this new global policy unit should be located. It was clear, however, that the proposal was intended to undercut the State Department's role. The recommendation was heavily weighted toward the theme that communications policy was primarily a trade issue, one in which the Commerce Department should have the lead.

Commerce's attempt to dominate global communications policy became more explicit three months later when the Reagan White House unveiled a plan for restructuring the agency as a Department of International Trade and Industry.[38] Among other implications, the proposal was a direct assault on the State Department's role in economic policy in general, and communications policy in particular.

State officials reacted briskly to the White House proposal, first by lobbying successfully against it and then by strengthening economy policy operations within the department. Although this reorganization included all trade issues, communications was singled out for special attention. In large part, this reflected the strong interest of Secretary George W. Schultz in the subject. He was an economist and a former executive in Bechtel, a global construction company that depended heavily on communications to coordinate its overseas operations. Overall, he had a better feel for the importance of a robust approach to U.S. communications issues than had any previous secretary.[39]

In April 1983, Schultz approved plans for a new office to coordinate communications and information policy, headed by Diana Lady Dougan. She brought to the job strong credentials as a communications industry executive. To give weight to her appointment, and to the importance he attached to the new office, Schultz asked the White House to grant her the personal rank of ambassador.[40]

Schultz's action raised the ante in the dispute over control of communications policy within the federal government. It was greeted by an anonymous Commerce Department spokesman as "a clever bureaucratic move," designed to block Commerce's claim to primacy in the field. State was no longer interested in coordinating policy, he declared: "Now they're taking over the whole executive branch. No one objects to a State Department role. But we don't want to entrust the commercial interests of a high-tech industry to the State Department."[41] Despite this sniping, Congress approved the Schultz proposal several months later.[42]

For the moment, the issue of responsibility for global communications policy was settled in the State Department's favor. Congressional proposals for a White House–level coordinating unit languished and died. The White House also backed off its plans for a new international trade department. To ease tensions between the State and Commerce departments, a memorandum of understanding was drawn up which outlined the respective responsibilities of the two agencies in communications policy. The understanding quickly broke down, a victim of semantic differences over its provisions.[43]

Meanwhile, the newly appointed Ambassador Dougan turned to the job of reducing a backlog of communications policy decisions. Her task, she told a Georgetown University seminar, was akin to hugging Jell-O. The workload included preparations for a dozen international conferences dealing with the radio spectrum, information-flow barriers and other issues. The new office also became involved in White House plans to incorporate services trades, including telecommunications and information, in a new global trade agreement, replacing the General Agreement in Trade and Tariffs (GATT). This initiative led to the creation of the World Trade Organization (WTO) in the mid-1990s.

Trade also played a key role in another policy decision facing the new coordinator's office. This was the future of global communications satellite development. Intelsat had been a spectacular success, linking every part of the earth. Traffic on the network was growing at 15 percent a year. Throughout the 1970s, American policy was firmly committed to maintaining the network's dominant role. In particular, Washington had supported Intelsat treaty provisions that gave the organization veto-power control over the entry of potential competitors. In effect, they had to get Intelsat's permission to compete.[44]

Economic and technical realities were, however, intruding on Intelsat's ability to maintain its monopoly position. The concept of a single global network was being eroded in much the same way that PTT telephone monopolies were being challenged. If Intelsat could provide a range of separate services for national, regional and global users, why couldn't competing networks do it just as well or better? This question, posed tentatively at first, marked the beginning of the end of Intelsat's role as the leading supplier of global satellite communications.

The most immediate threat to Intelsat's dominance came from Western Europe. By 1970, the European Community was actively promoting the idea of a regional satellite network, controlled by community governments. The project was seen as a practical example of economic integration within the region. Moreover, its advocates declared, it would advance the goal of a home-grown space industry that would challenge the American near-monopoly in satellite equipment and services. The Europeans also saw economic benefits in keeping revenues from the proposed network within the region rather than turning them over to Intelsat.

The Europeans submitted their plan for a regional network to Intelsat for approval in 1978. This move set off a four-year debate while Intelsat officials sought to limit the project's impact on their own network with what the Europeans regarded as petty restrictions. The European side of the exchange was led by a feisty Italian, Andrea Caruso, the first director of Eutelsat, the organization set up to run the regional network.[45] Caruso took up arms not only against Intelsat but also against the American satellite industry, claiming that it wanted to cripple European space efforts. Caruso and his colleagues finally won approval for their regional network, with support from the United States.[46] This American support was the first clear signal that Washington recognized the need for flexibility in dealing with potential competition to Intelsat.

While the Europeans touted the advantages of alternate satellite systems, they were not interested in commercial competition within their own region. This prospect arose when a group of Swedish investors proposed a private "European Business Satellite" network. The project was opposed by West European governments, fearful of the economic effect it would have on their Eutelsat project. The Swedish group eventually withdrew its proposal.[47]

A more potent series of projects to commercialize satellite communications came from the U.S. space industry. A robust domestic market had opened up as a result of an FCC decision to license commercial satellite operations. By 1981, conditions were ripe for a similar move into global markets. The newly installed Reagan administration was strongly pro-business and particularly intent on promoting competition in the telecommunications sector. The 1982 agreement to break up AT&T set a precedent for the more difficult task of opening up global markets. In the same year, the FCC lifted most of its regulatory limits on overseas networking, allowing AT&T to enter the global data market and also allowing data firms such as RCA and Western Union to compete for the first time with AT&T in the voice market.[48]

These FCC rulings applied only to terrestrial networking. Opening up space communications to global competition was another matter, given the American government's commitment to Intelsat's anticompetitive rules. The United States had reaped enormous political and economic benefits from its support of the global cartel. The Reagan White House was initially cautious in proposing any changes in the Intelsat arrangements, despite its ideological bias towards reducing regulatory restrictions on American business. It was, moreover, apparent that a proposal for reducing Intelsat's cartel power faced strong opposition among the network's other owners.[49]

The stage was set for confrontation over the issue of Intelsat's future role in global communications. At first it was an unequal contest, with Intelsat and most of its member countries having the upper hand.[50] The Europeans and Japanese, in particular, saw commercial satellite competition as another American move to dominate global communications. Opposition was even stronger among Intelsat member countries in Asia, Africa and Latin America. Using rhetoric borrowed from their earlier advocacy of a New World Information Order (described in Chapter 4), they saw commercialization as a threat to the expansion of Intelsat services in their regions. In particular, they benefited from Intelsat's tariff structure that in effect subsidized traffic to and from developing countries.

Meanwhile, the Reagan administration faced strong pressures to change what came to be called the "separate satellite issue," a circumlocution for ending Intelsat's protective rules against competition. In the Senate, a bill sponsored by Barry Goldwater, the Arizona Republican, supported commercial competition to Intelsat. Intelsat's defenders were led by the Comsat Corporation, whose role as U.S. representative at Intelsat was threatened by the prospect of private competition. In 1982, Comsat owned 24 percent of Intelsat stock and derived $250 million of its $409 million operating revenues from Intelsat traffic. Meanwhile, the space and telecommunications industries had launched a campaign to reduce Comsat's role in controlling all U.S. traffic in and out of the Intelsat network.[51]

The debate over commercialization was joined in March 1983. Two young Washington lawyers, Thomas McKnight and Christopher Vizas, applied to the FCC for permission to launch a pair of commercial satellites in the North Atlantic region, to be operated by their newly formed venture, Orion Communications. Four months later, a similar application was made by TRT Telecommunications, owned by United Brands, the banana company, which had long experience in managing communications networks in Central America.[52] Within a year, three other companies had similar applications pending before the FCC.

These moves forced a U.S. decision about whether to continue to support Intelsat's rules against private competition. The plans put forward by the five American companies posed a limited challenge to Intelsat's main business—telephone calls, which accounted for about 85 percent of the network's revenues at the time. The five FCC applicants proposed to limit their operations to the lease or sale of satellite capacity to large private users, primarily corporations, for their in-house communications. This would have threatened a relatively small portion (about 15 percent) of Intelsat's annual revenues.[53] Nevertheless, it was clear to everyone in the policy debate that the FCC applicants' proposals were the opening wedge in a process that would lead to full competition against Intelsat.

Intelsat officials moved quickly to defend their anticompetition rules. They asked the organization's 109 members to send letters (based on forms drafted by Intelsat lawyers) to the State Department urging rejection of the commercial satellite projects. Seventy countries did so, most of them from developing regions. European countries and Japan held back, waiting to see the specific details of the American government's decision on the FCC satellite applications. The Europeans in particular saw that they might benefit from the introduction of competition, both as users and as likely partners in commercial systems. Their reluctance to challenge the FCC applications immediately was the first indication of less-than-solid support within Intelsat for opposing private competitors.

Meanwhile, the State Department had to deal with domestic opposition to the FCC applications. The Comsat Corporation's objections were a foregone conclusion. Although the company was the designated U.S. government representative at Intelsat, it supported the network's strategy of opposing any commercial competition. More surprising was the opposition of the two leading U.S. satellite builders—Hughes Communications and Ford Aerospace. Both argued that their business would suffer in the likely event that the Europeans required the FCC applicants to buy European technology as a condition for cooperating with their ventures. The dispute was eventually settled by making open bidding a condition for approving the FCC applications. The policy debate was resolved in a November 1984 White House "presidential determination" that international satellite systems separate from Intelsat were required in the national interest.[54] The decision reflected more than the deliberations of federal bureaucrats. It also bore the strong mark of industry influences, managed by sobersided executives in corporate boardrooms.

The flamboyant standout in this group was Rene Anselmo, the head of PanAmSat, one of the five applicants for FCC permission to expand into international satellite services. The son of a Massachusetts postal worker, Anselmo linked up with Mexican investors as a young man to develop the first Spanish-language television network in the United States. The network (now called Univision) eventually expanded to 400 television and cable TV outlets. In the early 1980s, Anselmo put his own considerable fortune on the line to found PanAmSat with the intention of competing against Intelsat—a perilous proposition given the strong American government commitment to protect the network from competitors. As one observer noted at the time: "Rene Anselmo wanted nothing less than to go head-to-head with the big boys at Intelsat."[55]

He proceeded to do so with a campaign of maverick tactics that included a cartoon dog named Spot, usually shown lifting a hind leg in a less-than-subtle indication of Anselmo's attitude towards Intelsat. Spot's image was emblazoned on PanAmSat letterheads and on the rockets that put its satellites into orbit. The company's stock traded on the NASDAQ exchange under the Spot symbol. However unorthodox his tactics, Rene Anselmo caught the business community's attention with a message, repeated with mantra-like regularity, that pitted the glories of private enterprise against the machinations of international bureaucrats.

Partly as a result of his attention-getting antics, Anselmo played a key role in removing the biggest obstacle to American private sector competition in global satellite networking. This was the requirement that commercial firms get "landing rights" for their satellite signals in each of the countries where they hoped to do business. In every case, these rights were controlled by the local government. Intelsat's anticompetitive strategy centered around its ability to convince these governments not to cooperate with Anselmo and the other private networkers.

This roadblock was breached in April 1986. Peru's government-controlled telecommunications agency agreed to become, in the industry's phrase, a foreign correspondent for Rene Anselmo's proposed network in Latin America. Intelsat's officials scolded the Peruvians for their transgression, but the critical breakthrough had been made.[56] Bowing to the inevitable, Intelsat management pulled back from its stolid opposition to commercial competition. Negotiations were begun to coordinate PanAmSat's network operations with those of Intelsat.

By September 1985, the FCC had approved operational permits for four of the five satellite applicants, including PanAmSat. It was the beginning of the end of Intelsat's domination of global satellite communications. Within a decade, the organization accounted for only 30 of the 157 satellites providing communications services worldwide. By the turn of the century, the Intelsat organization had been transformed into a much leaner operation, competing on price and services with over a dozen commercial networks.

The American government's decision to reverse its policy on competition to Intelsat marked a turning point in digital diplomacy. It established trade considerations as the main focus of international communications policy after 1985, paralleling other efforts to reduce overseas barriers to American digital commerce. Challenging Intelsat's control of global satellite communications fitted into the new policy emphasis on open markets, particularly in the negotiations leading up to the creation of the World Trade Organization in 1993.

As we shall see in the next chapter, the decision to introduce competition in global satellite networking was a relatively small part of this initiative. It was, however, one of the factors that fueled the expansion of digitally based world trade at an annual rate of about 15 percent, a pace unmatched by any other economic sector. This growth helped to push electronics ahead of automobiles as the dominant world industry by the turn of the century.

The proliferation of digital diplomacy issues, especially those dealing with trade, raised the visibility of the new State Department policy coordinator's office. Under Diana Dougan's leadership, the unit played an activist role in calling attention to the strategic importance of communications and information issues. One of the office's early accomplishments was to set up a schedule of regular consultations with foreign governments and with the new private telecommunications companies overseas. Previously, such consultations were episodic and usually dealt with technical issues. Ambassador Dougan expanded them to include the political and economic implications of the new communications environment.[57] The result was to strengthen the State Department's primacy in global communications policy issues within the Washington policy community.

Despite these improvements, inter-agency tensions over communications policy persisted. The Commerce Department continued to press its claim for a leading role in negotiating trade-related policy. The dispute surfaced publicly in 1984 when Commerce challenged the State Department's chairmanship of the senior inter-agency group dealing with communications and information issues. After a testy exchange of correspondence between the two agencies, a decision was made that the group would be co-chaired by State and Commerce officials who would alternate in presiding. It proved to be an uneasy truce.[58]

The coordinator's office at State was at a disadvantage because it was a very small operation in a large agency, with none of the organizational clout available to the geographic and functional bureaus. Secretary Schultz took steps in February 1985 to give the Dougan office more resources and greater visibility. He informed Congress that he wanted to upgrade the coordinator's office to full-fledged bureau status.[59]

Despite ritualistic grumbling from congressional Republicans about expanding the department's bureaucracy, the proposal was approved. Diana Dougan was confirmed as an assistant secretary, heading a new Bureau for International Communications and Information Policy. She also kept the title of U.S. coordinator for all federal activities in the field. In line with Schultz's interest in trade issues, the new bureau was placed under the wing of the undersecretary of economic affairs.

Digital diplomacy now had a secure niche of its own within the State Department structure. It had strong leadership in the person of Ambassador Dougan and a staff of over 20 officers and support personnel. Overall, it was a major break with the department's previous practice of dealing with communications issues in separate policy compartments.

Trade issues dominated the new bureau's activities as part of the wider strategy to reduce barriers faced by American companies in their overseas operations. As noted earlier, barriers to electronics-based goods and services were particularly resistant to change, given the long-standing practice of most governments to protect their communications and information sectors from outside competition.

The intervening years have seen a series of important breakthroughs in the American strategy of reducing global trade barriers. We will take a closer look in the next chapter at how digital diplomacy contributed to this change.

NOTES

1. The evolution of this economic shift is described in *The information economy*, 9 vols. (Washington, DC: Office of Telecommunications, U.S. Department of Commerce, Special Publication 77-12, 1977).

2. Jonathan D. Aronson and Peter F. Cowhey, *When countries talk: International trade in telecommunications services* (Cambridge, MA: Ballinger Publishing Co., 1987).

3. The evolution of national communications at the time is discussed in Tho-

mas E. Will, *Telecommunications structure and management in the executive branch of government 1900–1970* (Boulder, CO: Westview Press, 1978), pp. 49–77. See also: Francis E. Rourk and Roger G. Brown, "The President and telecommunications policy: The failure of an advisory system," paper presented at the 1980 annual conference of the American Political Science Association, August 1980.

4. "President names panel to review communications," *New York Times*, 15 August 1967, p. 1. See also Will, op cit., pp. 79–94.

5. "Department of communications urged," *New York Times*, 12 March 1969, p. 12.

6. "Final report of the president's task force on communications policy" (Washington, DC: The White House, 7 December 1968), p. 36.

7. "Industry is upset by Rostow report," *New York Times*, 13 December 1968, p. 5.

8. Rourk and Brown, op cit., pp. 22–23.

9. The Office of Telecommunications Policy was activated in an executive order signed by President Nixon on 4 September 1970. Executive Order 11556, Section 2 (1), *Federal Register*, Vol. 35, No. 175, p. 14193.

10. "White House circulates new int'l communications act," *Electronic News*, 26 February 1973, p. 3.

11. The OTP's overall record is discussed in James Miller, "Policy planning and technocratic power: The significance of OTP," *Journal of Communication*, Winter 1982, pp. 174–178. See also: "A beleaguered Whitehead and a battered OTP," *Broadcasting*, 17 September 1973, pp. 16–18.

12. "White House plans to end office that set communications policy," *New York Times*, 26 June 1977, p. 1.

13. The early implications of this development are discussed in "Foreign policy choices for the 1970s and 1980s: Information resources, strategic weakness," Publication P-76-6, Program in Information Technologies and Public Policy, Harvard University, October 1976. The significance of packet-data networking is outlined in Ithiel de Sola Pool and Arthur B. Corte, "The implications for American foreign policy of low-cost non-voice communications," Research Program on Communications Policy, Department of Political Science, MIT, October 1977.

14. For the evolution of U.S. foreign policy in dealing with electronic data flows, see: "International policy implications of computers and advanced telecommunications in information systems" (Washington, DC: Bureau of Oceans, International Environmental and Scientific Affairs, Department of State, January 1979).

15. Quoted in *Telecommunications Report*, 18 July 1977, p. 5.

16. "International information flow: Forging a new framework," House report No. 96-135, Committee on Government Operations, House of Representatives, 96th Congress, 2nd session, 1980.

17. For a useful survey of the Carter administration's plans at the time, see: "Special report: Mr. Carter's communications policy—the stage is set," *Broadcasting*, 2 January 1978, pp. 115–118.

18. "Responsibilities, actions and coordination of federal agencies in international communications services," report of the Comptroller-General, CED-77-132, General Accounting Office, 1977.

19. The formal title of the group was the Commission on the Organization of

the Government for the Conduct of Foreign Policy. It was authorized in Public Law 92-352, 92nd Congress, H.R. 14734, 13 July 1972.

20. Ibid, p. 65.

21. Reorganization Plan Number One (42 FR 56101), 21 October 1977, and Executive Order 12406, "Relating to the transfer of telecommunications functions," (43 FR 13349), 26 March 1978. See also: M. Kent Sidel and Vincent Mosco, "U.S. communications policymaking: The results of executive branch policymaking." *Telecommunications Policy*, September 1978, pp. 211–217.

22. "Transfer of telecommunications functions," ibid., paragraph 2-204.

23. Anne W. Branscomb, "Bundling communications policy for the new administration," *Telecommunications Policy*, June 1977, pp. 212–219.

24. Zbigniew Brzezinski, *Between two ages: America's role in the technotronic era* (New York: Viking Press, 1970).

25. Ibid., pp. 292–293.

26. "No go for satellite sanctions against Iran," *Science*, 16 May 1980, p. 20.

27. "International communications policy," PRM/NSC 35, 12 March 1979.

28. The evolution of federal responsibilities for international communications policymaking at the time is documented in Anthony M. Rutkowski, "United States policymaking for the public international forums in communications," *Syracuse Journal of International Law and Communications*, Vol. 8, No. 29, 1980, pp. 95–157.

29. Robert Crandall, *After the breakup: U.S. telecommunications in a more competitive era* (Washington, DC: Brookings Institution, 1991).

30. This development is described in J. Gregory Sidak, *Foreign investment in American telecommunications* (Chicago: University of Chicago Press, 1997).

31. Wilson P. Dizard, "Europe calling Europe," in Alan W. Cafruny and Glenda G. Rosenthal (eds.), *The state of the European Community: The Maastricht debates and beyond* (Boulder, CO: Lynne Rienner Publishers, 1993), pp. 321–336.

32. "Proposed objectives and functions of an NCLIS task force on international relations," Appendix C, National Committee on Library and Information Sciences, Washington, DC, 9 May 1980.

33. The FCC's expanded activities in global communications are described in Lawrence J. Spiwak, "From international competitive carrier to the WTO: A survey of the FCC's international telecommunications policy initiatives 1985–1998," *Federal Communications Law Journal*, Vol. 51, No. 2, March 1999, pp. 519–539.

34. For an example, see: "International information flow: Forging a new framework," op cit., pp. 31–36.

35. Quoted in *Communications Daily*, 2 August 1981, p. 2.

36. "Hearings on the International Communications Reorganization Act (HR 1957) before the subcommittee on government and individual rights," Committee on Government Operations, House of Representatives, 2 April 1981.

37. "Long range goals in international telecommunications," National Telecommunications and Information Administration, Department of Commerce, 11 March 1983, p. 30.

38. "White House unveils plan for Commerce reorganization," *Washington Post*, 2 June 1983, p. D-1.

39. For a summary of Schultz's views on the subject, see: "The shape, scope and consequences of the age of information," address to the Stanford University

Alumni Association, reprinted in Current Policy No. 811, Bureau of Public Affairs, Department of State, March 1981.

40. "Personal rank of ambassador accorded Diana Lady Dougan," Department of State press release No. 112, 19 April 1983.

41. "Turf war over communications policymaking," *Broadcasting*, 6 June 1983, p. 40.

42. "Congress OK's new communications unit at the State Department," *Broadcasting*, 28 November 1983, p. 33.

43. "Commerce, State quickly disagree on roles under new agency accord," *Communications International*, 14 October 1983, p. 1.

44. The effect of this cartel power is described in Marcellus Snow, "Intelsat: an international example," *Journal of Communication*, Vol. 33, No. 2, pp. 147–156.

45. "Eutelsat news release aims square at Intelsat," *Satellite Week*, 18 October 1982, p. 1.

46. "Intelsat coordinates with European system," Intelsat press release 82-28-1, 8 October 1982.

47. Lee McKnight, "The deregulation of international satellite communications policy: U.S. policy and the Intelsat response," *Space Communications and Broadcasting*, No. 3, 1985, pp. 39–59.

48. "FCC removes limitations on international services," Federal Communications Commission press release, 9 December 1982.

49. For background on the evolution of American policy on competition to Intelsat, see: Andrea Kavanagh, "Star WARCs and new systems: An analysis of U.S. international satellite policy formation," *Telecommunications Policy*, June 1986, pp. 93–106.

50. Intelsat's defense of its policies on competition is outlined in Richard R. Colino, "The possible introduction of separate satellite systems: International satellite communications at the crossroads," *Columbia Journal of International Law*, Vol. 24, No. 1, 1985, pp. 13–35.

51. "Lobbying effort under way in Senate to undo Comsat," *Broadcasting*, 28 August 1983, p. 36.

52. "A storm that could snap Intelsat's monopoly," *Business Week*, 1 August 1983, p. 78.

53. Kavanagh, op cit., p. 98.

54. Presidential Determination 85-2, 28 November 1984, *Federal Register*, Vol. 49, No. 232, p. 46987.

55. Quoted in "The tale of a man, his dog and the industry they changed," *Satellite Communications*, November 1995, p. 27.

56. "Intelsat chides Peru for signing on with PanAmSat," *International Communications Week*, 2 May 1986, p. 3.

57. The bureau's expanded activities are described in "Ambassador Diana Lady Dougan: An open world policy for telecommunications," *Broadcasting*, 19 October 1987, pp. 33–40.

58. Kavanagh, op cit., p. 101.

59. "Schultz wants new communications bureau, congressional view uncertain," *International Communications Week*, 15 February 1985, p. 1.

Chapter 8

Negotiating Electronics Trade

Walter Wriston was an aspiring young executive in the 1950s when he went to work in Citibank's international division. He recalls that the company's rule at the time was that you never sent a cable to overseas clients if a letter would do—and the letter was often sent by ship. Citibank took its first halting steps towards the electronic age a few years later when it set up a telex line between its New York and London offices, a channel that transmitted a leisurely seven characters per second.

Wriston moved up the corporate ladder to become chairman of the company, and a pioneer in adapting advanced information resources to the firm's needs. Citibank (now part of Citigroup) is a leading global networker, routinely moving data at high speeds among its branches in more than 50 countries. Foreign operations represented a large share of Citigroup's market capitalization of $144 billion at the turn of the century; the company has more branch banks in Brazil than in the United States. The goal, as one Citibanker has noted, is to know where the company's money is, and what it is worth, at the end of every business day. Wriston made the firm one of the prime examples of how world trade is being shaped by a new standard—the information standard, replacing the old industrial measures.

This chapter looks at how this shift has had a major impact on American international strategy in general, and on digital diplomacy in particular, with every indication that it will continue to do so well into the future. Information technology (IT) in all its forms is, by some estimates, a $2 trillion global enterprise, the largest segment in an electronics sector which has replaced automobiles as the leading world industry.[1] Moreover, IT trade at the turn of the century was expanding at a rate of 11 percent annually, compared to 2.7 percent for chemicals and 1.8 percent for automobiles.

By any measure, the United States is the leader in this development. At the turn of the century, 16 of the top 20 information technology companies worldwide were American.[2] Inevitably, this lead is eroding as other economies adjust to information age realities. The United States still has some formidable advantages, notably in the ways that it has reshaped political, economic and social patterns to the needs of the new environment. Beyond the usual economic benchmarks of change, this includes the intangibles of what economist Everett Ehrlich calls "information liquidity," the openness to facts and ideas rooted in the First Amendment.[3] One result has been conflicting scenarios about America's digital future, ranging from Microsoft's Bill Gates' vision of life in the sunny uplands of what he calls friction-free capitalism to the darker warning of the Federal Reserve's Alan Greenspan that, over and above their undoubted advantages, the new technologies provide the mechanisms for mistakes to ricochet throughout the global financial system at lightning speeds.[4]

The shift to a digitized global economy accelerated during the 1990s, hastened by technology and economic forces. It was a decade that saw the introduction of a new generation of advanced communications, including the Internet. But it also reflected the reshaping of global politics in the wake of the cold war. As Edward Luttwak of Washington's Center for Strategic & International Studies points out, geopolitics has been edged out by geoeconomics as the focus of American strategic interests. It is a less dangerous environment but no less confrontational.[5]

Digital diplomacy has become a critical factor in sorting out the implications of this shift. Moreover, its impact extends beyond mundane trade concerns, touching on all other aspects of American strategic interests. The difference is in the scope and complexity of the current changes. Forty years ago, IBM and a few other multinationals set a new pattern for American trade expansion. That first wave has since been expanded and transformed by a wider corporate diaspora. It now involves tens of thousands of firms, well beyond the Fortune 500. The trend favors companies involved in IT goods and services. For many of them, including Microsoft, Intel and Dell, half or more of their revenues now come from overseas sales. Their common link with their competitors at home and abroad is their dependence on high-capacity global networks to integrate their management, production and sales operations.

The mirror-image to this American corporate expansion is the growing number of foreign IT companies entering the U.S. market, seeking access to what is still the largest free-trade area on earth. One of the most visible examples of this is the mobile phones Americans carry around with them. Most of these instruments bear the trademarks of Ericsson and

Nokia, both Scandinavian firms. Meanwhile, U.S. firms have forged alliances with overseas firms. Before its takeover of the Time Warner media conglomerate in January 2000, America Online had joint ownership agreements with foreign partners on five continents.[6]

This crosshatching of corporate interests across borders raises a question: What is an "American company"? Cross-border alliances smudge the old distinctions. Many U.S. firms operate out of corporate safe havens on fly-speck Caribbean islands, beyond the reach of tax and regulatory authorities back home. The question has particular relevance for electronic diplomacy, as IT firms take the lead in internationalizing their operations. It affects such quintessentially national companies as AT&T, which is involved in a cat's cradle of overseas deals that has included a $10 billion alliance with British Telecom. AT&T is still a Delaware-chartered corporation, but its corporate reach extends well beyond Wilmington.[7]

One consequence of this trend is that nations face the digital depowerment of their sovereignty. In many ways, the balance of power is tipping towards global corporations that have the mobility, technical expertise and management skills to exploit the new IT resources. Nowhere is this more evident than in the flow of money across borders. Every working day, electronic circuits move more than $1 trillion in digital transactions between banks and other financial institutions around the globe. Governments once had a monopoly on setting the value of their currency. This function has been largely displaced by electronic dealings between trading houses in New York, London and Tokyo.[8]

The erosion of sovereign authority over currency flows is only one example of the impact of digital resources on foreign policy. Policy options are narrowed as governments scramble to adapt to a digital environment in which they have fewer options to control what were once unquestioned prerogatives.

This trade policy dilemma is highlighted in the United States by the sheer size of an increasingly digitized economy, operating within a political structure in which power is disbursed down to the small-town level. Until a generation ago, global trade policy was largely determined by a small group of Washington agencies. There were often sharp differences among them, as we have seen throughout this survey, but there was usually a general consensus about the form and direction of policy. A major change in this pattern is the increasing assertiveness of Congress over the details of overseas trade policy, reflecting pressures from home-district industries.

The continuing example of this has been congressional foot-dragging in granting the White House negotiating flexibility (so-called "fast-track authority") in reaching international trade agreements.[9] A newer development is the role of state and municipal governments in promoting local economic interests abroad. By 2000, over 35 states had overseas trade offices, dealing directly with local industries and with government bureaus. These changes have also boosted the influence of private sector groups on trade policy, ranging from corporate lobbying to the no-less-benign influence of public interest advocacy groups. Whether they are working with government policymakers or in opposition to them, their influence is pervasive.

Although this new complexity of private interests offers many long-term strengths, it often frustrates government efforts to carry out a consistent trade strategy. Unlike other industrial democracies, the United States lacks a centralized bureaucracy for international trade issues. The classic overseas example is Japan's Ministry of International Trade and Industry (MITI), which has coordinated public and private sector trade initiatives for over 50 years. In Europe, most foreign ministries have been reorganized to give policy priority to trade promotion efforts. The 18-member European Union adds a regional note by presenting a common policy position in major trade negotiations, particularly in dealing with the United States. American trade policy, by contrast, operates within a much looser framework. Its focus is primarily domestic. An example of foreign trade subordination to domestic interests was a 1997 Clinton administration "presidential directive" on electronic commerce which relegated international considerations to one paragraph.[10]

Despite the apparent imbalance between domestic and overseas policy, U.S. electronic trade strategy has been better coordinated in recent years. The bureaucratic warfare over control of the subject, particularly between the State and Commerce departments, described in the last chapter, has largely subsided. Coordination among the major agencies, including Treasury and Defense, is carried on through standing committees. The 1983 Reagan administration plan to create a cabinet-level international trade department has never been revived. The Federal Communications Commission has become a major player, particularly after it set up a full-fledged international bureau in the 1980s.[11]

The major change in organizing foreign trade policy has been the progressive consolidation of responsibilities for the subject within the White House structure. This trend had humble origins 40 years ago in the Kennedy administration. American trade policy at the time was directed primarily at building up the West European and Japanese economies as part of an overall cold war strategy. This included tolerance for increasingly protectionist trade practices by the Europeans and the Japanese. The new European Community created a common external tariff policy and a common agricultural policy, both direct threats to American exporters in their largest overseas market. The Japanese approach was more subtle, but the effect was the same.

Responding to industry and congressional pressures, the Kennedy

White House adopted a strategy which, with variations, has been the hallmark of U.S. strategic trade policy ever since. The new emphasis was on negotiations to reduce tariff and non-tariff barriers to American exports. The Trade Expansion Act of 1962 gave the president stronger authority to negotiate more favorable trade agreements. The immediate result was the "Kennedy Round" of the postwar General Agreement on Tariffs and Trade (GATT), which cut tariff rates worldwide by an average of 36 percent.[12]

The 1962 legislation also called for a new bureaucratic approach to organizing trade policy. In hearings on the bill, congressional leaders attacked the State Department's handling of trade negotiations. Arkansas Democrat Wilbur Mills, head of the powerful House Ways and Means committee, castigated the department for "trading away our economic advantages for political advantages." Congressman Henry Reuss of Wisconsin declared that what was needed was a trade negotiator who was a good trial lawyer, "someone who smokes a cigar without lighting it and doesn't smile very often."[13] The resulting legislation explicitly mandated that the State Department would no longer be the lead agency in U.S. trade negotiations. The bill authorized a new White House unit, the Special Trade Representative (STR), charged with managing a more aggressive trade policy without, however, specifying how it would be done.

The creation of the STR office was a turning point in U.S. trade strategy. However, electronics trade in both goods and services was a relatively low priority in STR's early years. The policy focus was on textiles and agricultural trade—politically potent issues in many congressional districts. It would be 15 years before the White House trade office became involved in a major electronics dispute, involving alleged dumping of Japanese semiconductor products.

Meanwhile, the new trade office consolidated its control over strategic trade policy. Over four decades, its effectiveness has been enhanced by the fact that it resisted the bureaucratic urge to expand. At the turn of the century, it had fewer than 150 officials and staff. Another STR advantage was that, from the beginning, its directors were close political allies of the incumbent president. The quintessential example of this group was Robert Strauss, a flamboyant Texas lawyer, who ran the office in the late 1970s as a Carter administration appointee. Strauss changed STR's name to the more imposing Office of the United States Trade Representative (USTR). He also upgraded the agency's charter, identifying it more explicitly as "the principle locus" of trade policy coordination and negotiation.[14]

Strauss's most important contribution was to expand the focus of U.S. trade policy beyond manufacturing exports to the more elusive but growing services area.[15] The eventual result of this effort, 15 years later, was the creation of a new World Trade Organization in which trade in services was given equal status with manufacturing exports for the first time.

This new attention to services had a particular impact on digital diplomacy. Manufacturing and agricultural trade still represent the bulk of U.S. overseas trade, both in volume and in dollar value. However, electronic services increasingly dominated trade strategy for two reasons. First, they are an overseas extension of an economy that is increasingly oriented to the production and distribution of electronically based services. Secondly, services play a critical role in what is the most vulnerable aspect of American trade policy—the burden of a persistent annual trade deficit since the 1980s. The deficit began small—only $300 million in 1985—and has increased steadily ever since. By 2000, the deficit was $271 billion, an imbalance caused largely by a rising tide of "hard goods" imports, from steel ingots to television sets.[16] The imbalance would be spectacularly higher but for the fact that there is a healthy balance in services trade, reducing the merchandise deficit by about 40 percent. The services sector at the turn of the century accounted for 30 percent of all U.S. exports, a figure that expands annually.

It took a long time for American trade officials to accept the new importance of services exports. Traditionally, services had been lumped together as "invisible exports," a catch-all category for revenues from financial transactions, tourism, telecommunications, licensing fees and the like. It was a convenient, and inaccurate, way of getting around the fact that, unlike other exports, it was harder to identify services statistically by volume, size or dollar value. The London *Economist* once famously suggested a way to do this: if you drop a service on your foot, you don't feel anything. It was not until the mid-1980s that the Department of Commerce, the keeper of the nation's trade statistics, developed a reasonably accurate method of identifying and measuring services trade.[17]

Most American services exports depend, in varying degrees, on electronic resources, involving their content or the ways in which they are moved around. Both of these activities have become a newly critical part of digital diplomacy. In bureaucratic parlance, the subject is described as transborder data flow issues—TBDF, for short. The policy problem is to reduce the tariff and non-tariff obstacles to electronic information exports, from financial data to television broadcasts. In its broadest form, open transborder data flow is a digital extension of the longtime American commitment to free trade.[18]

Data flow issues have dominated American trade policy in recent decades. In the 1990s, it took on new importance with the growth of global Internet traffic, from ordinary e-mail traffic to the burgeoning field of electronic marketing ("e-commerce") on the World Wide Web and other channels. [19]

Electronic data traffic has been a factor in world trade since Cyrus Fields' first transatlantic telegraph cable in the 1850s. However, trans-border telegraphy remained a limited resource for over a century, because of its technological shortcomings. This changed with the expansion of advanced satellite and cable links in the 1960s. For the first time, the world's commercial centers were connected by high-speed circuits. A new dimension was added to international trade, not only in supporting the expansion of its infrastructure but also in creating a major industry in itself.

This development was dominated by American firms from the beginning, both as creators and users of the new high-tech networks. Their facilities were an overseas extension of the electronification of the U.S. economy after 1980, marked by the shift from a telephone network communications system, dominated by AT&T, to the multiservice competitive networks of the present day. The biggest change was in how Americans used these networks. A generation ago, voice telephone traffic dominated both personal and business communications. By the turn of the century, data transfers accounted for 70 percent of the traffic flowing through U.S. domestic circuits.[20]

The rest of the world is catching up with these changes. Because of their early lead in the field, American enterprises are the main players in global data networking. IBM, General Electric and Lockheed began expanding their domestic data networks to overseas points in the early 1970s, capturing the lion's share of the business. By 1985, seven of the top 10 data processing companies worldwide were American, led by IBM whose processing activities were greater than that of the other nine combined.[21]

As noted above, American policymakers were generally slow to recognize the new importance of electronic data exports.[22] Data transfers were generally regarded as a "back office" activity supporting the more important area of manufacturing and agricultural exports. The subject had little priority on the U.S. trade agenda before 1980. [23]

If American trade officials were slow to realize the policy implications of the new data networks, the Europeans and America's other trade competitors were even slower. In part, this reflected the fact that their telecommunications systems were government monopolies that were technologically weak and decidedly not market oriented. By and large, these overseas systems were reluctant to reform their networks in ways that would, among other changes, improve their data networking capabilities. As a result, they ceded the international data networking sector largely by default to American companies.

Two issues—telecommunications reform and trade liberalization—

played against each other to form the principal agenda of electronic trade diplomacy since 1980. Together they formed the basis for a new American strategy of bilateral, regional and international negotiations that have since changed the form and direction of global communications.

One of the earliest of these negotiations involved Canada, America's largest trading partner. Traditionally, information exchanges between the two countries had been largely unregulated. However, the exchange was heavily one-sided, with most information flowing north. As electronic traffic increased dramatically in the 1970s, many Canadians began to question this imbalance. Economically, their concerns focussed on cross-border data flows, and particularly on increasing Canadian dependence on U.S. data processing resources. A large share of the information about the Canadian economy was stored in American computers. On the cultural front, Canadian nationalist groups called for limits on the most visible of U.S. cross-border information exports—television, radio and other media products. Pressures rose to restrict this trade under the rubric of protecting Canada's cultural heritage in general and the country's media sector in particular.[24]

As these pressures mounted, Canadian official attitudes towards unrestricted cross-border flows hardened, aided by the fact that standing up to the United States has always been good domestic politics. The first overt move to limit cross-border information took place in the mid-1970s. It was a tax regulation denying Canadian taxpayers deductions on purchases of advertising services from U.S. TV and radio broadcasters if such ads were directed primarily at the Canadian market. Although the regulation's connection with promoting cultural sovereignty was a tenuous one, it set off long and often acrimonious negotiations, prodded on the American side by broadcasters' claims that they were losing $25 million in revenues a year.[25] The Canadian response was to extend the tax deduction restriction to ads in Canadian editions of American magazines. At one point, Canadians were threatened with criminal prosecution if their cable TV satellite terminals were receiving cross-border programs. The threat was never carried out.

On another front, Canadian officials moved to lower the country's dependence on more prosaic information—the storage and processing of data about the Canadian economy in the United States. A 1979 government report described this development in stark terms: "Of all the technologies that are developing so rapidly today, that of informatics (computer communications) poses possibly the most dangerous threat to Canadian sovereignty, in both its cultural and commercial aspects." The document (known as the Clyne Report) recommended immediate action to regulate transborder data flows.[26] Within a year, the Canadian parliament approved restrictive legislation in line with the report's recommendations.

More recently, there has been some easing up of Canadian information trade restrictions, in part as a result of the 1992 North American Free Trade Agreement. Nevertheless, Canadian nationalists remain wary of the continued encroachment of what they describe as the U.S. entertainment-industrial complex. In 1999, the House of Commons passed legislation, with strong multiparty support, which makes it a criminal offense for Canadians to place advertising in American or any other foreign-owned magazines.[27]

Japan has presented a special problem in negotiating electronic commerce. Although the Japanese have often displayed protectionist attitudes regarding transborder information flows, their policy focus in recent decades has been on expanding their global influence in electronics manufacturing. In large part, this reflected the dual-economy global strategy fostered by the Ministry of International Trade and Industry, the government's lead agency in trade matters. MITI's policies emphasized an aggressive manufacturing export sector while sheltering most of the rest of the economy from foreign competition. The electronics sector was a special target for this strategy. By the 1980s, Japan had become fully competitive in challenging the United States in most advanced information technology export areas.[28]

MITI's protectionist strategy led to a major dispute in the early 1980s focussed on an imbalance in semiconductor chip trade with the United States. The issues centered around American complaints that the Japanese were dumping chips on the U.S. market while limiting chip imports into Japan.[29] After several years of testy negotiations, a bilateral semiconductor trade agreement was signed in 1986 that informally established a 20 percent market share target in Japan for all foreign-made chips. The agreement's supporters hailed it as results-oriented trade diplomacy. Others saw the agreement as a major step towards managed trade, a potentially dangerous abandonment of traditional U.S. open-trade policy, particularly in its assumption that governments could determine what an appropriate share for a given product should be.[30]

The Japanese have since softened their hard-line protectionist policies in electronics trade, largely under pressure from Washington. This change has included a reluctant retreat from their practice of limiting American data network companies from marketing to Japanese customers. The Japanese government moved more slowly in allowing American firms to compete in telecommunications services against the state-controlled Nippon Telephone & Telegraph (NTT).[31] It was not until 1998 that an American company, MCI WorldCom, was authorized to build and operate a network in Japan offering both domestic and international services.[32] Meanwhile Tokyo officials stepped up their efforts in 2000 to deregulate the overall domestic communications system.[33]

These moves to introduce competition strengthened Japan's domestic markets, as well as made them more competitive in global markets.[34] It has also affected the agenda of U.S.-Japanese digital diplomacy as the Japanese shift from their longtime strength in high-technology manufacturing to a greater emphasis on software goods and services—a sector in which they have been generally weak competitors both in their domestic and export markets.[35] By the turn of the century, major Japanese electronic firms had shifted more of their resources to the production and marketing of software products. In 1998, these activities accounted for 28 percent of the revenues of Fujitsu, the country's leading producer of computer hardware.[36] The result, inevitably, will be a greater Japanese international presence in a sector that has long been dominated by American firms.

Digital trade issues with Canada and Japan have been dealt with largely in bilateral negotiations in the past 20 years. Western Europe, the other major American trading area, presents a different pattern. Although negotiations on a country-to-country basis continue to be important, the European Union has dealt with the United States as a bloc on trade issues in recent years. This has created a formidable challenge to American policymakers as they face representatives of a regional economy that by most economic indicators matches and often surpasses that of the United States. As a result, Western Europe represents the most important single target for Washington's trade diplomacy activities.

In part, this reflects a greater sense of urgency on the part of EU members to catch up with the United States in information technology. European weakness in this sector became glaringly apparent in the 1980s. Not only did community nations collectively have a large deficit with the United States and Japan in IT trade within the region, they accounted for only 15 percent of global trade in the sector. IT resources within the community were increasingly dominated by American companies that had set up shop in the region to take advantage of the community's free-trade rules.[37]

Unlike their European competitors, who were organized primarily to serve their national markets, American IT firms treated all of Western Europe as a single market. Their presence was particularly strong in information processing ventures. By 1980, U.S. data processing companies were operating across the region. According to one survey at the time, more than half of European use of database services involved American facilities.[38] The need to strengthen the region's IT capabilities was underscored by a French industry minister, Alain Madelin: "Europe has no choice but to become a third pole of equivalent weight to the U.S. and Japan. Or else, poor in raw materials, politically divided, technologically dependent, it will in fact become nothing more than a subcontractor for the other two."[39]

Similar statements made it clear that European-controlled information technology resources in EC countries were clearly inadequate to support the community's goal of regional economic integration. In addition to their weakness in data production and distribution, community nations lagged well behind the United States in their telecommunications practices. Although the two regions had roughly the same population, Americans used their telephone systems three times as much as Europeans.[40] Moreover, the overall reliability of data networking services in the region was poor, particularly for business users. A survey by the European Association of Information Services Users found that almost 25 percent of its members' international calls on public data networks were not completed.[41]

The major obstacle to correcting this situation was the power of the national telecommunications monopolies, known collectively as post-telephone-telegraph administrations (PTTs). Modifying these monopolies by privatizing them and introducing competition became a major goal of economic planners at European Community headquarters in Brussels. Their proposals had strong support from European industries, which were well aware of the penalties that second-rate communications had on their operations.

The idea of breaking up their national phone monopolies did not sit well with the community's member governments. The PTTs were political sacred cows—entrenched bureaucracies that were big contributors to national treasuries as well as major employers of unionized civil servants. By the mid-1980s, only one EC member, Great Britain, had taken steps to shut down its phone monopoly, transferring its assets to a private company. Despite attempts by most EC governments to slow down the process, the transition from monopoly to privatized, competitive telecommunications systems throughout the region was largely completed by January 1992, the target date set by EC planners.[42]

As noted in Chapter 6, a powerful influence on this European initiative was the breakup of America's own telephone monopoly, AT&T, in 1982. The competitive forces unleashed by this decision meant that European industry would face increasing trade pressure from the Americans not only within Europe but in world markets generally. One of the key provisions in the European Commission's telecom reform plan permitted foreign investors and operators to compete in the newly deregulated regional market. Although this idea was resisted initially by the old-line European PTTs, it survived as an integral part of the commission's overall reform program.[43]

American diplomacy quietly supported the commission's competition initiatives. At the same time, the U.S. communications sector began positioning itself to take advantage of the trade and investment opportunities opened up by the shift from monopoly to competitive markets. The result was a steady expansion of an American communications presence within Western Europe after the EC reform program took effect in the mid-1990s.[44] By 2000, for example, U.S. investment controlled 30 percent of Germany's telecommunications networks.

Although the liberalization of West European telecommunications favored American trade interests, one important obstacle remained. This was the increase in laws and regulations throughout the region restricting transborder data flows. New rules were ostensibly designed to protect citizen privacy. They were also intended, if only indirectly, to meet local criticisms that Americans dominated the storage and distribution of electronic data in the region. The perils of this digital invasion were first highlighted in an influential French government report, *The Computerization of Society*, which was widely distributed throughout Europe in the late 1970s. It described what it called "the IBM challenge" to French political, economic and cultural values, comparing the giant computer firm to the Vatican in its worldwide reach and influence.[45] This theme was repeated, with variations, in other forums throughout Western Europe.

Sweden was the first European country to set up rules regulating cross-border data transfers. A May 1973 law created a commission to screen all requests for exporting personal information about Swedish citizens over data networks. In an incident that became a classic case, the restrictions were applied to a computerized system maintained by the fire department in Malmo. The system allowed the department to respond more efficiently to fire alarms by giving it quick access to information about the location and the fire hazard factors of every building in the city. The data, however, was stored at a General Electric computer facility in Cleveland, Ohio. This set off a political debate that was resolved when the government decided that foreign storage of information about Swedish buildings was an invasion of citizen privacy.[46]

By the late 1970s, a dozen other European countries had taken similar steps to limit both incoming and outgoing data, under the rubric of protecting citizen privacy. For the first time, American firms saw a threat to their European operations. "It's simple," said one Bank of America executive at the time. "If we can't move information, we go out of business."[47] Their concerns were heightened by European initiatives to develop regional restrictions on data flow.[48] The European Commission in Brussels generally resisted efforts to restrict data flows, in line with its overall policy of liberalizing communications resources in the region. However, the Council of Europe adopted a binding convention in September 1980 containing strict privacy provisions that applied uniformly to data traffic throughout Western Europe. The restrictions placed on such flows clearly affected American trade interests.[49]

The U.S. government countered the European Council convention and other data-flow restrictions in Europe by proposing that the subject be dealt with through voluntary guidelines rather than legal regulations. It suggested that this be done under the auspices of the Paris-based Organization for Economic Cooperation and Development (OECD). With a membership of 29 industrialized countries, the OECD was the successor to the economic planning group that had coordinated West European postwar recovery efforts. Its staff of economists had, moreover, taken an early interest in the impact of data networks on global trade, forming a working group on the subject as early as 1972.[50] After seven years of negotiations, OECD members adopted a set of voluntary guidelines in April 1985 which affirmed the importance of open information access and the need for personal privacy protection along with the avoidance of "unjustified barriers" to data flows. The United States welcomed the guidelines as a major step towards assuring reasonable controls over global information flows.

The OECD guidelines were, however, just that—a set of general principles, with few details on how they were to be implemented. Major issues remain unresolved, with particular attention to regulations covering protection of personal information about citizens in electronic data transmissions. After years of negotiations, the European Union approved a directive that mandated strict privacy controls over electronic data. It also included a provision that foreign governments provide similar rigorous data protection or face a cutoff of data traffic from Europe. This set off a sharp round of negotiations between the EU and the United States, where data privacy is dealt with largely through voluntary industry standards. An agreement which set up compatible standards on both sides of the Atlantic was finally reached in June 2000.[51]

American digital trade strategy relies on a mix of bilateral, regional and global negotiations. The overall strategy is managed by USTR, with implementing roles assigned to State, Commerce and other federal agencies. As we saw in the previous chapter, the confusion over responsibility for communications and information issues within the State Department had been clarified somewhat with the creation of a separate bureau to deal with these subjects. For the first time, the department had adequate resources to coordinate trade and other issues in the increasingly complex communications sector.

Bilateral negotiations play a key role in this negotiating pattern. Under pressure from its business constituencies, Congress gave American negotiators strong support in the Omnibus Trade and Competitiveness Act of 1987. One of its articles, the so-called "super-301" provision, contained strong retaliatory trade penalties against countries that discriminated against American electronics exports. It was the first time that this business sector had been singled out in trade legislation. Super-301 became an important bargaining tool for U.S. trade officials, usually resulting in a favorable agreement before its provisions had to be invoked.

Beyond bilateral negotiations, the next phase in American services trade strategy involved agreements at the regional level, specifically with Canada and Mexico. The result, in 1992, was the North American Free Trade Agreement (NAFTA), the first multilateral accord in which specific provisions for services trade were included. The American negotiating team was led by USTR officials, including a group of young economists who had assembled detailed research on the newly strategic role of services in American trade policy. The USTR team also had strong support from a private sector advisory team that included the major service industries.[52]

Electronics-based services were a relatively small part of the NAFTA agenda. The primary focus in the negotiations was on the traditional trade issues—manufacturing and agriculture. Nevertheless, services came into their own as a critical sector in the negotiations. It was new territory for both sides, with few precedents to fall back on. NAFTA broke new ground by getting down to the details of managing cross-border services trade. Services emerged as a prominent part of the final document, which ran to 600 pages, with 1,400 pages of supplementary data.

The document covered a wide swathe of services issues between Canada and the United States, with one exception. The Canadians adamantly refused to discuss media services. Any concessions, no matter how small, in the area of so-called cultural exports would have been political suicide for any Canadian government. Once the media issue was set aside, U.S. and Canadian negotiators took a step-by-step pragmatic approach in dealing with other cross-border service subjects. Despite some difficult passages, the negotiations were successful in large part because a consensus was reached in three critical areas.

The first of these was to let stand existing laws and regulations in both countries that affected cross-border services trade, a practice known as grandfathering. Changing thousands of these rules at the federal, state and provincial levels would have fatally overloaded the negotiations. Grandfathering had the positive effect of implying a commitment that existing trade restrictions on both sides of the border would not be expanded in the liberalizing spirit of an overall agreement. In general, this has proved true in the first decade of the NAFTA agreement.

The second breakthrough involved what trade negotiators call the national treatment principle. This was an agreement that each country would treat citizens of the other country in trade matters in a way that was not less favorable than that accorded its own citizens. In many ways, this provision was the hinge on which a successful agreement was reached. It proved to be particularly important in electronics-based trade where cross-border trading rules and practices were either nonexistent or vague. The third negotiating breakthrough was to set up a binding consultative and dispute resolution mechanism to deal with the NAFTA agreement's many ambiguous provisions. Among other results, this gave the services sectors in Canada, Mexico and the United States a forum for dispute resolution.[53]

NAFTA was a critical turning point in U.S. digital diplomacy. It significantly lowered both trade and non-trade barriers for information technology products between the three countries involved. At another level, NAFTA had an important influence in opening up both the Canadian and Mexican telecommunications markets to greater competition. Mexico privatized its state telephone monopoly, Telmex, in 1990, the first of the big developing countries to do so. The deal was significant also in that the newly privatized Telmex included a major investment stake by two foreign companies, France Telecom and Southwestern Bell. It was the first breakthrough in what has since become a steady pattern of similar investments in Asia and Latin America.

Canada's telecommunications structure was also opened up to competition, in part because of NAFTA's influence. In the early 1990s, the Canadian phone system was dominated by Stentor, an alliance of provincial phone systems and the old national monopolist, Bell Canada. By the end of the decade, the alliance had eroded as the government permitted new firms to compete. Among the investors in these enterprises were American companies such as AT&T, MCI WorldCom and GTE. Although they were not allowed to own majority stakes or to otherwise control their Canadian ventures, they were an important part of the new electronic relationship with the largest U.S. trading partner.

NAFTA's major contribution to digital diplomacy was to develop a workable model for managing cross-border services trade. This set an important precedent for the parallel negotiations that led to the creation of the World Trade Organization in 1993. The WTO was the capstone of American efforts to promote an open global trading system after World War II. It built on the precedent set in the 1930s by the Roosevelt administration's advocacy of most-favored-nation agreements, emphasizing reciprocal tariff treatment. The WTO expanded this emphasis on tariffs by including enforceable rules on a wide range of non-tariff barriers. The impact of this change has since been particularly noticeable in the current expansion of electronics-based trade, both in goods and services.

Creating a global organization to lower all trade restrictions was a key element in the American strategy for restoring economic stability after World War II. During the war, Dean Acheson, then the assistant secretary of state for economic affairs, headed a team that drafted a plan for an International Trade Organization (ITO). The plan was eventually approved, with modifications, at an international conference in Havana in March 1948. U.S. Senate approval of the agreement was crucial to its

success, and this was not forthcoming. Congressional opposition, reinforced by protectionist industry lobbies, effectively ended the prospects
for a comprehensive postwar agreement on liberalized trading rules.[54]

What was left was the General Agreement on Tariffs and Trade
(GATT), which had been negotiated separately in 1947 before the Havana
ITO conference. (The ITO conferees planned to fold the GATT into their
more comprehensive structure.) When the United States withdrew its
support for the ITO, the GATT became the only international hook on
which to hang trade liberalization. Its focus was on tariff reduction, but
its writ extended only to trade in manufacturing and agricultural products. The GATT agreement was flawed in other respects. It said nothing
about investment, restrictive business practices, commodity agreements
or trade issues related to poorer countries. Its enforcement mechanisms
were weak. Overall, the GATT process went about as far as it could go
in the tight protectionist environment that marked international trade in
the early postwar years.

The GATT agreement's biggest weakness was that it had no jurisdiction over services trade—the fastest expanding area of international
trade in the postwar decades. American trade officials had never given
up the idea of a more comprehensive global trade regime, particularly
one which would include removal of the barriers to services exports. By
the mid-1970s, the office of the U.S. Trade Representative led a renewed
effort to create such a regime.[55] The project was given a strong push by
Congress, which was reacting to industry pressures for trading rules that
went beyond the GATT focus on tariff reduction. The result was the
Trade Act of 1974, which authorized the president to negotiate on non-
tariff barriers. The law expanded the term "international trade" to include, for the first time, services exports.

The first opportunity to press this new approach took place in the 1974
Tokyo Round of GATT negotiations, which were already under way
when the trade act was passed. Mindful of the congressional tendency
to kill international agreements by adding amendments, the White
House insisted on so-called "fast-track" authorization for the Tokyo
Round, limiting the Senate to an up-or-down vote on the round's final
decisions.

Armed with this authority, the U.S. Trade Representative, Robert
Strauss, orchestrated strong business support for the Tokyo negotiations,
including the U.S. Chamber of Commerce, the National Association of
Manufacturers and the Business Roundtable. Significantly for digital diplomacy, this group was expanded to include, for the first time, information technology lobbyists representing the Electronic Industries
Association and the Coalition of Service Industries.

Despite these efforts, the American services trade proposal did not sit
well with other delegations in Tokyo. The best the U.S. delegation could

get was a promise by other industrialized countries to study the issues involved in expanding the GATT into the services area. Based on this tentative commitment, the White House authorized a full-scale policy review of the subject. An inter-agency task force, headed by USTR, focussed on the transborder data flow issues, among other service trade concerns. Within the State Department, responsibility for data-flow policy was transferred from the Bureau of Oceans, Environment and Science (where it had been dealt with primarily as a technical issue) to the economic and business bureau, where the subject came into its own as a trade issue. Several years later, data-flow policy was integrated into the overall communications responsibilities assigned to the new Bureau for Communications and Information Policy, described in the previous chapter.

American strategy in the mid-1980s was focussed on a full-scale review of services trade issues at the next GATT round, scheduled to take place in Uruguay. Although this decision included all services, it was heavily weighted towards electronics-based trade, particularly in banking, the media and telecommunications. For the first time digital diplomacy issues were integrated into a larger American trade policy.

The Uruguay round of negotiations opened in 1984 and continued, with frequent recesses, for over seven years. The result was an agreement that has become the capstone of American trade policy, with special significance for digital diplomacy. For the first time, electronic goods and services were negotiated together at the global level. The 70 countries that signed the 1993 World Trade Agreement, which created the World Trade Organization, collectively represented 95 percent of the world's information technology markets.

The Uruguay Round focussed largely on traditional GATT trade subjects, specifically those involving manufacturing and agricultural goods. The United States had a large stake in these negotiations, particularly in electronics-based manufacturing, where American exports were expanding rapidly. But the round's uniqueness lay in the willingness of GATT members to consider the totality of cross-border trade by adding services transactions to the agenda.

Predictably, the inclusion of services in a global trade agreement was the most contentious issue on the Uruguay Round agenda. A major problem for most delegations was the absence of any firm precedents for services trade rules. The closest model was the negotiations taking place at the same time between the United States and Canada, which included services in a sweeping review of cross-border trade. The result, as we have seen, was the North American Free Trade Agreement that, in its final stages, also included Mexico. NAFTA was a working example of the opportunities and difficulties of negotiating an all-inclusive trade agreement. It involved many elements relevant to the problems faced by the Uruguay Round negotiators. The U.S.-Canadian negotiations were not, however, a cookie-cutter model for a global agreement. They involved two countries that, despite some differences in trade policy, were politically and socially compatible in ways that encouraged close economic integration. By contrast, the Uruguay Round involved the gamut of political, geographic, economic and cultural diversity. Its delegations were headed by trade officials who were comfortable with the slow-moving GATT pace of dealing with discrete manufacturing and agricultural disputes. The proposal to expand into the untested area of services trade rules was unsettling to many of them.

Moreover, most GATT signatories resisted a change they regarded as primarily advantageous to the United States, the largest services-oriented economy in the world. In particular, they did not welcome the idea of more competition in their own national services sectors, particularly financial services and telecommunications.

Eventually, agreement was reached on a services trade regime that reflected overall U.S. objectives. This happened in large part because America's industrial partners, notably the West Europeans and the Japanese, overcame their suspicions about negotiating rules that would, initially at least, benefit U.S. exports. As the Uruguay negotiations proceeded, they lowered their guard, accepting the fact that robust services trade rules would boost their own economic interests, in particular their efforts to challenge the American lead in information technology services.

The developing countries were more resistant to services trade liberalization. They were a mixed group, from the so-called Big Emerging Markets like Brazil and Korea to the basket-case economies of Africa. Most of them had joined the GATT because the agreement's rules had been relaxed over the years to give them special concessions designed to boost their exports. The Uruguay Round proposals to develop rules for services trade did not include any significant concessions for developing countries. The services sector in these countries, most notably in communications, were highly protectionist for both economic and political reasons. The 90 or so Third World signatories to the GATT were basically unwilling to make the jump to multilateral services rules. Fewer than a dozen of them signed the services section of the World Trade Organization agreement in 1993.[56]

In the end, the Uruguay Round negotiators made decisions that broke new ground for American digital diplomacy. These decisions involved a package of separate agreements that restructured the 50-year-old GATT and expanded the responsibilities of GATT's successor, the World Trade Organization (WTO). Electronic issues permeate the thousands of pages, including annexes and other documents, containing the round's final decisions.

Given the misgivings of most delegations about including services in the agreement, the rules governing them were negotiated separately from the old GATT framework. The result was a new General Agreement on Trade in Services (GATS). Basically, GATS extended many of the GATT manufacturing trade provisions to the services area, prohibiting WTO members from discriminating among themselves or from treating other members less favorably than any other. Moreover, both the restructured GATT and the new GATS included dispute resolution provisions that had regulatory teeth, including enforceable trade sanctions against violations of WTO trading rules. For the first time, the American information services industry—the fastest expanding sector in the economy—had a global regulatory forum for challenging protectionist laws and practices that limited its exports in many overseas markets.

The final package of Uruguay Round agreements contained other provisions that benefited the U.S. electronics sector. One of these involved protection of intellectual property—patents, copyrights and the like. These exports became the subject of multilateral trading rules for the first time. The resulting WTO agreement, known as TRIPS (trade-related intellectual property rights) did not go as far in protecting such rights as American negotiators would have liked, but it was nonetheless an important breakthrough in a trade sector in which the United States is dominant.

Another part of the final Uruguay Round package favoring the U.S. electronics sector was a provision that the WTO would oversee an agreement on reducing technical barriers to international trade. A nongovernmental group, the International Organization for Standardization (IOS), had been setting global technical standards since 1947. Working in almost total obscurity, it made recommendations on a wide range of standards, from screw threads to the height of automobile bumpers. Although most countries formally accepted the IOS recommendations, they were not above manipulating the details in ways that resulted in a nontariff barrier, restricting or prohibiting foreign imports, particularly in electronics.

WTO's new jurisdiction over the use of technical standards to limit trade was an important boost for the American information technology sector. One result was a U.S.-European agreement in June 1997 to curb the use of technical standards as a trade protection device. Known as a mutual recognition agreement, it specifically dealt with telecommunications equipment, allowing a product in each market to be technically certified according to the regulations of the other.[57] These Uruguay Round decisions marked a new recognition of the importance of electronics-based goods and services by the world trading community. However, the record was incomplete. The 1993 World Trade Organization did not include trade rules covering the most ubiquitous electronic service—ordinary telephone voice and data traffic, accounting for over 80 percent of all telecommunications usage worldwide.

Writing trade rules for telephone services ran up against some intractable politics. Agreeing to such rules meant that WTO members would have to open up their carefully preserved government phone monopolies to local competition and foreign investment—a development that was only beginning to take hold in a few industrialized countries when the Uruguay Round negotiations began in the mid-1980s. Opening up the PTTs to competition under WTO rules would be a major breakthrough in removing one of the largest obstacles to a fully competitive global electronics market.[58]

The U.S. delegation pressed the issue throughout the Uruguay Round negotiations with little success. The American motives were mixed. Telephone-based services were too important to be left out of any expanded free-trade agreement. The world telecommunications market was big and growing, involving $600 billion a year, according to a World Bank estimate at the time. Moreover, it was clear that the largest beneficiaries of expanded trade in this sector would be U.S. telecommunications firms, which were cash rich, technologically advanced and already moving into foreign markets where they could.

Having failed to agree on the issue by the time the Uruguay final act was ready for signature in April 1994, the Uruguay Round delegates agreed to further negotiations on basic telecommunications services (BTS), with a two-year target date for completion. "Basic telecommunications" meant just that—the ordinary uses of telephone lines for voice and data services. Pointedly excluded from the negotiations were so-called value-added services, telecommunications for which suppliers add value to the customer's information by enhancing its form or content or by providing for its storage or retrieval. The omission was significant, since value-added services were the fastest growing sector within telecommunications services, and one in which American firms had a decided competitive edge.

The BTS negotiations stretched out for almost three years, marked by hard bargaining sessions in which the American delegation, managed by USTR officials, argued for full compliance with basic WTO trading rules. This meant opening up local markets to foreign competitors in a global sector dominated by closed public monopolies. In effect, it meant the beginning of the end of these monopolies.

American strategy was centered on an informal caucus of OECD delegations whose economies dominated global telecommunications facilities in terms of resources and traffic volume. Known as the Quad Members, their governments were already committed, in varying degrees, to deregulating their phone systems. The Americans were the most advanced in this area, following the 1982 decision to break up AT&T, its own version of a national monopoly. The Europeans, through the European Union, were already deregulating their national systems, under an EU mandate.

Two Quad members balked at full implementation of BTS rules to their communications systems. The Canadians initially would not agree to allowing majority foreign investment in their network. The Japanese offered to permit foreign investment of up to 20 percent in new networks but not in the dominant government-controlled network, Nippon Telephone & Telegraph, at the time the world's largest telephone network in terms of capital assets.[59]

Meanwhile, most delegations outside the Quad Group balked at the idea of opening up their phone monopolies to full competition, using a variety of arguments. The Jamaican delegation, for example, cited the sanctity of contracts, noting that its government had signed an agreement that limited competition to the local phone monopoly until the year 2013. Brunei said it would wait until 2010 to decide whether to permit competition to the local phone monopoly. Other Third World delegations cited national security, cultural integrity and sovereign rights in defense of their monopolies.

After two years of rear-guard attempts to thwart telecom services liberalization, the United States walked away from the negotiations in April 1996. The move had the intended shock effect. The negotiations were resumed a few months later, ending in February 1997 with an agreement in which 55 countries, owners of most of the world's telecommunications resources, committed themselves to opening up their markets to international competition by the end of the year. Fifteen other countries made partial commitments.[60]

It would be difficult to underestimate the impact on American digital diplomacy of the WTO in general, and the basic telecommunications services agreement in particular. They were critical steps towards creating a global communications system along lines that the United States had long championed—competitive, integrated and readily accessible to ordinary consumers. The agreements' achievement was the inclusion of services, for the first time, in a global trade regime, effectively ending a long-standing myth about services—namely that "if you can't taste it, touch it, or smell it, it ain't tradeable." In fact, by the turn of the century, services represented over half of the gross domestic product of the world's major trading partners, including a growing role for information technology products.

In addition to promoting overall competition in national phone systems, the basic telecommunications agreement opened the door to wider foreign investment in these systems. This was an indispensable condition for assuring that competition would actually take place. Foreign telephone monopolies relied primarily on local government funding for their expansion; private investment in telecommunications was largely unknown outside the United States. Private funds, both domestic and foreign, would be needed to finance the new competitive networks abroad. In the basic telecommunications negotiations, the American delegation pressed hard for rules that would remove obstacles to foreign investment in the sector, stressing that the pro-competitive intent of the agreement would be seriously compromised without such rules.

Despite initial heavy opposition, liberalized cross-border investment rules were included in the final BTS agreement. The 48 countries that signed the agreement pledged to allow 100 percent foreign investment in local network enterprises. Other countries promised a gradual phasing in of regulations that would open up sectoral investment from abroad. These commitments had their intended effect. By the late 1990s, cross-border investment in information technology ventures soared in Europe, Asia and Latin America, led by American financial firms. It also led to renewed efforts by America's industrial partners, particularly in Europe, to restructure their own information sectors.[61]

In summary, the 1993 WTO agreement represented a sharp turning point in American digital diplomacy. It defined basic standards for trade in both electronic goods and services, together with dispute resolution procedures for enforcing them. It also encouraged a series of follow-up agreements that reflected a more open approach to electronics trade. One of these was a 1995 agreement between the United States and the European Union to negotiate a phasing out of all tariffs and trade barriers to all information technology products.[62] A more generalized agreement to speed up the phasing out of IT trade barriers was approved at the WTO's first ministerial gathering in Singapore the following year.

However useful these political actions were, they are being overmatched by two more powerful developments in electronics trade. One is the swift pace of technological change in the sector. The other is the restructuring of the electronics industry to accommodate these technologies. No political entity could fully anticipate, much less control, these changes. Digitization is bending, if not breaking, the political, economic and legal assumptions underlying IT development in recent decades. The most visible example of this is the Internet—a rogue technology that undercuts all of the old rules and most of the new ones. "We are now entering a strongly political phase in the evolution of the Internet as it becomes a globally distributed economy," says communications executive Einar Stefferud.[63]

One result is that Internet issues now dominate the transborder dataflow agenda. Internet-based commerce at the turn of the century was the fastest growing sector of global trade, expanding 120 percent in 1999 to a total of $111 billion.[64] The United States and the European Union, both anxious to promote Internet use, agreed in 1997 that the Internet should be a "tariff-free environment" when it is used for trade in goods and services.

The Internet has raised other policy issues, including data privacy. In 1998, the European Union approved a directive that guaranteed its citizens strict control over the distribution of electronic data on their private lives. The directive included a provision that foreign governments provide data protections every bit as rigorous under a similar regulatory structure or face a cutoff of data traffic from Europe. This set off a sharp round of negotiations between the EU and the United States, where data privacy is dealt with largely through voluntary industry standards.[65] Meanwhile, the WTO and its member governments have only begun to sort out the Internet's impact on the conventional voice, data and video networking covered under WTO rules.

The other factor affecting global communications trade has been the opportunities opened up by the privatization of national phone systems in the past decade. The pattern is similar to the one which took place in the United States in the mid-1980s following the breakup of the AT&T monopoly, when hundreds of new domestic networks began to compete with the old-line phone companies for market share. By the mid-1990s, all of the Bell regional companies ("Baby Bells") and many of their local competitors were involved in overseas investments, mergers and marketing agreements. The three big international carriers—A&T, MCI and Sprint—each successfully sought overseas partners to strengthen their global operations. MCI became MCI WorldCom, combining its resources with those of a company that in less than a decade moved from being a small start-up operation in Louisiana to running a high-technology global network.

This American push into overseas markets resulted in countermoves in Western Europe and Japan. Newly privatized phone monopolies scrambled to make similar investment and marketing arrangements to protect their own domestic interests and to ease their way into foreign markets, including the United States. In 1998 alone, the Federal Communications Commission granted over 40 licenses to foreign telecom firms to operate in the United States.[66]

The following year, a British wireless phone company, Vodophone, bought a California-based counterpart, Airtouch, for $55 billion—at the time, the biggest ever European buy-out of an American firm.[67] Other cross-border deals involved joint marketing or operating agreements. British Telecom, Europe's largest carrier, agreed to a $10 billion venture with AT&T in 1998 in a move designed to strengthen both firms' global business. A year later, two other regional telecom giants, Deutsche Telekom and Telecom Italia, moved towards a $70 billion merger that created an entity with more than 50 percent market share in Western Europe. Countering competition from U.S. firms was a critical part of their calculations. "American and Japanese companies have left Europe trailing in the dust in the computer industry," Deutsche Telekom chief Ron Sommer declared at the time. "This cannot be allowed to happen in telecommunications. Europe missed out on Silicon Valley. We don't want to miss Telecom Valley."[68]

Despite this warning, Europe as a whole lagged behind the United States in applying new information technologies on a mass basis.[69] A telling statistic at the turn of the century was that only 12 percent of families in EU countries were hooked up to the Internet, compared to 50 percent of American families.[70]

The global telecommunications sector currently is in splendid disarray. Twenty years ago, its resources were controlled by national monopolies, intent on maintaining their power. Technology, economics and politics combined to undermine their authority. The idea of control over electronic communications as a sovereign right was a throwback to a simpler age when kings and clerics could enforce their authority over books and other information sources. It is an anachronism in an age when information moves over high-speed digital channels whose content cannot be monitored and controlled.

The second justification for government control was that only a centralized authority could ensure technical integrity and management efficiency. Any alternative, the argument went, would be chaotic. This claim has been overtaken in the new age of advanced information services, both domestic and international, that crisscross many networks, using common technical standards.[71] More than any single event, the decision to break up AT&T in the early 1980s eroded these assumptions by demonstrating the economic and technological advantages of competitive networks. As a result, government monopolies no longer control 95 percent of the world's communications traffic. The minority holdouts can be found largely in Latin America and Africa.

The new multi-billion-dollar mergers between giant telecom companies clearly will play a dominant role in the new pattern. It is probable than a half-dozen of these international combines will set the pace and growth of global communications in the coming years. However, there is a countervailing growth of smaller enterprises that have the managerial flexibility and technical skills to exploit niche markets in a rapidly expanding sector. All of these networks, large and small, will be part of an integrated global system, in which digital standards are blurring the old distinctions between voice, data and video networks.[72]

These technological and economic changes dominate the new environment within which American digital diplomacy will operate from now on. It is complex and multilayered in ways that affect every other aspect of strategic policy. As international economist Ellen Frost points out:

The galloping expansion of the Internet has pulled globalization down to the level of ordinary citizens and groups, but it has pushed the demand for rules up to the multilateral level. In between these two levels is the government of the nation state, whose relative power is shrinking as both sovereignty and economic resources become more dispersed. This configuration of power not only makes the job of negotiating more complex, but it also multiplies the number of new issues subject to negotiation or coordination. [73]

The 1993 WTO agreement gave digital diplomacy new options to expand open trade strategies in a cyberspace environment. Despite its more flexible and enforceable rules, the agreement offers no ready-made solutions. The WTO is an international bureaucracy, involving over 130 nations, in which decision making is agonizingly slow. In many instances, its decisions are overtaken by economic and technological change before they come into force. The difficulties of coming to terms with fast-moving developments were dramatized in December 1999 when labor unions, environmental organizations and other groups used street demonstrations to close down a WTO conference in Seattle, called to consider further steps towards opening up world trade. [74]

NOTES

1. *Digital planet: The global information economy* (Arlington, VA: World Information Technology and Services Alliance, October 1999).
2. "The struggle for survival in an IT-dominated world," *Financial Times* (London), Special supplement on information technology, 3 March 1999, p. 14.
3. Everett Ehrlich, "Global integration and the service industries," in *The Service Economy* (Washington, DC: Coalition of Service Industries, July 1997), p. 4.
4. "Greenspan in warning on capital flow curbs," *Financial Times* (London), 5 October 1997, p. 4. Bill Gates' views are summarized in *The road ahead* (New York: Viking, 1995).
5. Edward N. Luttwak, *The endangered dream* (New York: Simon & Schuster, 1993).
6. "Giants' embrace threatens network of online alliances," *Financial Times* (London), 12 January 2000, p. 22.
7. For a survey of cross-border IT alliances, see: Mark Jamison, "Business imperatives," in *The new global telecommunications industry and consumers* (University Park: Institute for Information Policy, Pennsylvania State University, 1999).
8. The sovereignty implications of this development are discussed in Eric Helleiner, "Electronic money: A challenge to the sovereign state," *Journal of International Affairs*, Vol. 31, No. 2, Spring 1998, pp. 387–409.
9. Under fast-track authority, first agreed to by Congress in the Trade Act of 1974, trade agreements under its jurisdiction were subject to an up-or-down vote in the Senate, without any amendments that often had the effect of killing the

proposed agreement. Stephen Dryden, *Trade warriors: The U.S. Trade Representative and the crusade for free trade* (New York: Oxford University Press, 1995), p. 239.

10. Presidential directive on electronic commerce, The White House, 1 July 1997.

11. The FCC's role in recent international policy decisions is described in Lawrence J. Spiwak, "From international competitive carrier to the WTO: A survey of the FCC's international telecommunications policy initiatives 1985–1998," *Federal Communications Bar Journal*, Vol. 51, No. 1, March 1999, pp. 519–539.

12. John W. Evans, *The Kennedy Round in American trade policy* (Cambridge, MA: Harvard University Press, 1971).

13. Dryden, op cit. p. 52.

14. Ibid., p. 252.

15. For a survey of trade problems that were surfacing in the services area at the time, see: Wilson P. Dizard, "U.S. competitiveness in international information trade," *The information society*, Vol. 2, Nos. 3–4, 1984, pp. 179–216.

16. " '99 trade gap hit record $271 billion," *Washington Post*, 19 February 2000, p. E-1.

17. "Services statistics too important to ignore," *The Service Economy*, Coalition of Service Industries, Washington, DC, April 1995, p. 1.

18. For background, see: Anne W. Branscomb, "Global governance of global networks: A survey of trans-border data flow in transition," *Vanderbilt Law Review*, Vol. 30, 1983, pp. 985–1043.

19. Ellen Frost, "Horse trading in cyberspace: U.S. trade policy in the information age," *Journal of International Affairs*, Vol. 31, No. 2, Spring 1998, pp. 473–496.

20. "The next net," *Wired*, April 1999, p. 151.

21. "USA firms dominate list of data processors," *USA Today*, 6 March 1985, p. 1.

22. Joan Edelman Spero, "The policy void," *Foreign Policy*, No. 48, Fall 1982, pp. 139–156.

23. For useful surveys of the early development of electronic data trade policies, see: John M. Eger, "Emerging restrictions on transnational data flows: Privacy protection or non-tariff trade barriers?" *Law and International Business*, Vol. 10, No. 4, 1978, pp. 1055–1103; Ithiel de Sola Pool and Richard Solomon, "The regulation of transborder data flows," *Telecommunications Policy*, September 1979, pp. 179–191; William L. Fishman, "Introduction to transborder data flows," *Stanford Journal of International Law*, Vol. 16, Summer 1980, pp. 1–25; "Teleinformatics," a special issue of the *Cornell International Law Journal*, Vol. 14, Summer 1981, pp. 203–353.

24. Oswald Ganley, "The U.S.-Canadian communications and information relationship and its possible significance for worldwide diplomacy," Paper W-79-71, Program on Information Resources Policy, Harvard University, November 1979.

25. For a useful summary of the television issue, see: *Cultures in collision: The interaction of Canadian and U.S. television broadcast policies* (New York: Praeger Publishers, 1984).

26. "Report of the Consultative Committee on the implications of telecommunications for Canadian society," Department of Communications, Ottawa,

March 1979, p. 64. The chairman of the committee, John U. Clyne, was chancellor of the University of British Columbia.

27. "Canada's House votes to curb ad sales to foreign magazines," *Washington Post*, 16 March 1999, p. E-1.

28. "High technology: Clash of the titans," *The Economist* (London), special supplement, 23 August 1986.

29. For a summary of the U.S. chip industry's complaints, see: "The effect of government targeting on world semiconductor competition," research study issued by the Semiconductor Industry Association, Cupertino, CA, 1983.

30. These points are discussed in Stephen D. Cohen, Joel R. Paul and Robert A. Blecker, *Fundamentals of U.S. foreign trade policy* (Boulder, CO: Westview Press, 1996), pp. 275–283. For a critical view of high-technology export policy, see Laura D'Andrea Tyson, *Who's bashing whom? Trade conflict in high-technology industries* (Washington, DC: Institute for International Economics, 1992).

31. Richard E. Nohe, "A different time, a different place: Breaking up telephone companies in the United States and Japan," *Federal Communications Bar Journal*, Vol. 48, No. 2, March 1996, pp. 307–340.

32. "Japan awards licenses to foreign carriers," *Telecommunications Reports International*, 13 March 1998, p. 3.

33. "In Japan, the legacy of a phone monopoly," *New York Times*, 19 March 2000, p. Bu-1.

34. "The coming of the digital age: Challenges and opportunities for Japan and the United States," Report 98-JUS-2, Japan-U.S. Telecommunications Research Institute, San Diego State University, San Diego, CA, 1998.

35. The Japanese government's strategy for strengthening what it calls "the infocommunications sector" is described in *White Paper on Communications in Japan*, issued by the Ministry of Posts and Telecommunications in November 1999.

36. "Fujitsu becomes more focussed," *Financial Times* (London), 7 April 1999, special supplement on information technology, p. xvi.

37. For the evolution of Common Market communications policies, see: Morris W. Crawford, "The Common Market for telecommunications and information services," Report 90-6, Program on Information Resources Policy, Harvard University, July 1990.

38. James Coward, "Development of European data bases in a world context," *Information Privacy*, January 1980, p. 35.

39. Quoted in *European Trends*, No. 2, The Economist Intelligence Unit, 1989, p. 49.

40. Michel Carpentier, "The single European market and telecommunications in a world context," *Single Market Telecommunications Review*, January 1991, p. 28.

41. "Data networks disappoint," *Communications Week International*, 16 July 1990, p. 1.

42. The blueprint for this transition was set in a commission document, "On the development of the common market for telecommunications services and equipment," Report COM 87(260), Commission of the European Communities, Brussels, 1987. For an analysis of the EC's actions, see: Wilson Dizard, "Europe calling Europe: Creating an integrated telecommunications network," in Alan W. Cafruny and Glenda Rosenthal (eds.), *The state of the European Community: The*

Maastricht debates and beyond (Boulder, CO: Lynne Rienner Publishers, 1993), pp. 321–326.

43. Morris W. Crawford, *EC-92: The making of a common market in communications*, Publication I-88-2, Program on Information Resources Policy, Harvard University, July 1988.

44. The initial impact on the American presence in Europe after the EC communications reforms is described in Robin Gaster, Erik R. Olbeter, Amy Bolster and Clyde V. Prestowitz, Jr., *Bit by bit: Building a transatlantic partnership for the information age* (Armonk, NY: M. E. Sharpe, 1996).

45. Simon Nora and Alain Minc, *The computerization of society* (Cambridge, MA: MIT Press, 1980).

46. "U.S. worried by world efforts to curtail flow of information," *New York Times*, 26 February 1978, p. 1.

47. "Wire static," *Wall Street Journal*, 26 August 1981, p. 1.

48. For a useful survey of these restrictive measures, see: Rolf T. Wigand, Carrie Shipley and Dwayne Shipley, "Transborder data flow, informatics and national policies," *Journal of Communication*, Vol. 34, No. 1, Winter 1984, pp. 153–175.

49. The text of the council's draft convention "for the protection of individuals with regard to automatic processing of personal data" is given in *Transnational Data Report*, Vol. 2, No. 3, 1979, pp. 16–23. See also: James R. Maxeiner, "Freedom of information and the EU data protection directive," *Federal Communications Law Journal*, Vol. 48, No. 1, 1996, pp. 93–98.

50. For a description of early OECD activities in this field, see: "OECD computer-telecommunications policies," *Intermedia* (London), December 1976, p. 9.

51. "U.S., EU agree on privacy standard," *Washington Post*, 1 June 2000, p. E-1.

52. Dryden, op cit., pp. 369–371.

53. Gary C. Hufbauer and Jeffrey J. Schott, *NAFTA: An assessment* (Washington, DC: Institute for International Economics, 1993). See also: "Telecommunications services in the US-Canadian free trade agreement: Where do we go from here?" International Communications Studies Program, Center for Strategic and International Studies, Washington, DC, May 1989.

54. Dryden, op cit., pp. 9–32.

55. The early history of these efforts is described in Geza Feketekuty, *International trade in services* (Cambridge, MA: Ballinger Publishing Co., 1988), pp. 296–313.

56. Bruno Lanvin, "Participation of developing countries in a telecommunications and data services agreement: Some elements for consideration," in Peter Robinson, Karl P. Sauvant and Vishwas P. Govitrikar (eds.), *Electronic highways for world trade* (Boulder, CO: Westview Press, 1989), pp. 71–100.

57. For a useful survey of the overall impact of the Uruguay Round agreements on telecommunications and other IT sectors, see: Gary Clyde Hufbauer and Erika Wada (eds.), *Unfinished business: Telecommunications after the Uruguay Round* (Washington, DC: Institute for International Economics, 1995).

58. Tannya L. McLarty, "Liberalized telecommunications trade in the WTO:

Implications for universal service policy," *Federal Communications Bar Journal*, Vol. 51, No. 1, December 1998, pp. 1–59.

59. "NTT—Born again," *The Economist* (London), 3 July 1999, p. 55.

60. For a summary of the BTS negotiations, prepared by USTR, see: "The WTO and the negotiations on basic telecommunications," Appendix IV in William Garrison, Christopher P. Foss and Carol Charles (eds.), *The WTO telecom agreement: Engineering the global information highway* (Washington, DC: Center for Strategic and International Studies, 1997), pp. 78–83.

61. "EU to push growth in innovation, technology," *Washington Post*, 25 March 2000, p. E-1.

62. "U.S. and EU aim to end IT tariffs by 2000," *Financial Times* (London), 24 August 1995, p. 18.

63. Quoted in "Internet governance: The struggle over the political economy of cyberspace," *On the Internet*, January 1999, p. 9.

64. "Net is reshaping world business," *Financial Times* (London), information technology supplement, 24 September 1999, p. xx.

65. "Europe's privacy cops," *Business Week*, 2 November 1988, p. 49.

66. "Now that's long-distance," *Business Week*, 14 December 1998, p. 132.

67. "Deal mania," *Business Week*, 5 April 1999, p. 50.

68. "U.S. inroads prompted huge telecom merger," *Washington Post*, 23 April 1999, p. E-1.

69. "The transatlantic productivity race," *Financial Times* (London), 3 June 2000, p. 8.

70. "Gigabits behind," *Washington Post*, 15 January 2000, p. 1.

71. Lee McKnight and W. Russell Neuman, "Technology policy and national information infrastructure," in William J. Drake (ed.), *The new information infrastructure: Strategies for U.S. policy* (New York: Twentieth Century Fund Press, 1995), pp. 137–154.

72. Geza Feketekuty and Bruce Stokes (eds.), *Three strategies for a new era: Ensuring U.S. leadership in a global economy* (Monterey, CA: Monterey Institute of International Studies, 1998).

73. Frost, op cit., p. 494.

74. "The shipwreck in Seattle," *New York Times*, 5 December 1999, p. 5.

Chapter 9

The Future of Digital Diplomacy

This survey has covered almost 130 years of American foreign policy involvement with electronic communications. Symbolically the story begins on the day in 1868 when the State Department hired its first telegraph clerk. His duties were to pick up telegrams addressed to the department at the Western Union office in downtown Washington. From that modest beginning, the role of electronic communications has expanded fitfully in U.S. foreign affairs, both in its policy agenda and in the way it conducts its business. Having traced its origins from that unknown clerk, it is useful to look at digital diplomacy prospects at the beginning of a new century.

As we have seen throughout our survey, the American diplomatic community has generally lagged in adapting its policies and operations to electronic realities. The pace has quickened in recent years, but there are still lingering misunderstandings about the role of information technologies. In November 1998, the State Department issued an "international affairs strategic plan," outlining its policy priorities for the next decade and beyond. It included the standard list of issues (national security, trade, environment, human rights) without referring, except for a cliché nod towards the information age, to the role of electronic technologies in determining the form and content of these issues.[1]

This reluctance to acknowledge new digital realities reflects an organizational culture that still resists change. There is an element of a commendable caution in this attitude. As Lawrence Eagleburger, a former secretary of state, notes: "Will the speed at which we communicate drive out thought? I worry about that a lot. Instant answers to instant problems can get you in a hell of a lot of trouble."[2] However valid this caution, it can also be an excuse to cling to an older diplomatic culture whose practitioners were suspicious of threats, real or imagined, to their professional self-esteem. They operated in a hierarchical, closed environment that was increasingly at odds with the boundary-jumping technologies that define today's information society.

These digital pressures on the diplomatic process will increase in the coming years. Scientist Peter Goldmark, a pioneer in advanced information technology, has noted that we are still in the tom-tom stage of communications networking. There is no lack of self-appointed clairvoyants telling us where the new technologies will take us. Their projections range from gloom-and-doom scenarios of information overload turmoil to those that envision a steady climb to the sunny uplands of world peace and prosperity. Microsoft's Bill Gates sees a global era of what he calls friction free capitalism. On the other hand, computer agnostic Clifford Stoll predicts an "overpromoted, hollow world, devoid of warmth and human kindness . . . no birds sing."[3] Anatoly Voronov, a Russian scientist, views the Internet and similar developments as a dark Yankee plot, "the ultimate act of intellectual colonialism."[4]

The reality, as usual, lies somewhere in between. There is, however, one indisputable fact that will drive the subject in its many aspects, including digital diplomacy. It is that sometime within the next generation almost everyone on earth will be linked by multimedia electronic networks. Plain old telephone service (POTS, in the engineer's phrase) is driving much of this expansion. However, over 40 percent of the earth's population still has no regular access to a telephone. This phone gap is closing steadily: the number of telephones worldwide has doubled in the last 20 years, and will double again in the next decade.[5]

The result will be a high capacity "information pipe" providing universal access to a wide variety of voice, video and data resources, including the Internet. Linking everyone on an electronic network will be a turning point in human history, with multiplier effects that are unpredictable. The only comparable past event was the introduction of multiple-copy printing in the Renaissance. It was, however, an event whose influence has been spread out unevenly over 500 years, with one third the earth's population still functionally illiterate.[6] The new digital grid's reach, by comparison, is universal and instantaneous.

Our focus in this survey has been on how this change will affect America's global role, with particular attention to its diplomacy. We have seen how digital communications resources have begun to modify the nation-state system, including the new influence of transnational institutions and non-governmental groups, in large part the result of their mastery of information networking. Increasingly, the new ingredient in the comparative ranking of nations is soft power, denominated in invisible bits and bytes stored on fingernail-sized semiconductor chips.

The yardsticks for measuring these trends are elusive and subject to constant change. Inflated statistics are the rule. The most reliable summary of global trends is assembled in *Communications outlook,* a report replete with eye-glazing charts issued every two years by the Paris-based OECD. The publication's strength is its hard statistics on the new dominance of information-related activities in the OECD's 29 industrialized member countries. The survey has been particularly useful in tracking the expansion of Internet resources.[7]

A less accurate but interesting attempt to get a comparative ranking of global soft-power resources was made in the late 1990s by a Boston consultancy, International Data Corporation (IDC). Using 20 indices (telephones, home computers, etc.), IDC measured over 50 countries in three sectors—their social, information and computer infrastructures. The national rankings that resulted confirmed the long lead the United States had in each category. Its statistical score was 5,107 points. Second-place Sweden scored 4,003. The scores for other industrial democracies were largely in the 2,500 to 3,500 range. India, Indonesia, Pakistan and China, whose populations include half the human race, were at the bottom of the list.[8] However imperfect as a measure of soft power, the IDC survey highlights the U.S. role as the global information power—not in the hegemonic sense of preponderant influence over territory or other physical measures, but as a pervasive influence based on information resources.[9]

Inevitably, this strong American lead in information resources is temporary. The rest of the world is catching up, beginning with the Europeans, Canadians and Japanese. In the new technocentric order, the lead time for moving to an information-intensive society is narrowing. Technological isolationism of the kind that led Chinese emperors to decapitate subjects who sold secrets to foreigners is no longer possible. The research breakthrough made in a California laboratory shows up very quickly on production lines in Cologne or Osaka, often in an improved version. Increasingly, the American strength lies in what the London *Economist* calls the ultra-tech sector, where research innovations leapfrog over older technologies. Moreover, the American economy continues to have an edge in getting these innovations onto production lines and into the market quickly.

Most of this process is still dominated by big industrial conglomerates, but they are challenged (and often overmatched) by agile smaller enterprises. Many of these challengers had their origins in an informal fraternity of young computer buffs that formed on the West Coast a generation ago. They were bright, bearded, sandaled, educated and disdainful of careers that involved a conventional climb up the corporate ladder. Their attitudes were summarized by Steve Jobs, one of Apple Computer's founders: "We realized that we could build something ourselves that could control billions of dollars of infrastructure in the whole world. . . . We could build a little thing that could control a big thing."[10]

His comments reflect the multilayered restructuring taking place in the U.S. economy at the turn of the century, involving a mix of corporate giants and smaller start-ups. The information sector is in constant churn, its future open-ended, with no clear guidelines to set its pace and direction. Moreover, its activities continue to be challenged by political and economic forces attempting to defend remnants of an older, more familiar order.

As we have seen throughout this survey, public policy, including digital diplomacy, has often stumbled in keeping up with these developments. In part, this has involved a failure to understand the dimensions of the change. As computer pioneer John Von Neumann pointed out, modern technology increases the rate of change not so much by shortening the time involved but by expanding the areas—political, economic, social—that are affected. A Harvard University study has noted:

Decisions of vital importance—national, international, corporate and personal—are being fought out in dimly lit arenas under rules that are not clear even to the lawyers, engineers, economists and bureaucrats who devised them. Rosters and score cards are rare. Some of the players are unnumbered; others wear the wrong numbers. . . . There are many kinds of information technologies, but it is becoming clear that there is really only one information system, no matter how disconnected the parts may seem. Information is a basic resource, fully as important as materials or energy.[11]

Digital diplomacy is a small but important part of this pattern. It is an extension of the interplay among powerful domestic forces, each bent in influencing information age events. The issues are complex, often involving abstruse technical and economic subjects. Most of the deal making has taken place behind closed doors, involving groups of lawyers, bureaucrats and corporate lobbyists.

However, public awareness about information-age issues is changing rapidly. One defining event was the 1992 presidential campaign. In challenging the incumbent George Bush, Bill Clinton's campaign managers saw a chance to reach a new constituency—millions of voters who were newly involved with computers and other digital tools at work and at home. The election coincided with the expansion of the Internet, and particularly its World Wide Web resources. Given the national penchant for reducing big ideas to bumper-sticker simplicity, the Clinton campaign trumpeted the need to build a high-tech "information highway." It was a theme that resonated particularly well with younger voters as an extension of the traditional American faith in salvation-through-technology.[12] It also contrasted sharply with the lackluster set of issues pushed by the Bush strategists.

Once in office, the Clinton administration pressed its information highway proposals under the awkward title of the National Information Infrastructure (NII).[13] The project was led by Vice President Al Gore, who had promoted high-tech legislation, including the expansion of Internet resources, as a senator. For the first time, information policies and programs had high visibility at the White House level. Gore assembled a team of young technocrats and policy wonks to orchestrate the information highway program. In an administration bedeviled by controversy, these initiatives were popular and largely bipartisan. Republican Speaker of the House Newt Gingrich, a self-styled conservative futurist, announced: "We are beginning to invent the information age." In his enthusiasm for the new age, Gingrich suggested that laptop computers should be an automatically deductible expense on income tax returns—a proposal he later dropped.

The Clinton administration's initiatives also affected the way that information policy was organized in the federal government, including digital diplomacy. At the White House level, the vice president's office managed the project's overall strategy. Within the federal bureaucracy, an Information Infrastructure Task Force was formed, chaired by the secretary of commerce. The Commerce Department's role was enhanced by the fact that the agency was headed by two politically well-connected secretaries—Ronald H. Brown, a former chairman of the Democratic National Committee, and William M. Daley of the Chicago political dynasty. An advisory council, heavily weighted towards corporate interests, was set up to oversee the project.

The focus of these activities was the domestic economy. Eventually, however, the overseas implications of the information highway program were addressed. Its themes were outlined by Vice President Gore in a speech at an International Telecommunications Union conference in Buenos Aires in March 1994.[14] Gore called for the creation of a "global information infrastructure," with an emphasis on closing the resource gap between the industrialized and the emerging economies. This could be done, he suggested, by removing trade restrictions on information technology goods and services.

The Gore speech gave a global dimension to the Clinton information agenda. It also rearranged the ways in which digital diplomacy efforts were organized in Washington. The emphasis on trade policy strengthened the influence of the Commerce Department as the day-to-day manager of the Clinton initiatives within the federal bureaucracy. On the international side, it also enhanced the U.S. Trade Representative's role as the lead negotiator on information issues in the World Trade Organization and other multilateral forums.

These policy and operational shifts diminished the State Department's role. As we saw in Chapter 7, the department had consolidated its activities in a new bureau for communications and information policy in the 1980s. In its early years, the bureau (known by the acronym CIP) was generally successful in coordinating communications policy initiatives both within the department and with other agencies. However, its influence waned as the Commerce Department and USTR took the lead in promoting Clinton information highway policies at home and abroad. In effect, the State Department was reduced to a minor coordinating role in dealing with overseas information issues, particularly in the trade area. Its role was further weakened by general indifference to information policies in the upper reaches of the department.

The eventual result was the elimination of the information and communications policy bureau, which had been set up with much fanfare in 1985. The decision was taken in part to mollify Senator Jesse Helms, the North Carolina Republican who was chairman of the Foreign Relations Committee and a perennial critic of the department's alleged bloated bureaucracy. But it also involved the perception that active responsibility for major information issues, particularly those involving trade, had shifted to the USTR and the Commerce Department. Unlike the State Department, the two agencies each had the advantage of a strong private sector constituency to protect their bureaucratic interests.

The department bureau's functions were transferred to the third level of the economic and business bureau. The unit continues to play a useful but diminished role in digital diplomacy. The overall result, however, has been a setback in developing a comprehensive approach to dealing with American foreign policy interests in the new information-intensive global environment. At the turn of the century, there was little prospect that the organization of digital diplomacy within the federal bureaucracy would be changed.

The closing down of the CIP bureau in 1994 ended, for the time being at least, the State Department's attempt to assert a strong role in global communications policy. In the unlikely event that an inquest should be held to determine why this happened, it would lead inexorably back 35 years to State's failure to take the lead in crafting the strategy for the new communications satellites. Intelsat's creation was a turning point in confirming American leadership in world communications. It also created an opportunity for a more orderly policy approach in dealing with cross-border communications issues, led by the State Department. This did not happen. The department played a useful but subsidiary role in the events leading up to the creation of the Intelsat network. But there was a general lack of commitment to, and understanding of, the importance of communications issues by the department's leadership. The exception was Secretary George Schultz, who had raised the visibility of the subject by creating the CIP bureau in 1985 to deal with these issues.

As we saw in Chapter 6, the State Department has been more forthcoming in addressing another aspect of digital diplomacy—namely, the use of advanced information technologies in its day-to-day operations. By the early 1990s, the department had fallen disastrously behind in this area. One 1992 internal survey indicated that almost three quarters of its computer-based resources were obsolete in terms of the technologies then available.[15] In part, this was the result of a decision, a dozen years earlier, to choose a desktop computer manufactured by the Wang Corp. as the standard for the agency's operations at home and abroad. The Wang machines were quickly outmoded in the industry's rush to develop more advanced personal computers. Nevertheless, they remained the department's standard even after the company filed for bankruptcy.

By the late 1990s, pressures mounted to upgrade advanced electronic resources in the Department's day-to-day operations. Scattered responsibilities for this subject were consolidated in a full-fledged bureau, the Bureau of Information Resources Management, created in March 1998. For the first time, the Internet was incorporated into the department's operations through an "OpenNet" network linking employees with overseas posts. E-mail facilities were upgraded to the point where they were being used to transmit 20 million messages annually. Overall, by the turn of the century, new and upgraded facilities accounted for over $538 million of the agency's budget. Although problems remained, particularly in dealing with the storage and transmittal of classified materials, the State Department was moving towards an electronic capability that began to match its information age responsibilities.[16]

Despite these improvements, there are still questions whether the department is adequately equipped to take advantage of new information technology resources. These concerns were addressed in 1998 studies of State's operations in the new digital environment by two Washington think tanks—the Center for Strategic and International Studies and the Henry L. Stimson Center.[17] Earlier studies on reforming the department had stressed bureaucratic restructuring. The CSIS and Stimson reports put their emphasis on the need for a change in the department's organizational culture. The alternative, they suggested, was that State's role in forming and carrying out foreign policy would become increasingly irrelevant.

As the CSIS report pointed out:

The first and highest priority is to end the culture of secrecy and exclusivity, to embrace the notions of openness and trust. The sense that diplomacy can take place in a closed universe of privileged intellectuals must change. Diplomacy must move from a mandarinate system to one that recognizes the permeability of borders and information. Embassies must not become the monasteries of the twenty-first century.[18]

Both studies called for an overhaul of the department's traditional hierarchical ways of doing business. In particular, this meant removing the obstacles that inhibited the flow of information within Washington headquarters and with overseas posts. In proposing this, the reports were taking a leaf from the radical restructuring of communications patterns taking place within corporate America. As Helene Runtagh, a former General Electric executive, has pointed out: "Communications in a network are absolutely incompatible with a strict parochial hierarchy. . . . The worst of all worlds is clinging to hierarchical behavior while bringing in network-based communications. You're in for a decade of chaos, frustration and poor financial results."

The CSIS and Stimson surveys recognized that the department's communications needs are somewhat different from those of a corporation, in particular the requirement to protect sensitive information. They each recommended phasing out the agency's three separate communications networks and replacing them with what in business school jargon is called a fully integrated value chain. Its purpose would be to give every department employee in Washington and at overseas posts desktop direct access to information relevant to his or her duties. The network would also provide advanced online links to other offices within the department, to Washington foreign policy agencies, and to U.S. embassies and consulates in over 180 countries. Access to sensitive information on the network could be controlled by electronic "fire walls."[19]

The Stimson study emphasized the need for opening up the network to allow access to the private sector:

On many specific issues, they know more about the problems that confront the U.S. than do our government officials. This pool of knowledge should be tapped to make American foreign policy more insightful as well as to forge an inclusive diplomacy that expresses America's diverse interests to a world that is more complex than it was even just ten years ago.[20]

Both surveys recognized the new importance of the electronic mass media in the foreign policy process. The impact of televised images on American perceptions of overseas events, particularly those involving U.S. military resources, is well documented. The result is the phenomenon known as the CNN effect, where attitudes of both diplomats and the public at large are heavily influenced by fast-breaking (and often misleading) coverage of international crises.[21] This is despite the fact that overall coverage of foreign news by American media has declined sharply in recent decades. One survey found that such coverage by the

Big Three television networks dropped from more than 40 percent in the 1970s to less than 15 percent by 1995.[22] In part, the void has been filled by the Internet, with its interactive Web sites that deal with global developments at all levels.

Looking at the State Department's role in public diplomacy, the reports recognized the new importance of clarifying foreign policy issues credibly. They recommended greater use of the Internet in reaching both the general public as well as private groups that have specialized interests in foreign policy. The department's public affairs bureau has, in fact, made considerable progress in integrating these resources into its operations in recent years.[23] Its mandate was extended to international audiences in October 1999 when most of the activities of the formerly independent U.S. Information Agency were integrated with the bureau's domestic information activities.[24] At the same time, the department created a new unit, the International Public Information group with a mandate to control the overseas flow of official news output of federal government agencies, including the Defense Department. The project, designed to counter anti-American propaganda abroad, was criticized by some civil liberties groups as an attempt to filter information that should be freely available.[25]

Commenting on the overall need to upgrade the department's information technology resources, both the CSIS and Stimson studies acknowledged that there were pockets of technological excellence within the State Department, notably in the consular service, which has put complex computer-aided identification systems in place, including machine-readable visa systems and fingerprint recognition technology.

Strengthening information resources within the department has always been hostage to niggardly congressional attitudes about the agency's budget, backed by the populist tradition that its officers spend their time at cocktail parties in opulent embassies. The Stimson report called for a $400 million "information technology working capital fund" to close the technology gap. Recent secretaries of state, notably Warren Christopher and Madeleine Albright, have been successful in getting smaller but still respectable budget increases for advanced information facilities, including a $117 million allocation in the fiscal year 1998 appropriation.[26]

This new attention to electronic resources will strengthen the department's management capabilities in the new century. It should also have the useful effect of further sensitizing its personnel, from the secretary of state on down, to the pervasive effect of information technology on all foreign policy issues—the traditional ones as well as those spawned by the digital revolution.

Trade issues will dominate this agenda, given the outsized role information technology now plays in the American economy. The IT sector made up about 8 percent of domestic GDP at the end of the 1990s, but it accounted for one third of national economic growth, according to the Department of Commerce.[27] The sector's future growth rests heavily on further expansion into overseas markets. American firms are firmly placed as the leading players in the global IT sector. However, their share of the market is declining, particularly as other industrialized countries step up their transition to information-based economies. By the mid-1990s, more than half of the gross domestic product of OECD countries involved information-based goods and services.[28] U.S. high-tech companies have played a significant role in this expansion, exporting a record $181 billion in 1999, representing 26 percent of all goods exported.[29]

Meanwhile, there are new competitive threats from a group of Asian and Latin American countries—the so-called Big Emerging Markets—who have begun to challenge what had become a commanding U.S. lead in software production. India has led the way, producing for its own domestic market and exporting an estimated $3 billion in software products in 1999, most of it to the United States.[30] The bulk of these exports originally involved products produced by American companies that moved into India to take advantage of lower labor costs. More recently, a larger share of the industry's output is produced by Indian companies. Software exports overall are growing at a rate of 50 percent a year, with two thirds of them going to the United States.[31] At the turn of the century, information technology accounted for one third of India's total capitalization, equal to 10 percent of its gross domestic product.[32]

This new foreign competition now sets the pace and tone of U.S. electronic trade policy. As noted earlier, its overall aim is to help American business maintain its lead in IT trade. This involves aggressive marketing support, as well as negotiations to reduce the regulatory barriers that limit sales of U.S. digital products and services abroad. A secondary but critical objective is to leverage the strong surplus created by information exports in ways that will further reduce the large deficits that have marked American global trade patterns for over 20 years.

In this competitive environment, American trade policy faces a new challenge that promises to dominate electronic diplomacy in the coming yeas. It is electronic commerce, the fastest growing trend in world trade. Doing business over electronic circuits is hardly new. As we have seen throughout this survey, American companies have taken advantage of computers, satellites and other IT resources to expand their operations. The prime example has been the financial services sector, with its almost total reliance on electronic transactions.[33]

The new element is the Internet and the fact that, increasingly, it is a place to do business. The Net has emerged as a global marketplace in which goods and services can be transacted at any level, from big-time corporate deals down to consumers who buy a book online at Amazon.com. Increasingly, it is the way more and more business will be done in the new century, at home and abroad.[34]

This trend began in the early 1990s as American firms turned to the Internet to trade goods and services among themselves. The idea caught on primarily because trading over the Net cut paperwork and other costs. By the turn of the century, these companies were buying and selling $500 billion worth of goods and services annually to each other over Internet links. The practice spread to international inter-company trading. In 1995, a consortium of U.S. firms, including IBM, General Electric and Chase Manhattan, set up an Internet-based global network to trade goods and services among themselves. Known as IBEX (International Business Exchange), the service was open to any company, foreign or domestic. Web-based trade on IBEX and other networks is projected by Forrester Research, a Boston consultancy, to reach $1.3 trillion worldwide by 2005.[35]

Business-to-business transactions are now a permanent feature in Internet-based electronic commerce. However, they may be outpaced in both volume and revenues by a newer phenomenon—the growth of consumer sales on the Net. Domestic consumer transactions on the Internet are still a small part of the $7 trillion U.S. economy, but they are its fastest growing sector. Many estimates project that consumer Internet sales will exceed $100 billion by 2003.

Both business and consumer transactions on the network are expanding globally, led by American companies such as IBM, Microsoft, Dell, American Express, Citibank and America Online, all of whom are well-entrenched in Western Europe and other affluent areas. They are applying the lessons learned at home, namely that electronic sales can dramatically cut transaction costs. A consumer bank transaction over the Internet costs a penny compared to 27 cents at an ATM. An airline ticket can be processed for a dollar, compared to $8 at a travel agency office. Among the companies that have learned this lesson is IBM, which generated an estimated $15 billion in Net revenues at home and abroad in 1999, the result of 28 million visits by customers to the firm's Web pages.[36]

In the early years of Internet commerce, U.S. firms accounted for as much as 75 percent of the transactions. More recently, foreign competitors have begun to catch up as they saw themselves losing market share to American electronic trade.[37] In a global survey of senior executives by Booz Allen & Hamilton, over half of the respondents saw the Internet as having a major impact on their business, with almost as many declaring that it will transform their marketing strategies. There will be corporate winners and even more losers as this electronic marketplace expands. Andrew Grove, chairman of Intel, makes a flat prediction: in a few years all companies will be Internet companies, or they won't be companies at all.

Meanwhile, Internet-based trade has introduced a new set of digital diplomacy issues. Governments scramble to adapt policies and actions to Internet realities. For the United States, this means negotiating from a set of domestic policies that emphasize self-regulation of electronic trade by the industries involved with a minimum of government interference.[38] This approach contrasts with the policies and practices of most governments abroad which, in varying ways, want to regulate electronic trade both domestically and internationally.

The United States deals with these issues in three sets of international forums. At the global level, this involves the Geneva-based World Trade Organization. Internet trading was in its infancy when the WTO was founded in 1993. Since then, American efforts have focussed heavily on getting the organization's support to reduce barriers to electronic commerce, including Internet transactions. U.S. negotiators scored an important breakthrough with the 1997 WTO agreement to lower barriers to telecommunications trade, described in the last chapter. Since then, they have had a more difficult time convincing other WTO members to open up their markets to electronic trade. It was one of the reasons for the failure to agree on a WTO agenda for future negotiations at the organization's December 1999 ministerial meeting in Seattle.[39]

The second negotiating level involves discussions with America's industrial partners in the Paris-based Organization for Economic Cooperation and Development. As in earlier trade negotiations, the OECD has been a useful forum for reaching agreements on so-called voluntary guidelines on trade issues. This approach has generally worked well in negotiations with the European Union, the largest regional market for American electronic exports.[40]

The final segment of this electronic trade negotiating triad is bilateral negotiations with individual countries. Largely as a result of pressures from the American electronics industry, the State and Commerce departments continually press these countries about their treatment of American exports, involving a wide range of tariff and non-tariff barriers. It is a subject of continuing disputes with China, which has been fiercely protective of its electronics industry in the negotiations leading up to that country's admission to the World Trade Organization.[41]

Trade will continue to be the most visible issue in digital diplomacy for the indefinite future. It is measurable, it affects most Americans as a pocket-book issue and it is carefully monitored by powerful corporate lobbies. However, information issues cut across all other foreign policy concerns in varying degrees. Three of these issues stand out—national security, human rights, and American involvement with developing countries.

The latter is part of the larger problem of the global maldistribution of information age resources. As Robert Keohane and Joseph Nye point out: "Contrary to the expectations of some theorists, the information revolution has not equalized power among states. If anything, it has had the opposite effect."[42] The gap is most glaringly noticeable along the North-South axis. By rough count, 80 percent of the populations of Asia, Africa and Latin America have access to less than 20 percent of global electronic information resources.

Despite considerable efforts to narrow this difference, it remains a stubborn reality. Moreover, further progress is made difficult by the fact that an estimated 95 percent of all population growth in the coming decade will occur in developing countries.[43]

The problem is not new to American digital diplomacy, but it has taken on a wider dimension in recent years. The information deficit is now seen more clearly as a factor in global instability. Information advances in most emerging economies have generally benefited a relatively small group of urban elites. It has also given new power to destructive elements such as terrorists and drug dealers, each adept at using high-tech electronics in their operations.[44] In most countries, rural villagers and city slum dwellers have seen relatively few benefits from the new resources. The result is to widen domestic information gaps that fuel political and social tensions.

Beyond these political factors, the United States has compelling economic reasons to step up the pace of communications development in Asia, Africa and Latin America. Collectively, the emerging economies are the largest market for American information technology goods and services. The long-term health of the U.S. electronic sector will depend on how this market expands. It is already a highly competitive one, attracting European and Japanese firms as well as local entrepreneurs.

The American approach to the North–South information gap was ambiguous in the postwar decades. On the one hand, the U.S. government has been the largest donor of economic aid in this sector, directly and through the World Bank and other international agencies. At another level, the United States has had to fend off demands that it and other OECD countries fund a massive effort to narrow information inequalities. As we have seen in Chapter 5, this resulted in a Third World campaign for financial support of what its sponsors called a New World Information Order. Their effort largely failed, but not without leaving a legacy of recriminations on all sides.

Attitudes on the issue began to change in the late 1980s. In part this was the result of an influential 1984 study, known as the Maitland Report, sponsored by the International Telecommunications Union. The study argued cogently that there would be no significant improvement in Third World communications resources until governments loosened political controls over local communications resources, allowing for more private investment and ownership.[45] The Maitland Report provided the framework for what has become a significant turnaround in the way that telecommunications and information resources are organized in Third World countries.

The major pressure for change, however, came from local business interests in the emerging economies, fearful of falling behind in the new global trade competition because of poor communications. By the turn of the century, governments in almost 100 developing countries had made their communications networks more competitive as part of a general movement towards open market economies. In a few cases, the results have been spectacular: Hungary increased the number of telephone access lines per 100 inhabitants from 10 to 32 in the seven years after 1990.

American policy has been to encourage these developing country initiatives. In particular, it has encouraged World Bank communications development programs that support private sector projects.[46] In the mid-1990s, the Bank set up an Information for Development Program (InfoDev) to coordinate its lending and grant programs in this sector. In 2000, it also set up a $200 million fund to finance Internet start-ups in 100 developing countries.[47] American digital diplomacy also urges developing countries to agree to World Trade Organization rules for opening up trade in information technology goods and services.

These initiatives have had the general effect of expanding communications and information resources in emerging economies. The effort has been aided by the introduction of two new technologies—cell phones and the Internet. Wireless phone systems are the fastest growing communications resource in Asia, Africa and Latin America. The reasons are that they can be installed easily and they lessen dependence on creaky wired phone systems. The Internet is experiencing similar expansion in these regions, despite the fact that its requirements—modem-equipped computers and reliable phone systems—are still in short supply. Overall, developing countries account for less than 2 percent of global Internet users. This figure is skewed by the fact that Internet use is expanding most rapidly in so-called Big Emerging Markets like Mexico, Argentina and India. The number of Internet users in Brazil reached 3 million by the turn of the century, with an annual growth rate of 130 percent since then. In part, this is the result of an intensely competitive market, in which local firms vie with IBM, Microsoft and Yahoo! for Web customers.[48]

Several imaginative programs to harness the Internet to development needs have been launched in recent years. One of the largest is sponsored by the U.S. Agency for International Development in Africa, which is supplying hardware, technical advice and training with the aim of getting 20 countries online early in the new century. The project has been hampered by the reluctance of local governments to open up their phone monopolies to competitive Internet traffic.[49] A more hopeful approach is the 1999 decision of San Jose–based Cisco Systems Inc., a major provider of computer networking software, to promote Internet use in partnership with the U.N. Development Program (UNDP). The result could be the world's biggest Internet site (NewAid.org), reaching out to the more than 150 countries where UNDP operates.[50]

Military security is another area where digital diplomacy will play a more active role in the coming years. The Defense Department has moved steadily to integrate advanced information technologies as a central element in its operational plans. The subject has created its own vocabulary of clichés—cyberdeterence, digital battlefields, netwars and information warfare. As a Pentagon study has noted: "The computer chip and digital systems for ground combat are as radical as the machine gun in World War I and the blitzkrieg in World War II; they will permit standoff attacks rather than closure to rifle range, decreasing U.S. casualty rates and increasing the tempo and breadth of the battlefield."[51]

The result has been the emergence of a new strategic doctrine—the revolution in military affairs (RMA). Its core concept has been aptly described by Rand Corporation researchers looking at what they call cyberwar:

The information revolution implies the rise of a mode of warfare in which neither mass nor mobility will decide outcomes; instead the side that knows more, that can disperse the fog of war yet enshroud an adversary in it, will enjoy decisive advantages. At a minimum, cyberwar represents an extension of the traditional importance of obtaining information in war: having superior command, control, communication and intelligence and trying to locate, read, surprise and deceive the enemy before he does the same to you.[52]

The military's emphasis on cyberwar resources continues a longstanding tradition of involvement in strategic communications. As we saw in Chapter 2, the U.S. Navy played a leading role in assuring a strong American presence in global communications by thwarting a British plan to monopolize wireless communications early in the last century. Strategic communications policy was largely handled by the War and Navy departments (later the Defense Department) until the 1960s. Among other issues, this involved coordinating military needs with the U.S. civilian network, at home and abroad. This task was simplified at the time by the fact that one company, AT&T, controlled most of the civilian facilities. The company maintained a small military liaison office to deal with coordination problems and to plan communications requirements in case of war.[53]

By the 1980s, this simple arrangement became more complicated. AT&T had to give up over 60 percent of its domestic assets to resolve a Justice Department antitrust case. Instead of one company, the military now had to coordinate its communications needs with seven regional Bell Company systems and the dozens of other commercial networks that sprang up in the newly deregulated industry. At the same time, Defense Department planners were being pressed to incorporate an emerging generation of advanced technologies—satellites, fiber-optic cables and computers—into their plans. It was the first step towards the much-publicized Revolution in Military Affairs with its emphasis on electronic warfare. Beginning in the Reagan administration, military budgets were expanded to include greater emphasis on high-speed networks, surveillance satellites and computers that could provide direct command and control from the Pentagon to distant combat areas. The Defense Communications Agency was expanded and later supplemented by a Defense Information Systems Agency.[54]

A major problem for information warfare planners is the vulnerability of global communications systems to attacks on military computers by terrorists and freelance hackers. In one test, a team of Defense Department in-house hackers were able to take control of 88 percent of 8,400 Pentagon computers, with only 4 percent of the penetrations noted by their operators. A related problem is the vulnerability of civilian computers on which the military depends. By the mid-1990s, 50 percent of Fortune 1000 companies reported that they had been subject to information attacks.[55] Electronic break-ins on the Internet are also a problem for the military services. By 2000, hacker interference with Internet military traffic had become serious enough for the Pentagon to make plans to move its unclassified messages from the Internet to its own internal system.[56]

The State Department faces similar threats to its computer systems. In April 2000, it was forced to reorganize its security systems following the disappearance of a laptop computer which contained thousands of pages of top-secret information. Meanwhile, it has a continuing problem with hackers who attempt to break into its databases. Noting this problem, Georgetown University computer expert Dorothy Denning points out:

Hackerism brings the methods of guerilla theater and graffiti to cyberspace. It can be conducted by individuals acting alone or, as is more often the case, in groups and coalitions. It can exhibit elements of art and theater. It can even be humorous. But it is not benign, and it threatens U.S. embassy computers and diplomatic missions. It can compromise sensitive or classified information and sabotage or disrupt operations. At the very least, it can be an embarrassment to those attacked and erode public confidence in the U.S. government.[57]

Computer security is only part of the problem digital diplomacy must deal with in protecting global networks on which governments, the military and businesses depend. Private computers and networks are also vulnerable to manipulation by terrorists and hackers. Most negotiations between governments in this area are handled quietly, since the subject usually involves sensitive counter-operations by police authorities and intelligence agencies.[58] In January 2000, the Clinton administration took steps to tighten up coordination of electronic threats with plans for creating a federally funded Institute for Information Infrastructure Protection.[59]

Human rights is another policy area where digital diplomacy will take on new importance in the coming years. The United States took the lead after World War II in establishing human rights as a viable global issue, beginning with the U.N. Declaration of Human Rights, adopted in 1948. Since then, a growing body of laws and practices has emerged which, if it has not always curbed human rights violations, has made them more visible to world scrutiny.[60]

At the same time that the United States has promoted human rights, it has been ambivalent about agreements that committed it to specific actions. In large part, this has reflected fears of alleged international meddling in American domestic affairs. It took the U.S. Senate 40 years to ratify the Genocide Convention, 28 years for the Convention Against Racial Discrimination and 26 years for the International Covenant on Civil and Political Rights. America is not among the 160 countries that have ratified a convention banning discrimination against women. Even when it has approved similar treaties, the Senate has often attached extensive reservations, which have cancelled or modified the agreements' effectiveness.

In practice, however, the U.S. record in promoting worldwide communications and information rights has been positive. In the early postwar decades, the focus was on rights dealing with free speech, including the media. More recently, freedom-of-information rights have taken on a new cast, one which involves digital communications of all kinds. The sheer volume of electronic information moving across borders has increased exponentially. Much of it bypasses conventional government attempts to control information flows, such as radio jamming or censorship of printed materials. Despite rear-guard attempts to limit digital flows, the new circuits are a liberating force of unprecedented power. The most visible, of course, is the World Wide Web, where literally billions of pages of information are available instantaneously, globally and generally free of official constraints.[61]

The Web and the networks that transmit it are hastening the day when universal access to all kinds of information could be available from the village level on up. This conjures up visions of a nirvana of global information richness, with data resources of all kinds available from the village level on up. The reality is somewhat more sobering. As noted earlier, about half the earth's inhabitants do not have the tools, beginning with a telephone connection, which provide access to digital information resources. It is, in many ways, the most pervasive denial of the right to communicate. A second inhibition on information flow is official censorship. Although digital communications are difficult to control, governments use intimidation to limit access. In countries like Iran and Burma, it can involve a prison sentence. In Saudi Arabia, Internet users get around official monitoring of Web sites through a phone connection to a "free" Web site in neighboring Bahrain.[62]

The most interesting changes in the right to communicate are taking place in Russia and China—both bastions of official information repression only a dozen years ago. Many of these restraints remain in both countries, but they are eroding in the face of new social and economic pressures. Russia presents a mixed picture at the turn of the century—a lively opposition press, open Internet networks and street-corner freedom of speech. On the other hand, the most powerful media instruments, television and radio, are largely manipulated by government and corporate interests.

China presents a more intriguing pattern. Official controls over information flow remain largely in place. However, the Communist leadership faces an uncomfortable dilemma in reconciling strict censorship with the need to upgrade the national communications network in ways that match the demands of an expanding economy. The party leadership took steps, tentatively at first, to modernize the network. By the mid-1990s, the expansion was in full operation, spilling out beyond economic sectors into the homes of ordinary citizens. Mobile telephones account for a large share of this expansion. Kalba International, a Boston consultancy, estimated in 2000 that within a decade China will have almost a quarter of a billion mobile subscribers, more than any other country in the world.[63] Overall China's communications system will be the largest of its kind anywhere by the end of the decade. In the process, the country's leaders are losing control over their ability to manage information—an essential element in maintaining their grip on political power. Although the basic network is firmly in government hands, it now includes too many new gadgets (mobile phones, fax machines, Web sites, etc.) to permit the kind of monitoring that had previously allowed a vast surveillance bureaucracy to identify and punish violators of information controls.[64]

The Internet presents special problems for Beijing officials. On the one hand, the network is an increasingly important tool for economic development. However, it is almost impossible to control its use for other purposes, including providing a channel for political dissidents.[65] Officials have dealt with the problem ambiguously, periodically cracking down on dissidents while promoting Internet expansion generally. In the late 1990s, U.S. companies were given permission to compete in an Internet market that had grown to over 25 million users. American firms such as American Online, Intel, Yahoo! and Goldman Sachs formed joint ventures with Chinese entrepreneurs to provide services. By 1999, Yahoo's two sites, in English and Chinese, accounted for over 40 percent of all Internet "hits."[66] In what is probably a fruitless attempt to reassert control over the network, the Communist Party issued a directive in January 2000, requiring all Internet service providers to get a "security certification" in order to operate. The directive outlined penalties for Internet dissemination of "state secret information"—a phrase that covers almost anything not officially released to the public, from crop reports to news about an earthquake.[67]

Global digital communications also threatens information rights at another level—the erosion of individual privacy. Electronic storage and distribution of personal information (e.g., medical records) make it increasingly easy to get access to personal data normally regarded as confidential.[68] As we saw in Chapter 5, the United States and other Western democracies have moved actively into this largely uncharted area of protecting personal privacy.

They have only begun to discuss a more subtle threat—the organized manipulation of information moving through digital circuits. Is it a violation of human rights to spread false information that may harm social and cultural rights? This is a subject for ethicists and lawyers. But it is clear that the speed and efficiency with which information is digitally distributed can cause serious harm to individuals and to societies. An example is the vulnerability of global markets to manipulation on electronic circuits. One of the factors propelling the Asian financial crisis in the late 1990s was the ways in which financial speculators caused a domino-effect destabilization of local currencies. The result was a regional economic recession, with heavy job losses.[69]

It is appropriate that this survey end by discussing the right (and the capability) to communicate, to hear and be heard, to see and be seen, to write and be written about, with due allowance for libel and privacy concerns. The First Amendment is the bedrock principle of U.S. information policy at home and abroad. It was a revolutionary idea in the late eighteenth century. It still is today. Americans did not invent the concept of information freedoms: it is an idea that resonates in many forms throughout recorded history and into the digital age. The American contribution has been the working out of many rules and practices that translate the concept into day-to-day reality.

This principle of open information flow faces many challenges in the new century. To repeat a theme made throughout this survey, we are only at the edge of the changes digital technologies will bring about in future years. Until now these resources have largely benefited powerful interests, particularly governments and corporations. These institutions have had the money, and the will, to take advantage of electronic resources for their own purposes. As a result, they are primarily responsible for creating and exploiting the present basic ("backbone") network at home and abroad.[70] This backbone facility is now being widened and its purposes transformed as it reaches out to mass audiences through a web of smaller networks. In effect, the network is being consumerized, beginning in the OECD countries and extending, at various speeds, into other societies. Moreover, its capabilities reach far beyond telephone services to include a full range of information services that can be plugged into a digital circuit.

The changeover has turned up many unpredictable twists and turns. The most visible example is the astonishing growth of the Internet. From small origins as a data network for a few thousand computer buffs 20 years ago, it is now a multimedia resource, available to hundreds of millions of users worldwide. Vinton Cerf, one of the Internet's early pioneers, predicts that the network will soon surpass global telephone systems in size and usage.

These changes are creating the conditions for an unprecedented event in human history. It is the prospect of an electronic network that will allow everyone on earth to communicate with one another. The implications are open-ended, multilayered and with few precedents to measure their impact. As noted above, the closest early-warning signs about this shift are found in the United States with its long lead in moving towards a universal information utility, increasingly available to most of its citizens.

Despite this progress, there is a dark side to this national evolution. It is most evident in a growing sense of information imbalances within U.S. society, separating a digitally savvy elite group from the rest of the country. Reviewing information age prospects, Brandeis University economist Robert Reich points out:

No longer are Americans rising and falling together, as if in one large boat. We are, increasingly, in different, smaller boats. The new elite is linked by jet, modem, fax, satellite and fiber-optic cable to the great commercial and recreational centers of the world, but it is not particularly connected with the rest of the nation.[71]

This digital imbalance is a critical part of the American agenda in the new century. Another element is the subject of this survey (i.e., the implications of the information revolution for American geopolitical interests). We have seen the evolution of digital issues, from small beginnings to a subject increasingly integrated into overall global policies. We still do not have a clearly defined view of the medium-range impacts of this change.

In recent years, a small cottage industry, peopled by academics and strategic planners, has been studying these implications. Among the early practitioners in this field were two Canadian scholars—Harold Innis and Marshall McLuhan. Innis challenged the idea that communications would lead to a democratic diffusion of power. He saw what he called the tragedy of modern culture as the influence of the electronic media in undermining space and time in the interests of commercial and political power.[72] McLuhan, whose name will forever be tied to the global village cliché, took a similarly skeptical view of the new electronic age. He was a pragmatic realist who recognized the threat as well as the promise of the new technologies. He pointed out that a global network could lead to a new tribalism, hindering rather than helping the open exchange of information and the mediation of human differences. In today's world of ethnic and creedal conflicts, his warning seems at least as important as his vision of an inclusive global village.[73]

Building on research about the emerging U.S. information economy, other scholars have begun to pin down some of the global implications of the shift. The discussion has been led largely by the economists, including Nobelist George Stigler, Peter Drucker and William Baumel. Stephen Cohen and John Zysman of the Berkeley Roundtable on the International Economy have warned that "hard goods" industrial production remains a critical part of the American ability to compete in the new international economy. The choice, they point out, is not between phasing out the traditional manufacturing base in favor of information-dependent services. The two sectors are inextricably linked in setting an American strategy for the new global economy. Instead of ceding industrial production to other countries, public policy should actively aim to convert low-production, low-skill production processes into high-technology, high-skill, high-wage activities, whether they are included in the manufacturing sector itself or counted largely as service activities.[74]

Other disciplines have been slower to probe the effect of information age changes on U.S. strategic interests. Peter Hugill, a geographer at Texas A&M, has made a useful broad-brush attempt to fit the new information realities into a world-system theory. Others have addressed the new digital environment's impact on the nation-state system. One group sees a rapid deterioration of the system in the new century. Others are more aware of the staying power of the system as the main repository of loyalty and legitimacy in a dangerous world. Half of the 190 countries in the United Nations were created in the last 40 years, based on a mix (often a precarious one) of ethnic, religious or other cultural identities.

Nevertheless, the nation-state system is under pressure from many sides. A major factor is the erosive influence of non-governmental activities on traditional sovereign prerogatives. The most visible of these is the loss of control over the value and movement of national currencies, now increasingly controlled by multinational financial groups using digital circuits to move over $1.2 trillion every day without hindrance. It is one example, among many others, of the ubiquitous influence of the new electronic information resources in limiting sovereign rights.

What pattern of nation-state relations will emerge in the new century? Political scientists such as Harvard's Joseph Nye are prepared to give information equal status with older economic and military resources in the new equation of power. In his perceptive work, *The end of the nation state*, French diplomat Jean-Marie Guéhenno views the information age as imperial in the sense of a virtual society too vast to constitute a political entity, a world that is at once unified and without a center. Global relationships, he argues, will be increasingly dominated by commercial institutions, using the power of information technology.[75]

James Rosenau of George Washington University sees traditional national boundaries replaced by what he calls "the Frontier," a new political space in which networking organizations are as important as hierarchical ones, in large part involving advanced information technologies. The underlying dynamic is a process in which the world is not so much a system dominated by nation-states as by congeries of spheres of authority that overtake the old divisions of territorial space. The result will be what Rosenau calls imagined communities, emerging as "engines of change, redesigners of boundaries and sources of power in the years ahead."[76] A fascinating foretaste of this was a 1999 decision by the Internet's international coordinating group to assign a Net domain name (.ps) to the Palestine National Authority, in effect giving the authority its own piece of real estate in cyberspace before it had achieved status as a full-fledged government.[77]

Whatever scenario of national sovereignty emerges in the new digital environment, it will be very different from today's realities. As Jessica Mathews, head of the Carnegie Endowment, points out:

National governments are not simply losing autonomy in a globalizing economy. They are sharing powers—including political, social and security roles at the core of sovereignty—with businesses, with international organizations, and with a multitude of citizen's groups, known as non-governmental organizations (NGOs). . . . The most powerful engine of change in the relative decline of states and the rise of nonstate actors is the computer and telecommunications revolution, whose deep political and social consequences have been almost completely ignored. Widely accessible and affordable technology has broken the governments' monopoly on the collection and management of large amounts of information and deprived governments of the deference they enjoyed because of it.[78]

As a result, Mathews notes, the new information resources multiply the number of players and reduce the number who command authority: "The effect on the loudest voice—which has been the government's—has been the greatest."

These projections of a digital future increasingly set the tone and direction of U.S. diplomacy. Their assumptions, and the issues with which they deal, are an increasingly important part of American geopolitical strategy in the new century.[79] Moreover, their impact cuts across every other foreign policy issue from nuclear proliferation to the environment. The result will be a different type of diplomacy, both in the problems it deals with and the way it is organized. It is a new, challenging orientation, one which fits comfortably with American ideals and interests. This includes, first and foremost, a commitment to an open information culture, at home and abroad, as we play our role in creating a post-industrial democratic world order.

NOTES

1. "Planning for the 21st century," *State Magazine*, June 1999, p. 46.

2. "The FSO who did it all," *Foreign Service Journal*, June 1998, p. 32.

3. Clifford Stoll, *Silicon snake oil* (New York: Doubleday, 1995), p. 128.

4. "World, wide, web: 3 English words," *New York Times*, 14 April 1996, p. E-1.

5. Wilson P. Dizard, *Meganet: How the global communications network will connect everyone on earth* (Boulder, CO: HarperCollins/Westview Press, 1997), p. 2.

6. Elizabeth L. Eisenstein, *The printing press as an agent of change* (New York: Cambridge University Press, 1979).

7. *Communications outlook 1999*, Science, Technology and Industry Directorate, Organization for Economic Cooperation and Development, Paris, March 1999.

8. For a summary of the IDC survey, see: "A world standard for measuring societies," *On the Internet*, March/April 1997, p. 15.

9. The evolution of the American hegemonic role in international communications is explored in Peter J. Hugill, *Global communications since 1844: Geopolitics and technology* (Baltimore, MD: Johns Hopkins University Press, 1999).

10. Interiew in "The revenge of the nerds," Public Broadcasting System documentary film, July 1996.

11. *Information resources policy: Arenas, players and stakes*, annual report of the Program in Information Resources Policy 1975–1976 (Harvard University, 1976), p. 4.

12. This uniquely American trait is explored in Leo Marx, *The machine in the garden* (New York: Oxford University Press, 1964).

13. The overall themes of the NII were outlined in a 36-page statement, "Technology for America's economic growth: A new direction to build economic strength," issued by the White House on 23 February 1993. For a useful survey of the early period of the project, see: Jonathan D. Blake and Lee J. Tiedrich, "The national information infrastructure initiative and the emergence of the electronic

superhighway," *Federal Communications Law Journal*, Vol. 46, No. 1, June 1994, pp. 397–432.

14. "Text of speech by Vice President Al Gore prepared for delivery at the International Telecommunications Union meeting in Buenos Aires, Argentina," White House Press Office release, 21 March 1994.

15. "Major program to 'migrate' to more modern computers is launched," *State Magazine*, March 1993, p. 15.

16. For a useful survey of State's information management reforms, see "Information resource management: A new bureau for a new era," *State Magazine*, October 1998, p. 36.

17. The CSIS study is *Reinventing diplomacy in the information age*, a report of the CSIS Advisory Panel on Diplomacy in the Information Age, Center for Strategic and International Studies. The Stimson study is *Equipped for the future: Managing U.S. foreign affairs in the 21st century*, report of the Project on Advocacy of U.S. Interests Abroad, Henry L. Stimson Center. Both studies were issued in Washington in December 1998.

18. CSIS report, op cit., p. 53.

19. The need to upgrade the State Department's communications system to deal specifically with terrorist threats to its installations abroad was stressed in *America's overseas presence in the 21st century*, report of the Overseas Presence Advisory Board, Department of State, 5 November 1999.

20. Stimson report, op cit., p. 6.

21. Warren P. Strobel, *Late-breaking foreign policy: The news media's influence on peace operations* (Washington, DC: U.S. Institute of Peace Press, 1997); also Nik Gowing, *Media coverage: Help or hindrance in conflict resolution?*, report to the Carnegie Commission on Preventing Deadly Conflict, Carnegie Corporation of New York, September 1997.

22. Claude Moisy, "Myths of the global information village," *Foreign Policy*, Summer 1997, p. 82.

23. For a description of these changes, see "Public affairs: Taking the 'foreign' out of foreign policy," *State Magazine*, January 1998, pp. 23–29.

24. "USIA merger moves public diplomacy closer to the policy center," *State Magazine*, September 1999, pp. 23–25. See also: "Thoughts on public diplomacy and integration," *State Magazine*, February–March 2000, pp. 12–17.

25. "U.S. creates news agency," *Washington Post*, 13 August 1999, p. A-23.

26. "Officials describe growth, modernization efforts at State," *State Magazine*, February 1998, p. 8.

27. "Digital economy has arrived, Commerce Department says," *New York Times Cybertimes*, 6 June 2000, p. 1.

28. Candice Stevens, "The knowledge-driven economy," *OECD Observer* (Paris), June/July 1996, p. 6.

29. "U.S. firms spin a Web worldwide," *Washington Post*, 13 March 2000, p. A-2.

30. "A growing force and going places," special supplement on South Asian software and services, *Financial Times* (London), 2 June 1999, p. 1.

31. "The elephant and the Pekinese," *The Economist* (London), 18 March 2000, p. 25.

32. "Climbing the value ladder," *Institutional Investor*, September 1999, p. 186.

33. "The new world of banking," *Finance & Development*, June 2000, pp. 41–44.

34. The growth of Internet-based electronic commerce is described in "The net imperative: A survey of business and the Internet," special supplement, *The Economist* (London), 26 June 1999.

35. "Internet's E-conomy gets real," *Washington Post*, 20 June 1999, p. A-17.

36. "Internet remarks boost IBM stocks," *Washington Post*, 14 May 1999, p. E-1.

37. "Tycoons spread Net fever to Europe," *Financial Times* (London), 7 July 1999.

38. This basic position, enunciated by the Clinton administration, is described in "A framework for global electronic commerce," issued by the White House in May 1996. The text can be found at www.iitf.nist.gov/eleccomm/ecomm.

39. For background on these electronics-related negotiations, see "USTR eyes commitments to open telecommunications markets," *International Telecommunications Report*, 12 November 1999; "International jurisdiction in cyberspace," *Federal Communications Law Journal*, Vol. 50, No. 1, December 1997, pp. 117–178; *The Internet and global telecommunications: Exploring the boundaries of international coordination* (Washington, DC: Aspen Institute, 1999).

40. The basic American and European negotiating positions, as well as that of Japan, are described in *Enabling electronic commerce: The U.S., E.U. and Japanese white papers* (Washington, DC: International Communications Studies Program, Center for Strategic and International Studies, July 1997).

41. "China braces for open trade bid," *Washington Post*, 11 September 1999, p. E-1.

42. Quoted in "The road to 2050," special supplement, *The Economist* (London), 31 July 1999, p. 9.

43. Heather E. Hudson, "Development and the globalization of cyberspace," *Annual Review of the Institute for Information Studies* (Washington, DC: Aspen Institute, 1998), pp. 129–147.

44. "Dirty money goes digital," *Business Week*, 20 September 1999, p. 128.

45. *The missing link*, report of the Independent Commission for Worldwide Telecommunications Development, International Telecommunications Union, Geneva, 1984. Sir Donald Maitland, a retired British diplomat, was chairman of the commission.

46. This represented a change in the bank's practices, which had focussed on funding government telecommunications projects. For background on the bank's earlier activities, see: "Telecommunications: World Bank experience and strategy," Discussion Paper No. 192, March 1993. More recent developments are described in the bank's *World development report 1998/99* (New York: Oxford University Press, 1999).

47. "World Bank to join in Internet startup finance," *New York Times*, 14 February 2000, p. C-6.

48. "Brazilians take to the Web with uncommon speed," *New York Times*, 28 June 1999, p. C-2.

49. "Africa offline," *Wired*, May 1998, p. 82.

50. "An unlikely net alliance," *Washington Post*, 12 August 1999, p. E-1.

51. *War in the pits*, Report No. 61, Institute for National Strategic Studies, National Defense University, Washington, DC, February 1996, p. 1.

52. John Arquilla and David Ronfeldt, "Cyberwar and netwar," in *Rand Research Review* (Santa Monica, CA: Rand Corporation, Fall 1995), p. 8.

53. Both the Defense Department and AT&T discouraged any discussion of this arrangement at the time for security reasons. A useful overview of the subject can be found in "Basic telecommunications offerings affecting U.S. national security and survival," SRI Project 1232, Strategic Studies Center, SRI International, Arlington, VA, September 1980.

54. The literature on information warfare is vast, and constantly expanding. For an overview, see: James Adams, *The next world war: Computers are weapons and the front line is everywhere* (New York: Simon & Schuster, 1998); Ryan Henry and C. Edward Peartree (eds.), *The information revolution and national security* (Washington, DC: CSIS Press, 1998).

55. "Conflict in the digital age," *CSIS Chronicle* (Washington, DC: Center for Strategic and International Studies, February 1997), p. 2.

56. "Hackers spur Pentagon to bolster its security," *Washington Post*, 2 June 1999, p. A-2. See also: "Bringing down the Internet," *Scientific American*, May 1998, p. 45.

57. "Hacktivism: An emerging threat to diplomacy," *Foreign Service Journal*, September 2000, p. 43.

58. "Diplomatic consquences of the coming revolution in military affairs," *Foreign Service Journal*, September 1998, p. 24.

59. "Clinton plan targets 'cyber-terrorism'," *Washington Post*, 8 January 2000, p. E-8.

60. For a useful survey of international human rights, see: "The world is watching: A survey of human-rights laws," special supplement, *The Economist* (London), 5 December 1998.

61. For a discussion of the Internet's role in human rights, see: Andrew L. Shapiro, "The Internet," *Foreign Policy*, Summer 1999, pp. 14–26.

62. "In a spin over the Web," *Washington Post*, 26 July 1999, p. A-13; "The Internet changing dictatorship's rules," *New York Times*, August 1999, p. WK-1.

63. "3G mobile multimedia," research report, Kalba International, Waltham, MA, January 2000.

64. Milton Mueller and Zixiang Tan, *China in the information age: Telecommunications and the dilemma of reform* (Westport, CT: Praeger Publishers, 1996).

65. "China trying to crack down on vocal liberal intellectuals," *New York Times*, 8 May 2000, p. A-1.

66. "Betting Beijing can't control cyberspace," *Business Week*, 4 October 1999, p. 38.

67. "China puts clamp on Internet," *Washington Post*, 27 January 2000, p. 1.

68. Anne W. Branscomb, *Who owns information?* (New York: Basic Books, 1994).

69. These implications of the Asian financial crisis are discussed in David J. Rothkopf, "The disinformation age," *Foreign Policy*, Spring 1999, pp. 83–96.

70. These developments are discussed in Hugill, op cit., pp. 223–251.

71. "Secession of the successful," *New York Times Magazine*, 20 January 1991, p. 16.

72. Harold Innis, *Empire and communications* (Toronto: University of Toronto Press, 1972).

73. Marshall McLuhan, *The Gutenburg galaxy* (Toronto: University of Toronto Press, 1962).

74. Stephen S. Cohen and John Zysman, *Manufacturing matters: The myth of the post-industrial economy* (New York: Basic Books, 1987).

75. Jean-Marie Guéhenno, *The end of the nation state* (Minneapolis: University of Minnesota Press, 1995).

76. James Rosenau, *Along the domestic-foreign frontier: Exploring governance in a turbulent world* (New York: Cambridge University Press, 1997).

77. "Web domain to be assigned for Palestinian territory," *New York Times*, 6 December 1999, p. PC-10.

78. Jessica T. Mathews, "Power shift," *Foreign Affairs*, January–February 1997, p. 51.

79. *Cyberocracy, cyberspace and cyberology: Political effects of the information revolution*, Report P-7745 (Santa Monica, CA: Rand Corporation, 1991). See also: "The future of the state," special supplement, *The Economist* (London), 20 September 1997.

Selected Bibliography

Academy for Educational Development. *The United States and the debate over the world information order*. Washington, DC, June 1979.

Adams, James. *The next world war: Computers are the weapons and the front line is everywhere*. New York: Simon & Schuster, 1998.

Alleyne, Mark D. *News revolution: Political and economic decisions about global information*. New York: St. Martin's Press, 1996.

Aronson, Jonathan and Peter F. Cowhey. *When countries talk: International trade in communications services*. Cambridge, MA: Ballinger Publishing Co., 1987.

Aspen Institute. *A national information network: Changing our lives in the 21st century*. Washington, DC, 1992.

————. *The knowledge economy: The nature of innovation in the 21st century*. Washington, DC, 1994.

————. *The future of community and personal identity in the coming electronic culture*. Washington, DC, 1995.

————. *The emerging Internet*. Washington, DC, 1998.

————. *Towards sustainable competition in global telecommunications: From principle to practice*. Washington, DC, 1999.

————. *New world, new realities: The remaining roles of government in international telecommunications*. Washington, DC, 2000.

Barghoorn, Frederick C. *Soviet foreign propaganda*. Princeton, NJ: Princeton University Press, 1964.

Barrett, Edward W. *Truth is our weapon*. New York: Funk & Wagnalls, 1953.

Beniger, James R. *The control revolution: Technological and economic origins of the information society*. Cambridge, MA: Harvard University Press, 1989.

Betz, Cynthia. *The borderless economy: Global trade, rules and the Internet*. Washington, DC: AEI Press, 1999.

Blatherwick, David E. S. *The international politics of telecommunications*. Institute of International Studies, University of California, Berkeley, 1987.

Boli, John and George W. Thomas. *Constructing world culture: International non-governmental organizations since 1875.* Stanford, CA: Stanford University Press, 1998.

Boyle, James. *Shamans, software and pleens: Law and the construction of the information society.* Cambridge, MA: Harvard Business School Press, 1994.

Bradley, Stephen P., Jerry F. Hausman and Richard L. Nolan (eds.). *Globalization, technology and competition: The fusion of computers and telecommunications in the 1990s.* Cambridge, MA: Harvard Business School Press, 1999.

Branscomb, Anne (ed.). *Towards a law of global communications networks.* New York: Longman Publishers, 1986.

———. *Who owns information? From privacy to public access.* New York: Basic Books, 1994.

Browne, Donald R. *International radio broadcasting: The limits of the limitless medium.* New York: Praeger Publishers, 1982.

Bruce, Robert R., Jeffrey P. Cunard and Mark Director (eds.). *From telecommunications to electronic services: A global spectrum of definitions, boundary limits and structures.* Report of the Study of Telecommunications Structures. International Institute of Communications. London: Butterworth Publishers, 1986.

Brzezinski, Zbigniew. *Between two ages: America's role in the technotronic era.* New York: Viking Press, 1970.

Burnham, David. *The rise of the computer state.* New York: Random House, 1983.

Cable, Vincent and Catherine Distler. *Global superhighway.* London: Royal Institute of International Telecommunications Policy, 1995.

Cafruny, Alan W. and Glenda M. Rosenthal. *The state of the European Community: The Maastricht debates and beyond.* Boulder, CO: Lynne Rienner Publishers, 1993.

Carey, James (ed.). *Communications as culture: Essays on media and society.* Boston: Unwin Hyman, 1989.

Carnegie Endowment for International Peace. *Personnel for the new diplomacy.* Report of the Committee on Foreign Affairs Personnel, Washington, DC, December 1962.

Carnoy, Martin, Manuel Castells, Stephen S. Sohen and Fernando Henrique Cardoso. *The new global economy in the information age: Reflections on our changing world.* University Park, PA: Pennsylvania State University Press, 1993.

Cass, Ronald A. and John Haring. *International trade in telecommunications.* Washington, DC: American Enterprise Institute Press, 1998.

Center for Strategic and International Studies. *Enabling electronic commerce: The U.S., E.U. and Japanese white papers.* International Communications Studies Program. Washington, DC, July 1997.

———. *Cybercrime, cyberterrorism, cyberwarfare: Averting an electronic Waterloo.* Report of the CSIS Global Organized Crime Project, May 1998.

———. *Reinventing diplomacy in the information age.* Report of the CSIS Advisory Panel on Diplomacy in the Information Age. Washington, DC, December 1998.

Charles, Carol. *Building the global information economy.* Washington, DC: Global Information Infrastructure Commission, Center for Strategic and International Studies, September 1998.

Christensen, Clayton M. *The innovator's dilemma*. Cambridge, MA: Harvard Business School Press, 1997.

Clark, Keith C. and Laurence J. Legere (eds.). *The president and the management of national security*. "A report by the Institute for Defense Analysis." New York: Frederick A. Praeger, 1969.

Clarke, Arthur C. *Voices across the sea*. London: William Luscombe Publishers, 1958.

Codding, George A., Jr. and Anthony M. Rutkowski. *The International Telecommunications Union in a changing world*. Dedham, MA: Artech House, 1982.

Collins, Richard. *New media, new policies: Media and communications for the future*. New York: Polity Press, 1996.

Commission on the Organization of the Government for the Conduct of Foreign Policy. *Final report*. Washington, DC: U.S. Government Printing Office, June 1975.

Compaine, Benjamin M. and William H. Read (eds.). *The information resources policy handbook*. Cambridge, MA: MIT Press, 1999.

Conner, Edward (ed.). *The political economy of communications*. London: Macmillan, 1994.

Coyle, Diane. *The weightless world: Strategies for managing the digital economy*. Cambridge, MA: MIT Press, 1998.

Crandall, Robert. *After the breakup: U.S. telecommunications in a more competitive era*. Washington, DC: Brookings Institution, 1991.

Darling, Arthur B. *Central Intelligence Agency: An instrument of government*. University Park: Pennsylvania State University Press, 1996.

Deibert, Ronald. *Parchment, printing and hypermedia: Communications in world order transformation*. New York: Columbia University Press, 1986.

Demac, Donna (ed.). *Tracing new orbits: Cooperation and competition in global satellite development*. New York: Columbia University Press, 1986.

Deutsch, Karl W. *The nerves of government: Models of political communications and control*. Glencoe, IL: Free Press of Glencoe, 1963.

Didrich, Jason and Kenneth L. Kraemer. *Asia's computer challenge: Threat or opportunity for the United States and the world?* New York: Oxford University Press, 1998.

Dizard, Wilson P. *Strategy of truth: The story of the U.S. Information Agency*. Washington, DC: Public Affairs Press, 1961.

———. *Television: A world view*. Syracuse, NY: Syracuse University Press, 1966.

———. *Gorbachev's information revolution: Controlling glasnost in a new electronic era*. Significant Issues Series, Vol. 9, No. 8, Center for Strategic and International Studies. Boulder, CO: Westview Press, 1987.

———. *The Coming information age*. 3rd ed. New York: Longman Publishers, 1989.

———. *Meganet: How the global communications network will connect everyone on earth*. Boulder, CO: HarperCollins/Westview Press, 1997.

———. *Old media, new media: Mass communications in the information age*. 3rd ed. New York: Longman Publishers, 2000.

Doob, Leonard. *Public opinion and propaganda*. London: Cresset Press, 1949.

Dordick, Hebert S., Helen G. Bradley and Bert Nanus. *The emerging network marketplace*. Norwood, NJ: Ablex, 1981.

Drake, William J. (ed.). *The new information infrastructure: Strategies for U.S. policy*. New York: Twentieth Century Fund Press, 1995.

Dryden, Stephen. *Trade warriors: The U.S. trade representative and the American crusade for free trade*. New York: Oxford University Press, 1995.

Dye, Thomas R., S. Robert Lichter and L. Harmon Ziegler. *American politics in the media age*. New York: Brooke/Cole Publishers, 1997.

Eban, Abba. *Diplomacy for the next century*. New Haven, CT: Yale University Press, 1999.

Edelstein, Alex S. *Total propaganda: From mass culture to popular culture*. Mahwah, NJ: Lawrence Erlbaum Associates, 1997.

Ellis, Frank. *From glasnost to the Internet: Russia's new infosphere*. New York: St. Martin's Press, 1998.

Estabrooks, Maurice. *Programmed capitalism: A computer-mediated society*. Armonk, NY: M. E. Sharpe, 1988.

Etheridge, Lloyd S. *Politics in wired nations: Selected writings of Ithiel de Sola Pool*. New Brunswick, NJ: Transaction Publishers, 1998.

European Community. *Towards a competitive community-wide telecommunications market in 1992*. Document COM (88) 48. Commission of the European Communities. Brussels, February 1988.

Everard, Jerry. *Virtual states: The Internet and the boundaries of the nation state*. New York: Routledge, 1999.

Eward, Ronald S. *The deregulation of international telecommunications*. Dedham, MA: Artech House, 1985.

Feketekuty, Geza. *International trade in services: An overview and blueprint for negotiations*. Cambridge, MA: Ballinger Publishing Co., 1988.

Feketekuty, Geza and Bruce Stokes (eds.). *Three strategies for a new era: Ensuring U.S. leadership in a global economy*. Monterey, CA: Monterey Institute of International Studies, 1998.

Forester, Tom. *The information technology revolution*. Cambridge, MA: MIT Press, 1985.

Frankel, Max. *Media madness: The revolution so far*. Communications and Society Program. Washington, DC: Aspen Institute, 1999.

Friedman, Thomas L. *The Lexus and the olive tree*. New York: Farrar, Straus & Giroux, 1999.

Gaddis, John Lewis. *Strategies of containment*. New York: Oxford University Press, 1982.

Ganley, Oswald and Gladys Ganley. *To inform or control? The new communications networks*. New York: McGraw-Hill Publishers, 1982.

Garrison, William B., Christopher P. Foss and Carol Charles (eds.). *The WTO telecom agreements: Engineering the global information highway*. Washington, DC: Center for Strategic and International Studies, 1997.

Garrison, William B. and Peter S. Watson. *National conformity assessment schemes: Non-tariff trade barriers in information technology*. Washington, DC: Center for Strategic and International Studies, November 1999.

Gaster, Robin et al. *Bit by bit: Building a transatlantic partnership for the information age*. Armonk, NY: M. E. Sharpe, 1996.

Georgetown University Law Center. *Issues in international telecommunications*. Washington, DC, May 1983.

Gerbner, George and Marsha Siefert (eds.). *World communications: A handbook*. New York: Longman Publishers, 1984.

Gershon, Richard A. *The transnational media corporation: Global messages and free market competition*. Mahwah, NJ: Lawrence Erlbaum Associates, 1996.

Global Information Infrastructure Commission. *National information infrastructures for social and economic development in Asia*. Washington, DC: Center for Strategic and International Studies, November 1995.

————. *Globalizing electronic commerce*. GIIC report on the international forum on electronic commerce, Beijing, November 1996.

————. *Preparing India for the global information infrastructure*. March 1997.

————. *Building the global infrastructure*. October 1998.

Gonzalez-Manet, Enrique. *The hidden war of information*. Norwood, NJ: Ablex, 1988.

Gowing, Nik. *Media coverage: Help or hindrance in conflict resolution?* Report to the Carnegie Commission on Preventing Deadly Conflict. Carnegie Corporation of New York, September 1997.

Graff, Robert D. *Communications for national development*. Cambridge, MA: Oelgeschlager, Gunn & Hain, 1983.

Granger, John V. *Technology and international relations*. San Francisco: W. H. Freeman & Co., 1979.

Gross, Peter. *Continuing the inquiry: The Council on Foreign Relations from 1921 to 1996*. New York: Council on Foreign Relations, 1996.

————. *Operation rollback: America's secret war behind the iron curtain*. New York: Houghton Mifflin, 2000.

Guéhenno, Jean-Marie. *The end of the nation state*. Minneapolis: University of Minnesota Press, 1995.

Hafner, Katie and Matthew Lyons. *Where wizards stay up late: The origins of the Internet*. New York: Simon & Schuster, 1996.

Hague, Barry N. and Brian D. Loader. *Digital democracy*. New York: Routledge, 1999.

Hansen, Allen C. *Public diplomacy in the computer age*. New York: Praeger Publishers, 1989.

Harlow, Giles D. and George C. Maerz (eds.). *Measures short of war: The George F. Kennan lectures at the National War College*. Washington, DC: National Defense University Press, 1991.

Harper, Christopher. *And that's the way it will be: News and information in a digital world*. New York: New York University Press, 1998.

Headrick, Daniel R. *The invisible weapon: Telecommunications and international politics 1851–1945*. New York: Oxford University Press, 1991.

Henry, Ryan and C. Edward Peartree (eds.). *The information revolution and national security*. Washington, DC: CSIS Press, 1998.

Henry L. Stimson Center. *Equipped for the future: Managing U.S. foreign affairs in the 21st century*. Washington, DC, October 1998.

Herman, Edward S. and Robert W. McChesney. *The global media: The new missionaries of corporate capitalism*. London: Cassell, 1997.

Hills, Jill. *Deregulating telecommunications: Competition and control in the U.S., Japan and Britain*. London: Frances Pinter, 1986.

Hills, Jill and Stylianos Papathassopoulos. *The democracy gap: The politics of infor-

mation and communications in the United States and Europe. Westport, CT: Greenwood Press, 1991.

Hixson, Walter L. *Parting the curtain: Propaganda, culture and the cold war 1945–1961.* New York: St. Martin's Press, 1985.

Hoffman, Arthur S. (ed.). *International communications and the new diplomacy.* Bloomington: Indiana University Press, 1968.

Holt, Robert T. and Robert W. van de Velde. *Strategic psychological operations and American foreign policy.* Chicago: University of Chicago Press, 1960.

Horton, Philip C. *The Third World and press freedom.* New York: Praeger Publishers, 1978.

Hudson, Heather. *When telephones reach the village.* Norwood, NJ: Ablex, 1983.

————. *A bibliography of telecommunications and socio-economic development.* Norwood, MA: Artech House, 1988.

Hufbauer, Gary C. and Jeffrey J. Schott. *NAFTA: An assessment.* Washington, DC: Institute for International Economics, 1993.

Hufbauer, Gary Clyde and Erika Wada. *Unfinished business: Telecommunications after the Uruguay Round.* Washington, DC: Institute of International Economics, 1997.

Hugill, Peter J. *Global communications since 1844: Geopolitics and technology.* Baltimore, MD: Johns Hopkins University Press, 1999.

Innis, Harold A. *Empire and communications.* Toronto: University of Toronto Press, 1972.

Institute for Defense Analysis. *The national security process.* Report R-150. Vols. 1 & 2. Washington, DC, November 1968.

Institute for the Study of Diplomacy. *The foreign service in 2001.* Washington, DC: School of Foreign Service, Georgetown University, August 1992.

International encyclopaedia of communications. 4 vols. New York: Oxford University Press, 1988.

International Law Institute, Georgetown University Law Center. *Issues in international telecommunications: A source book.* Washington, DC, May 1983.

International Telecommunications Union. *The missing link.* Report of the Independent Commission for Worldwide Communications Development. Geneva, 1984.

Jervis, Robert. *The logic of images in international relations.* New York: Columbia University Press, 1989.

Journal of International Affairs. "Technology and international policy: Essays on the information age." Special issue, Vol. 51, no. 2, Spring 1998.

Jussawalla, Meheroo. *Information technology and global interdependence.* Westport, CT: Greenwood Press, 1988.

Jusssawalla, Meheroo, Donald Lamberton and Neil Karanaratne. *The cost of thinking: Information economies of ten Pacific countries.* Norwood, NJ: Ablex, 1988.

Katz, Daniel (ed.). *Public opinion and propaganda: A book of readings.* Society for the Psychological Study of Social Issues. New York: Dryden Press, 1954.

Katz, Raul. *The information society: An international perspective.* New York: Praeger Publishers, 1988.

Keck, Margaret E. and Kathryn Sikkink. *Activists beyond borders: Advocacy networks in international politics.* Ithaca, NY: Cornell University Press, 1998.

Kerry, Richard J. *The star-spangled mirror*. Savage, MD: Rowman and Littlefield, 1990.

Kovach, Bill and Tom Rosentiel. *Warp speed: America in the age of mixed media*. New York: Century Foundation Press, 1999.

Kubichek, Herbert, William H. Dutton and Robin Williams (eds.). *The social shaping of information highways*. New York: St. Martin's Press, 1997.

Lancaster, Carol. *Aid to Africa: So much to do, so little done*. Chicago: University of Chicago Press, 1998.

Laurie, Clayton D. *The propaganda warriors: America's crusade against Nazi Germany*. Lawrence: University Press of Kansas, 1996.

Lawton, Thomas. *Technology and the new diplomacy: The creation and control of EC industrial policy for semiconductors*. Brookfield, VT: Ashgate Publishers, 1997.

Leeson, Kenneth. *International communications: Blueprint for policy*. New York: North Holland Press, 1984.

Lerner, Daniel. *The passing of traditional society: Modernizing the Middle East*. Glencoe, IL: The Free Press, 1958.

Levinson, Paul. *Digital McLuhan: A guide to the information millenium*. New York: Routledge, 1999.

Libicki, Martin C. *What is information warfare?* Washington, DC: National Defense .University Press, 1995.

Lilly, Edward P. "The development of American psychological operations 1945–1951." In *Declassified documents reference systems*. Vol. 1. Washington, DC: Carrollton Press, 1989.

Lippmann, Walter. *Public opinion*. New York: Harcourt Brace & Co., 1922.

Luttwak, Edward. *Turbo capitalism: Winners and losers in the global economy*. New York: HarperCollins, 1999.

Maddox, Brenda. *Beyond Babel*. New York: Simon & Schuster, 1972.

Manheim, Jarol B. *Strategic public diplomacy and American foreign policy*. New York: Oxford University Press, 1994.

Mansell, Robin and Roger Silverstein (eds.). *Communications by design: The politics of information and communications technologies*. New York: Oxford University Press, 1996.

Mansell, Robin and Uta When (eds.). *Knowledge societies: Information technology for sustainable development*. New York: Oxford University Press, 1998.

Marvin, Carolyn. *When old technologies were new*. New York: Oxford University Press, 1988.

Massachusetts Institute of Technology. *Proceedings of the symposium on world telecommunications policy*. Department of Political Science, Cambridge, MA, January 27–28, 1988.

Mattelart, Armand and Hector Schmucler. *Communications and information technologies: Freedom of choice for Latin America?* Norwood, NJ: Ablex, 1985.

Mazarr, Michael. *Global trends 2005: An owner's manual for the next decade*. Washington, DC: CSIS Press, 1999.

McChesney, Robert W. *Corporate media and the threat to democracy*. New York: Seven Stories Press, 1997.

———. *Rich media, poor democracy: Communications politics in dubious times*. Champaign: University of Illinois Press, 1999.

McChesney, Robert W., Ellen Meiksins Wood and John Bellamy Foster. *Capitalism and the information age: The political economy of the global communications revolution*. New York: Monthly Review Press, 1997.

McDowell, Stephen P. *Globalization, liberalization and policy change: A political economy of India's communications sector*. New York: St. Martin's Press, 1997.

McKnight, Lee W. and Joseph P. Bailey. *Internet economics*. Cambridge, MA: MIT Press, 1997.

McPhail, Thomas L. *Electronic colonialism: The future of international broadcasting and communication*. Beverly Hills, CA: Sage Publications, 1981.

Merritt, Richard L. and Bruce M. Russett. *From national development to global community: Essays in honor of Karl W. Deutsch*. London: Allen & Unwin, 1981.

Mestmacher, Ernst-Joachim. *The law and economics of transborder communications*. Baden-Baden, Germany: Nomos Vertagsgesellschaft, 1997.

Miller, Teven E. and Thomas L. Stone (eds.). *Civilizing cyberspace: Policy, power and the information superhighway*. Reading, MA: Addison-Wesley, 1996.

Millikan, Max F. and Donald L. M. Blackmer. *The emerging nations: Their growth and United States policy*. Boston: Little, Brown & Co., 1961.

Milner, Helen V. *Interests, institutions and information*. Princeton, NJ: Princeton University Press, 1997.

Miscamble, Wilson D. *George F. Kennan and the making of American foreign policy 1947–1950*. Princeton, NJ: Princeton University Press, 1992.

Mitchell, J. M. *International cultural relations*. London: Allen & Unwin, 1986.

Mitrovich, Gregory P. *Undermining the Kremlin: America's strategy for subverting the Soviet bloc 1947–1950*. Ithaca, NY: Cornell University Press, 2000.

Mody, Bella, Johannes Bauer and Joseph D. Straubhaar (eds.). *Telecommunications politics: Ownership and control of the information highway in developing countries*. Mahwah, NJ: Lawrence Erlbaum Associates, 1995.

Molander, Roger C., Andrew S. Riddile and Peter A. Wilson. *Strategic information warfare: A new face of war*. Santa Monica, CA: Rand Corporation, 1996.

Mosco, Vincent and Janet Wasko (eds.). *The political economy of information*. Madison: University of Wisconsin Press, 1988.

Mosley, Leonard. *Dulles*. New York: Dial Press, 1978.

Mowlana, Hamid. *International communications: A selected bibliography*. Dubuque, IA: Kendall/Hunt Publishing Co., 1971.

———. *Global communications in transition: The end of diversity?* Thousand Oaks, CA: Sage Publications, 1996.

Muravchik, Joshua. *Exporting American democracy: Fulfilling America's destiny*. Washington, DC: American Enterprise Institute, 1991.

Muskens, George and Jacob Pruppelaar (eds.). *Global communications networks: Strategic considerations*. Norwell, MA: Kluwer Academic Publishers, 1988.

National Academy of Science. *The unpredictable certainty: Information infrastructure through the year 2000*. Computer Science and Telecommunications Board. Washington, DC: National Academy of Science Press, 1996.

———. *The evolution of untethered communications*. Computer Science and Telecommunications Board. Washington, DC: National Academy of Science Press, 1997.

Neuman, Johanna. *Lights, camera, war: Is media technology driving international politics?* New York: St. Martin's Press, 1996.

Ninkovich, Frank A. *The diplomacy of ideas: U.S. foreign policy and cultural relations 1938–1950*. New York: Cambridge University Press, 1981.

Nora, Simon and Alain Minc. *The computerization of society: A report to the president of France*. Cambridge, MA: MIT Press, 1981.

Norman, Albert. *Our German policy: Propaganda and culture*. New York: Vantage Press, 1951.

O'Donnell, James J. *Avatars of the word: From papyrus to cyberspace*. Cambridge, MA: Harvard University Press, 1999.

O'Hanlon, Michael. *Technological change and the future of warfare*. Washington, DC: Brookings Institution Press, 1999.

Organization for Economic Cooperation and Development (OECD). *Proceedings of the conference on communications/telecommunications policy: February 4–6 1975*. Paris, 1976.

———. *Organization for economic cooperation and development*. Vol. 12, Information, Communications and Computer Series. New York: Elsevier Science Publishers, 1987.

———. *The role of telecommunications and information infrastructure in advanced electronic commerce*. Working paper for the 1998 OECD Ottawa conference. Paris, 1998.

———. *Communications outlook*. 5th ed. March 1999.

Page, Caroline. *U.S. official propaganda during the Vietnam War: The limits of official persuasion*. London: Leicester University Press, 1996.

Pells, Richard. *Not like us: How Europeans have loved, hated and transformed American culture since World War II*. New York: HarperCollins, 1997.

Pelton, Joseph N. *Intelsat: Politics and functionalism*. Mt. Airy, MD: Lomond Books, 1974.

———. *Global talk*. Rockville, MD: Sijthoff & Noordhoff, 1981.

Pelton, Joseph N. and Marcellus Snow. *The economic and policy problems in satellite communications*. New York: Praeger Publishers, 1977.

Pettrazini, Ben A. *The political economy of telecommunications reform in developing countries: Privatization and liberalization in comparative perspective*. Westport, CT: Praeger Publishers, 1995.

Pierce, William and Nicholas Jequier. *Telecommunications for development*. Geneva: International Telecommunications Union, 1983.

Pletcher, William and Nicholas Jequier. *The diplomacy of trade and investments: American economic expansion in the hemisphere 1865–1900*. Columbia: University of Missouri Press, 1998.

Ploman, Edward W. *International law governing communications and information*. London: Frances Pinter, 1982.

Pool, Ithiel de Sola. *The technologies of freedom*. Cambridge, MA: Harvard University Press, 1983.

Prados, John. *Presidents' secret wars*. New York: Morrow & Co., 1986.

Price, Harry Bayard. *The Marshall Plan and its meaning*. Ithaca, NY: Cornell University Press, 1955.

Pye, Lucian W. (ed.). *Communications and political development*. Princeton, NJ: Princeton University Press, 1962.

Read, William. *Foreign policy: The high and low politics of telecommunications*. Publication P-76-3. Cambridge, MA: Program on Information Technologies and Public Policy, Harvard University, 1976.

Reich, Cary. *The life and times of Nelson A. Rockefeller: Worlds to conquer 1908–1958.* New York: Doubleday, 1996.

Remington, Thomas W. *The truth of authority: Ideological communications in the Soviet Union.* Pittsburgh, PA: University of Pittsburgh Press, 1988.

Riegal, O. W. *Mobilizing for chaos: The story of the new propaganda.* New Haven, CT: Yale University Press, 1934.

Riordan, Michael and Lillian Hoddeson (eds.). *Crystal fire: The birth of the information age.* New York: W. W. Norton & Co., 1997.

Robinson, Peter, Karl P. Sauvant and Vishwas P. Govitrikar (eds.). *Electronic highways for world trade: Issues in telecommunications and date services.* Boulder, CO: Westview Press, 1989.

Rosenau, James N. *Along the domestic-foreign frontier: Exploring governance in a turbulent world.* New York: Cambridge University Press, 1997.

Sapolsky, Harvey M., Rhonda J. Crane and Eli M. Noam (eds.). *The telecommunications revolution: Past, present and future.* New York: Routledge, 1993.

Saunders, Robert, Jeremy Warford and Bjorn Wellenius. *Telecommunications and economic development.* Baltimore, MD: Johns Hopkins University Press, 1984.

Sauvant, Karl P. *International transactions in services: The politics of transborder data flows.* Boulder, CO: Westview Press, 1986.

Savage, James G. *The politics of international telecommunications regulation.* Boulder, CO: Westview Press, 1989.

Schapiro, Andrew L. *The control revolution: How the Internet is putting individuals in charge and changing the world we know.* New York: Public Affairs Press, 1999.

Schiller, Dan. *Digital capitalism: Networking the global market system.* Cambridge, MA: MIT Press, 1999.

Schramm, Wilbur. *Mass media and national development.* Stanford, CA: Stanford University Press, 1964.

Schwartzstein, Stuart J. D. (ed.). *The information revolution and national security: Dimensions and directions.* Washington, DC: Center for Strategic and International Studies, 1996.

Seib, Philip. *Headline diplomacy: How news coverage affects foreign policy.* New York: St. Martin's Press, 1996.

Sell, Susan K. *Power and ideas: North-south politics of intellectual property and antitrust.* Albany, NY: SUNY Press, 1998.

Serfaty, Simon. *The media and foreign policy.* New York: St. Martin's Press, 1990.

Shulman, Holly Cowan. *The voice of America: Propaganda and democracy 1941–1945.* Madison: University of Wisconsin Press, 1990.

Sidak, J. Gregory. *Foreign investment in American telecommunications.* Chicago: University of Chicago Press, 1997.

Simpson, Christopher. *Science of coercion: Communications research and psychological warfare 1945–1960.* New York: Oxford University Press, 1994.

Skolnikoff, Eugene B. *The elusive transformation: Science, technology and the evolution of international politics.* Princeton, NJ: Princeton University Press, 1994.

Slack, Jennifer D. and Fred Fejes (eds.). *The ideology of the information age*. Norwood, NJ: Ablex, 1987.

Small, Melvin. *Democracy & diplomacy: The impact of domestic politics on U.S. foreign policy 1789–1994*. Baltimore, MD: Johns Hopkins University Press, 1996.

Smith, Delbert D. *International telecommunications control: International law and the ordering of satellite and other forms of international broadcasting*. Leyden, The Netherlands: A. W. Sijthoff, 1969.

Smith, Paul A. *On political war*. Washington, DC: National Defense University Press, 1989.

Smith, Peter L. and Gregory Staple. *Telecommunications sector reform in Asia: Towards a new pragmatism*. Washington, DC: The World Bank, 1994.

Snow, Marcellus S. (ed.). *Marketplace for telecommunications: Regulation and deregulation in industrialized democracies*. New York: Longman Publishers, 1985.

Snow, Marcellus S. and Meheroo Jussawalla. *Telecommunications economics and international regulatory policy: An annotated bibliography*. Westport, CT: Greenwood Press, 1986.

Soley, Lawrence C. *Radio warfare: OSS and CIA subversive propaganda*. New York: Praeger Publishers, 1989.

Stanford Research Institute. *Study on international telecommunications policies, technology and economics*. SRI project 5400. Stanford, CA, May 1966.

Staple, Gregory (ed.). *Telegeography 2000: Global telecommunications traffic and commentary*. Annual series. Washington, DC: Telegeography Inc., 1999.

Steele, Richard W. *Propaganda in an open society: The Roosevelt administration and the media 1933–1940*. Westport, CT: Greenwood Press, 1985.

Stephens, Oren. *Facts to a candid world: America's overseas information programs*. Stanford, CA: Stanford University Press, 1955.

Sterling, Christopher (ed.). *Telecommunications and information policy*. Washington, DC: Communications Press, 1984.

Stewart, Frances. *Technology and underdevelopment*. New York: Macmillan, 1977.

Strange, Susan. *The retreat from the state: The diffusion of power in the world economy*. New York: Cambridge University Press, 1996.

Strobel, Warren. *Late-breaking foreign policy: The news media's influence on peace operations*. Washington, DC: USIP Press, 1997.

Taylor, Philip M. *Global communications, international affairs and the media since 1945*. New York: Routledge, 1997.

Tehranain, Majid. *Global communications and world politics: Domination, development and discourse*. Boulder, CO: Lynne Rienner Publishers, 1999.

Thomson, Charles A. H. *Overseas information services of the United States government*. Washington, DC: Brookings Institution, 1948.

Tomlinson, John. *Cultural imperialism: A critical introduction*. Baltimore, MD: Johns Hopkins University Press, 1991.

Toulouse, Chris and Timothy W. Locke. *The politics of cyberspace*. New York: Routledge, 1998.

Traber, Michael (ed.). *The myth of the information revolution*. Newbury Park, CA: Sage Publications, 1986.

Troy, Thomas F. *Donovan and the CIA*. Frederick, MD: University Publications of America, 1981.

United Nations Development Program (UNDP). *Human development report 1999.* New York: Oxford University Press, 1999.

United States Congress. General Accounting Office. *Information highway: An overview of technical challenges.* Report GAO/AIMD-95-23, January 1995.

United States Congress. Office of Technology Assessment. *Critical connections: Communication for the Future.* Report OTA-CIT-407, January 1990.

———. *Electronic enterprises: Looking to the future.* Report OTA-TCT-600, May 1994.

———. *Global communications: Opportunities for trade and aid.* Report OTA-ITC-642, September 1995.

United States Institute for Peace. *Keynote addresses from the Virtual Diplomacy conference.* Peaceworks No. 18. Washington, DC, September 1997.

United States International Trade Commission. *Global competitiveness of the U.S. computer software and service industries.* Staff research study no. 21, June 1995.

U.S. Department of Commerce. National Telecommunications and Information Administration. *Telecommunications in the age of information.* NTIA Special Publication 91-26, October 1991.

———. *Globalization and the mass media.* NTIA Special Publication 93-290, January 1993.

———. *20/20 vision: The development of a national information infrastructure.* NTIA Special Publication 94-28, March 1994.

U.S. Department of Commerce. Office of Telecommunications. *The U.S. and the ITU in a changing world.* OT special publication 75-6, December 1975.

———. *The information economy.* 9 vols. OT Special Publication 77-12, 1977.

———. *Review of international telecommunications industry issues, structure and regulation problems.* OT Special Publication 77-16, 1977.

U.S. Department of State. *The computer and foreign affairs: Some first thoughts.* Center for International Systems Research. Occasional Paper No. 1, November 1966.

———. *Intelligence establishment.* Foreign Relations of the United States series. Washington, DC: U.S Government Printing Office, 1986.

———. *The Marshall Plan: Origins and implementation.* Office of Public Communications, Bureau of Public Affairs, 1987.

———. *Diplomacy for the 21st century: The IRM underpinning.* Office of Public Affairs, September 11, 1996.

U.S. Trade Representative. *U.S. national study on trade in services: A submission by the United States government to the General Agreement on Tariffs and Trade,* 1988.

Veronis, Suhler & Associates. *Communications industry forecast: 1998–2002.* New York, October 1998.

Wallenstein, Gerd D. *International telecommunication agreements.* 3 vols. Dobbs Ferry, NY: Oceana Publications, 1983.

Warner, Michael (ed.). *The CIA under Harry Truman: CIA cold war records.* Washington, DC: Government Printing Office, 1996.

Wellenius, Bjorn. *Telecommunications: World Bank experience and strategy.* Discussion Paper 192. Washington, DC: The World Bank, 1993.

Wellenius, Bjorn and Peter Stern (eds.). *Implementing reforms in the telecommunications sector*. Washington, DC: The World Bank, 1993.

Whitaker, Urban G. (ed.). *Propaganda and international relations*. San Francisco: Chandler Publishing Co., 1962.

Whitfield, Stephen. *The culture of the cold war*. Baltimore, MD: Johns Hopkins University Press, 1996.

Whitten, James B. *Propaganda and cold war: A Princeton University symposium*. Washington, DC: Public Affairs Press, 1963.

Wilhelm, Donald. *Global communications and political power*. New Brunswick, NJ: Transaction Press, 1990.

Winkler, Allan M. *The politics of propaganda: The Office of War Information 1942–1945*. New Haven, CT: Yale University Press, 1978.

World Information Technology and Services Alliance. *Digital planet: The global information economy*. Alexandria, VA, 1999.

Yurow, Jane. *Issues in international telecommunications policy: A source book*. Washington, DC: Federal Communications Bar Association and the International Law Institute, George Washington University, 1983.

Zacher, Mark W. *Governing global networks: International regimes for transportation and communications*. New York: Cambridge University Press, 1996.

Zhiveynov, Nicolai Ivanovich. *Operation PW: The psychological warfare of the American imperialists* (English translation). Moscow: Publishing House of Political Literature, 1966.

Index

Acheson, Dean, 14, 31, 149
Agency for International Development (AID), 9, 103, 178
Airtouch Corp., 157
Albright, Madeleine, 10, 109, 173
Alliance for Progress, 78
America Online, 175
American Express, 175
Anselmo, Rene, 128–29
Apple Computer Co., 167
Arms Control and Disarmament Agency, 103
Arthur D. Little Inc., 68
AT&T, 9, 13, 74, 115, 126, 149, 179–80; breakup of, 120; develops first communications satellite, 37–39; early role in global communications, 19
Australia, 122

Bahrain, 182
Ball, George W., 41
Bell Canada, 149
Bertlesmann Co., 74
Bloomberg news service, 8
Booz Allen & Hamilton, survey of Internet use by international corporations, 175
Brandt, Willy, 69

Brazil, 152
Bretton Woods Agreement, 11
British Telecom, 122, 137
Brown, Ronald H., 169
Browning, John, 13
Brzezinski, Zbigniew: criticizes State Department lack of computer resources, 105; emphasizes U.S. advantage over Soviet Union in information technology, 105; institutes National Security Council study of international communications policy, 119–20
Buckley, James, 89
Business Roundtable, 150

Cable & Wireless Ltd., 121
Cable News Network (CNN), 10, 106, 172
Campaign to Ban Use of Land Mines, employs World Wide Web as link with overseas organizations, 10
Canada, 83, 122; bilateral negotiations with United States on communications and information issues, 142–43; negotiates North American Free Trade Agreement (NAFTA) with United States and Mexico, 148–49

Cargill International, use of advanced electronic networks in global operations, 9

Carter, Jimmy, authorizes creation of National Telecommunications and Information Agency (NTIA), 116–17

Carter, William G., 41

Caruso, Andrea, 125

Cate, Fred, 80

Center for Strategic and International Studies (CSIS), report on future of digital diplomacy, 171–73

Central Intelligence Agency, 27, 32

Cerf, Vinton, 184

Chamber of Commerce, U.S., 8, 150

Charter 77 Organization in Czechoslovakia, 90

China, People's Republic of: applies for membership in World Trade Organization, 176; attempts to maintain controls over domestic communications channels, 182; critical of American role in creating Intelsat, 48; decision to expand national communications network, 91–92; opposition to U.S. global information flow policy, 75–76

Christopher, Warren, 173

Cisco Systems Inc., 179

Citigroup, 135, 175

Clarke, Arthur C., 53

Clinton, Bill, 138; emphasizes information highway theme in 1992 campaign, 168–69; proposes Institute for Information Infrastructure Protection, 181

Coalition of Service Industries, 150

Cohen, Bonnie, 109

Colchester, Nicholas, 12

Columbia University, 27

Commerce, Department of, 7, 169; organizes National Telecommunications and Information Administration, 118–19; role in early radio broadcasting, 63; seeks role in managing international telecommunications and information policy, 63

Commission on the Organization of the Government for the Conduct of Foreign Policy (Murphy Commission), 117–18

Commonwealth Conference on Satellite Communications, 45

Communications Satellite Act of 1962, 42–43

Communications Satellite Corporation, 115; creation of, 42–44; dispute with State Department over organization of Intelsat operations, 50–51; opposes private competition to Intelsat, 127; role in permanent Intelsat organization, 47–48

Communications satellites, 33: creation of Intelsat organization to manage global system, 43–54; early history of, 37–39

Compton, Wilson, 31

Conference on Security and Cooperation in Europe (Helsinki Accords), 90–91

Congress, U.S.: attempts to coordinate communications policies of federal agencies, 117, 123; interest in radio spectrum policy, 68; objects to financing UNESCO operations, 89; resistance to funding State Department telecommunications network, 108; role in authorizing international trade agreements, 137

Coordination Committee for Multilateral Export Controls (COCOM), 77

Coordinator for Inter-American Affairs (CIAA), 22

Council of Europe, adopts strict regulations to protect citizen privacy, 146

Council on Foreign Relations, 7

Cuban missile crisis, role of electronic communications in, 101

Daley, William M., 169

Data privacy: Council of Europe regulations on, 146; European-American agreement on standards, 147

Davy, Richard, 91

Defense Communications Agency, 180

Defense Communications Board, 20
Defense, Department of, 6, 7, 23, 138; interest in radio spectrum policy, 65; role in communications satellite development, 38, 51; use of advanced information and telecommunications technologies, 179–80
Defense Information Systems Agency, 180
Dell Corp., 136
Denning, Dorothy, 180
Deutsche Telekom, 157–58
Developing countries, 13; impact of Intelsat on, 60; membership in ITU, 64–65; opposition to U.S. global information flow policy, 78; participation in 1979 World Administrative Radio Conference, 69–70; role in Intelsat negotiations, 51–52; use of local radio and television broadcasting in social and economic development, 79
Diebold, John, 103–4
Digital technology developments, 62
Dingman, James, 39
Direct broadcasting satellites (DBS): negotiations on radio spectrum requirements, 67–68; United Nations negotiations on regulation of, 81–83
Dobrynin, Anatoly, 101
Dougan, Diana Lady, 124, 129–30
Dow Jones news service, 8
Dulles, John Foster, 29–30, 31

Eagleburger, Lawrence, 165
"Early Bird" communications satellite, 49–50
Economist, 12, 88, 140
Edelson, Bert, 50
Ehrlich, Everett, 136
Electronic Industries Association, 150
English, Glenn, 123
European Community, 77, 125, 138; decision to liberalize regional telecommunications practices, 122; early interest in communications satellites, 44–45; electronics trade

negotiations with the United States, 144–45; interest in radio spectrum negotiations, 70; role in creating Intelsat network, 46–47
European Conference on Satellite Communications (ECSC), 44
European Space Research Organization, 45
European Space Vehicle Launcher Development Organization (ELDO), 45

Farley, Philip, 41
Fascell, Dante, 68
Federal Communications Commission (FCC), 7, 32, 116, 138; authorizes domestic private satellite networks, 126; creates office of international communications policy, 122
Federal Radio Commission, 63
Fiber optic technology, role in expanding international telecommunications networks, 54
Field, Cyrus, 19
Financial networks, role in expanding global communications facilities, 137
Flanigan, Peter, 115
Ford Aerospace, 127
Ford Foundation, 79
Ford Motor Company, early use of multinational production of its products, 11
Foreign Affairs Information Management System (FAIMS), initial State Department attempt to create unified internal information network, 103
Foreign exchange networks, use of advanced information technologies, 12
France: early dominance in global communications, 19; government report warning of American domination of global information sector, 146; information technology policy, 77; plans for national communications satellite system, 49

France Telecom, 149
Frost, Ellen, 158

Gates, Bill, 136, 166
Gay Liberation movement, 117
Geller, Henry, 118
General Accounting Office, 3, 117
General Agreement on Tariffs and
    Trade (GATT), 84, 125, 139; post-
    war record of, 150; replaced by
    World Trade Organization, 151–54;
    "Tokyo Round" negotiations, 150
General Agreement on Trade and
    Services (GATS), 153
General Electric Co., 141, 146
Georgetown University, 101, 180;
    study on future of diplomacy, 2–3
Gingrich, Newton, 169
Ginzburg, Alexsandr, 90
Global information flows: American
    policy opposed by overseas cultural
    elites, 73; growing role of American
    information exports, 93; growth of
    commercial international data net-
    working, 116; origins of U.S. post-
    war free flow policies, 79–81; U.S.
    commitment to freedom of, 73
Goldmark, Peter, 166
Goldwater, Barry, 68, 126–27
Gore, Albert, role in managing Na-
    tional Information Infrastructure
    Project, 169
Graham, Philip L., 43
Great Britain, 145; attempt to monop-
    olize world wireless networks, 19;
    early dominance in global commu-
    nications, 19; privatizes national
    telecommunications network, 145
Greenspan, Alan, 136
Grove, Andrew, 175
GTE Corp., 149
Guéhenno, Jean-Marie, 186

Hammett, Dashiell, 31
Harbi, Mohamed, 70
Harvard University, 27, 168
Havel, Vaclav, 90
Heath, Don, 4

Helms, Jesse, 170
Helsinki Accords. See Conference on
    Security and Cooperation in Europe
Henry L. Stimson Center, report on
    restructuring State Department for
    information-age tasks, 171–72
Hertz, Heinrich, 62
Hollings, Ernest, 117
"Hotline" communications link be-
    tween Washington and Moscow,
    102
Howe, Fisher, 104–5
Hughes Aircraft Corp., 49, 128
Hugill, Peter, 185
Hull, Cordell, 22, 100

IBM, 9, 77, 136, 141, 175, 178
Ickes, Harold, 21
Independent Commission for World-
    wide Telecommunications Develop-
    ment (Maitland Report), 177
India, growth of software production
    in, 174
Information technology, global
    growth of, 135–36
Innis, Harold, 185
Intel Corp., 136
Intelsat. See International Telecommu-
    nications Satellite Organization
Interagency Radio Advisory Commit-
    tee (IRAC), 65
International Data Corp., survey of
    postindustrial economies, 167
International Institute of Communica-
    tions, 69
International Organization for Stan-
    dardization (IOS), 153
International Telecommunications
    Satellite Organization (Intelsat):
    challenge to its monopoly position,
    125–28; creation of, 47–50; 1969
    conference to develop permanent
    network, 52–53; resists moves to
    introduce private competition,
    127
International Telecommunications Un-
    ion (ITU), 63–64, 69; postwar role
    of, 23–24, 45; sponsors Maitland Re-

port on telecommunications in developing countries, 177–78
International Telegraph Union, 19, 63, 169
International Trade Organization (ITO), 149
Internet, 93, 181; early history of, 3; expansion in developing countries, 178; growth in Russia and China, 182–83; growth of Internet-based trade, 156–57, 174–76
Intersputnik (Soviet satellite organization), 49
Iran, 19

Jackson, Charles D., 30
Jackson, Wiliam D., 30, 32
Japan: negotiations with United States on electronics trade, 143; role of Ministry of International Trade and Industry (MITI) in electronics exports, 136
Jefferson, Thomas, 100
Jobs, Steve, 167
Joffe, Joseph, 14
Johnson, Lyndon: authorizes task force on communications policy, 114; orders greater use of computers in federal government offices, 102
Johnson, Robert L., 31
Justice, Department of, 114, 121

Katzenbach, Nicholas, 43
Kennan, George, 27–29
Kennedy, John F.: authorizes White House Office of Telecommunications Management, 50; establishes office for strategic trade policy, 139; role in satellite communications policy, 40–44
Kennedy, Robert, 41, 114
Keohane, Robert, 177
Kissinger, Henry, 87, 102
Konrad Adenauer Foundation, 69
Korea, 152

Lang, Jack, 75
Lenin, V. I., 26

Lerner, Daniel, 78
L. M. Ericsson Co., 136
Lockheed Corp., 141
Luttwak, Edward, 136

MacBride, Sean, 87
MacLeish, Archibald, 24
Madelin, Alain, 144
Maitland Report. *See* Independent Commission for Worldwide Telecommunications Development
Malraux, Andre, 86
Marconi, Guglielmo, 19, 62
Marks, Leonard, 52, 89
Massachusetts Institute of Technology, 27, 78
Matthews, Jessica, 11, 186
Mattingly, Garrett, 1
M'Bow, Amadou-Mahter, 86
McCarthy, Joseph, 25, 31
McCormack, James, 53
McGhee, George, 42
MCI World Com, 143, 149
McKnight, Thomas, 127
McLuhan, Marshall, 185
Media industry, U.S.: coverage of foreign news, 172; growth of export markets, 85–86; role in forming public opinion on international events, 106
Mercury Communications Ltd., 122
Mexico, included in NAFTA agreement, 148–49, 151
Microsoft Corp., 9, 136, 175, 178
Mills, Wilbur, 139
Modernization doctrine in U.S. foreign policy, 78
Motion Picture Association of America, 86
Murdoch, Rupert, 11, 83
Murphy, Robert D., 117
Murrow, Edward R., 48

National Aeronautical and Space Council (NASC), 40
National Aeronautics and Space Administration (NASA), 81–82

National Association of Manufacturers (NAM), 8, 150
National Committee on Library and Informational Sciences, 122
National Democratic Institute for International Affairs, 9
National Security Act of 1947, role in authorizing unconventional psychological warfare, 27
National Security Council, 27, 119; creation of, 27; includes psychological warfare in strategic plans, 29; issues report on international communications policy, 119
National Telecommunications and Information Agency (NTIA), 116; issues report on U.S. communications goals, 123; tensions with State Department over information policy responsibilities, 118, 122
Navy, U.S., 19
Neuman, Joanna, 106
New World Economic Order (NWEO), 89
New World Information and Communications Order (NWICO), 86, 126, 177
Newsweek, 84
Nippon Telephone and Telegraph Co., 143
Nixon, Richard M.: decision to create Office of Telecommunications Policy in the White House, 115; initiative in opening contacts with the People's Republic of China; role in Intelsat negotiations, 52
Nokia Inc., 74
Non-governmental organizations (NGOs), increasing influence in foreign relations, 7–8
Nortel Inc., 74
North American Free Trade Agreement (NAFTA): as model for World Trade Organization negotiations, 151–52; negotiations leading to first major regional trade agreement, 148–49
Nye, Joseph, 3, 177, 186

OECD. See Organization for Economic Cooperation and Development
Office of Strategic Services (OSS), 22, 27
Office of Telecommunications Policy (OTP), 115–16
Office of War Information (OWI), 22–25
Omnibus Trade and Competitiveness Act of 1987, 147
Organization for Economic Cooperation and Development (OECD), 147, 167, 176
Orion Communications, 127
Owens, William, 3

Palestine National Authority, assigned Internet domain name, 186
Palmerston, Lord Henry John, 5
PanAmSat Co., 128–29
Pastore, John, 53
Peace Corps, 78
Peacesat communications satellite, 82
Peru, 128
Pool, Ithiel de Sola, 1, 105
Post, telegraph and telephone organizations (PTOs), 121, 145, 157
Psychological Strategy Board, 29, 30, 32
Psychological warfare operations, 27–30

Radio Act of 1912, 19
Radio Corporation of America (RCA), 20
Radio Free Europe, 28, 77
Radio in the American Sector (RIAS), U.S. radio station in postwar Berlin, 30
Radio Liberty, 28, 77
Radio Moscow, 26
Radio spectrum: importance of, 62; ITU regulation of, 66–67
Rand Corporation, 179
Reader's Digest, 84
Reagan, Ronald: decision to break up the Intelsat monopoly, 126; pro-

poses Department of International Trade and Industry, replacing Department of Commerce, 123–24; supports expansion of military communications resources, 180

Reich, Robert, 184

Reinicke, Wolfgang, 19

Reuss, Henry, 139

Reuters news agency, 8, 74

"Revolution in military affairs," 179

Robinson, Glen O., 69

Rockefeller, Nelson A., 21–22, 24

Roosevelt, Eleanor, 80

Roosevelt, Franklin D., 22, 79

Rosenau, James, 186

Rosenberg, Emily, 76

Rostow, Eugene, 114

Runtagh, Helene, 172

Rusk, Dean, 102, 103

Russia, post-Soviet information and communications developments, 182

Saudi Arabia, 182

Scheransky, Anatoly, 90

Schlesinger, Arthur, Jr., 29

Schmidt, Harrison, 68

Schultz, George W., 124

Schumpeter, Joseph, 4

Selin, Ivan, 108

Semiconductor chips, 61

Servan-Schreiber, Jacques, 77

Shining Path guerilla group, 9

Siemens Co., 121

Small, Cornelia, 4

Smith Mundt Act of 1948, 26

Solidarity movement in Poland, 91

Sommer, Ron, 158

Sony Corp., 74, 121

South Vietnam, 79

Southwestern Bell Co., 149

Soviet Union, 59; attempts to circumvent information provisions of the Helsinki Accords, 90–91; Cold War information programs, 26–27; development of communications satellites, 39; objections to American direct broadcast satellites, 83; opposition to U.S. global information flow policy, 75–76; role in Intelsat negotiations, 48–49

Special Trade Representative (STR): created by Kennedy administration, 139; name changed to Office of the U.S. Special Trade Representative, 140

Sputnik space satellite, 33, 59

Sri Lanka, 9

Stalin, Josef, 30

Staple, Gregory, 10–11

State, Department of: adopts DOSTN telecommunications network plan, 108; assigned to take over responsibilities of Office of War Information, 24–25; cautious approach to adopting computer technology, 103–5; creates bureau for information resources, 2; creates Bureau for International Communications and Information Policy, 130; creates Bureau of Information Resources Management, 109; early attempts to organize communications policies procedures, 113–15; early role in communications satellite policy, 41, 45; early use of cable communications, 5; efforts to restructure internal communications network, 99–109; increasing importance of trade issues, 173–74; information and communications policy bureau closed down, 170; opposes Reagan administration plan for separate department to handle foreign trade negotiations, 123–24; organizes overseas information and cultural programs, 21; preparations for radio spectrum conferences, 68–69; problems with computer security, 180; role in World Trade Organization negotiations, 151; role of Policy Planning Staff in postwar psychological operations, 27; use of com-

puters in international negotiations, 69
Stettinius, Edwards, 24
Stoll, Clifford, 166
Stowe, Ronald, 70
Strategic Arms Limitation Talks, 102
Strauss, Robert, 139, 150
Submarine cables, 32
Sweden, 83, 146

Talbot, Strobe, 106
Telecom Italia, 157
Telecommunications Act of 1966, 74
Telephones, worldwide expansion of, 166
Television Program Export Association, 86
Telstar communications satellite, 37–39, 41, 49, 59
Time magazine, 84
"Tokyo Round" of GATT negotiations, 150
Toqueville, Alexis de, 7
Trade Expansion Act of 1962, 139
Trade in information services, 139–41
Transnational corporations: American corporations' leadership in information trade, 141; United Nations study of their influence on information trade, 81
Treasury, Department of the, 7, 138
TRT Telecommunications Co., 127
Truman, Harry, 24, 27

United Nations: considers role of communications satellites, 48, 68, 81; creates commission on transnational corporations, 84; debates free-flow-of-information issues, 78–84; monitors public policy networks, 10
United Nations Development Program (UNDP), 179
United Nations Educational, Scientific and Cultural Organization (UNESCO), 25, 68, 69; attempts to impose regulations on international information flows, 84–89

Universal Declaration of Human Rights, 80, 90, 181
University of Hawaii, 82
"Uruguay Round" of Wold Trade Organization negotiations, 151–52; inclusion of services trade in, 152; role of developing countries in, 152
U.S. Information Agency (USIA): creation of, 31; 1999 transfer to State Department, 173; role in public diplomacy, 6
U.S. National Commission for UNESCO, 85
U.S. Trade Representative, 7, 148, 169; established services trades as subject of global negotiation, 139–40; organizes private sector support for WTO negotiations, 150–51

Versailles peace conference, 20
Vertzberger, Yaacov, 100
Vietnam War, 79
Vizas, Christopher, 127
Vodophone Ltd., 157
Voice of America radio, 22, 32, 77

Walesa, Lech, 91
Wang Corp., 105, 171
War Information Board, 22
"Wars of national liberation," 79
Weisner, Jerome, 40, 43
Welch, Leo D., 43
Western Union International, 116, 126
Whitehead, Clay (Tom), 115–16
Wisner, Frank, 28
Wolf, Francis Colt De, 41
World Administrative Radio Conference (WARC), 50, 68–70, 107
World Bank, 178
WorldCom Inc., 149
World Press Freedom Committee, 88
World Trade Organization (WTO), 8, 84, 125, 129, 176; disruption of 1999 planning conference in Seattle, 159; inclusion of services trade in final agreement, 151–55; special negotiations on basic telecommunications services (BTS), 154–55; "Uruguay

Round" of WTO negotiations, 151;
U.S. strategy for replacing GATT,
149–51
Wriston, Walter, 135

Yahoo!, 178
Yugoslavia, 9

Zakaria, Fareed, 4

About the Author

WILSON DIZARD, JR. is a Senior Associate in the International Communications Program at the Center for Strategic and International Studies (CSIS) in Washington, DC. Prior to joining CSIS, he was a senior foreign service officer specializing in international communications policy. He has participated in numerous international negotiations and conferences on communications issues. Dizard is a former writer and editor for Time, Inc., and is the author of six books: *The Strategy of Truth* (1961), *Television: A World View* (1966), *The Coming of the Information Age* (1985), *Gorbachev's Information Revolution: Controlling Glasnost in the New Electronic Era* (1988), *Old Media, New Media* (1993), and *Meganet* (1997).

About CSIS

The Center for Strategic and International Studies (CSIS), established in 1962, is a private, tax-exempt institution focusing on international public policy issues. Its research is nonpartisan and nonproprietary.

CSIS is dedicated to policy impact. It seeks to inform and shape selected policy decisions in government and the private sector to meet the increasingly complex and difficult global challenges that leaders will confront in this new century. It achieves this mission in four ways: by generating strategic analysis that is anticipatory and interdisciplinary; by convening policymakers and other influential parties to assess key issues; by building structures for policy action; and by developing leaders.

CSIS does not take specific public policy positions. Accordingly, all views, positions, and conclusions expressed in this publication should be understood to be solely those of the author.